Unwavering Convictions

Unwavering Convictions

Gao Zhisheng's Ten-Year Torture and Faith in China's Future

Gao Zhisheng

Published by

THE AMERICAN BAR ASSOCIATION
SECTION OF INTERNATIONAL LAW

and

CAROLINA ACADEMIC PRESS
Durham, North Carolina

ISBN 978-1-5310-0471-2
LCCN 2016960229

Carolina Academic Press, LLC
700 Kent Street
Durham, NC 27701
Telephone (919) 489-7486
Fax (919) 493-5668
www.cap-press.com

Printed in the United States of America

Contents

Translator's Note

This book is the result of the efforts of several translators and editors apart from myself. I would like to thank Kevin Carrico, Paul Mooney, and Robert Kawtz, as well as others who for various reasons prefer not to be named, for contributing their invaluable skills to making Gao Zhisheng's narrative accessible to the English-reading public. I would also like to thank Bob Fu and the China Aid Association as well as Albert Ho Chun-yan in Hong Kong for providing the financial support for this translation.

Stacy Mosher
April 29, 2016

Foreword

Gao Zhisheng will inevitably be a key voice in the democratic future of China, the world's most populous country, which today is still ruled by the most murderous regime in history.

Gao was one of Beijing's most successful lawyers. Self-taught and brought up in poverty, he came to prominence through his defense of individuals persecuted by the regime for their religion and practice of Falun Gong.

These pages are not an easy read, because they detail the regime's attempts to break one of the greatest spirits of our time. Despite this, Gao Zhisheng's unwavering convictions, profound beliefs, and commitment to humanity shine through.

Escaping house arrest briefly, Gao once told me on a borrowed mobile phone that he had been tortured to the point of death. On regaining consciousness, he saw men in white coats around him. One said, "We don't want you to die: we want to make you want to die."

This book contains his prediction that the regime will fall in 2017. This echoes the prediction made to me in 2010 by China's great artist Ai Weiwei, who said of Gao (the video is available on YouTube) that his continued detention would be impossible in a civilized country, and that the present Communist totalitarian regime is doomed.

In 2005, Gao investigated the persecution of Falun Gong, a popular new Buddha-school exercise practice that at its height in 1999 had some seventy to hundred million practitioners. In early 2006, he gave evidence to the UN's torture *rapporteur*, Dr. Manfred Nowak, who estimated that some two-thirds of the seven to eight million detained in China's re-education through labor system were practitioners of Falun Gong. Thousands of them perished from the illegal harvesting of their vital organs as part of the People's Liberation Army's lucrative organ transplant trade.

I encountered Gao Zhisheng in Beijing in May 2006, where I met former prisoners who had been tortured. We often talked through an interpreter in the coming months, whenever he could find a safe mobile phone.

I was able to use my position in the European Parliament to keep Gao's name in public and political consciousness through debates, resolutions, and campaigns, and nominating him for the Nobel Peace Prize, which one day he will receive.

His many supporters followed Gao's arrest in August 2006, his release into house arrest, re-arrest and show trial to the condemnation of the international community and then his long disappearance.

This book, a sequel to his 2007 *A China More Just*, was written secretly in the humble home where he was brought up and is still today cared for by his beloved elder brother. It is a saga of suffering but it is also a detailed charge sheet for the international prosecutors of tomorrow. It lists as well the occasional acts of humanity from some of his jailers, toiling in the service of a tyranny.

I have met many great human beings such as Nelson Mandela or Aung San Suu Kyi who have suffered for their principles and fellow citizens, but none has come through ten years of such unending and extreme torture, with no concessions of principle. Gao's conversion to a robust, unshakable Christian faith is recounted in the book and credited by Gao with strengthening him to endure the agony of torture while showing compassion to his captors.

Gao Zhisheng is ready to serve the 1.3 billion Chinese when the time comes and is unwilling to leave China to join his wife and children in their US exile. He is a hero of our time.

Edward McMillan-Scott was a British vice-president of the European Parliament, responsible for Democracy & Human Rights 2004–2014, and is a board member of China Aid.

Edward McMillan-Scott

Introduction

2017 marks the hundredth anniversary of Communism. I believe that by Heaven's decree, this will also be the year in which the Chinese Communist Party (CCP) will be defeated and overthrown. At that time, having reached its ninety-sixth anniversary in China and having tyrannized China for sixty-eight years, the CCP will become just another horrible memory as it is swept into the dustbin of history. Evil regimes come and go, but the Chinese people abide forever!

The extinction of the world's communist regimes entered its final countdown in the 1980s, but to China's shame, one-fifth of humanity still crawls along this hard road. Human limitations cause civilization to move forward through repeated heroic attempts and bloody experiments. In this sense, Russia's embrace of Communism in 1917 was not blameworthy in itself, but once the communist system's evils became obvious, the wicked capabilities it had built up were then used to muffle dissent and coercively promote this evil to all of humanity, resulting in unnatural death on a massive scale and a suppression of basic freedoms.

Communism has gone through thirty years of flourishing and expansion, followed by thirty-odd years of sustaining its life through violence and lies. The current third period of thirty-odd years marks its steady decline, including its necrosis over wide expanses of territory from the 1980s to the early 1990s.

Communism's global defeat and extinction shows God's plan, first in that while all communist regimes seized power through violence, they have been vanquished through the peaceful opposition of their own citizens. Second, not a single one of the world's communist regimes has gained rebirth through self-transformation. Once the CCP collapses, the demise of the remaining communist regimes, such as North Korea's, will be a mere technicality. I believe that in 2017, China will be merged into humanity's universal civilization, and that in this new era of freedom and democracy, the Chinese people will become a constructive force in civilization's advancement.

I

The Unnamed Hell: Abduction, Detention, and Torture

The road to China's political modernization is filled with the blood and tears of our forebears, and violent abduction, torture, and imprisonment remain the backdrop to this road even today. My experience is just one part of the boundless suffering of the Chinese race under one of the cruelest regimes in human history.

At present I can move freely within the bounds of a village in northern China, but in the context of the greater world, I am still in prison—it is just that my cell has become larger.

Over the years, many people inside and outside of China have been following my situation, and I would like here to express my deep gratitude for their concern, through which God has protected me and by which God has sustained me in my time of trouble, and nurtured the faith that has allowed me to carry on. In particular, the unwavering attention of the foreign media is a crucial reason why China's dark powers have not dared to persecute me to death. This played a particularly important role in my surviving the abduction that happened in September 2009.

I am unable to provide a detailed account of all my abductions over the past decade, but will record some key incidents here.

1. My First Abduction, November 2004

The Chinese Communist Party's (CCP) secret police abducted me for the first time around late October or early November 2004. This first time came so suddenly that I had no idea what was happening. Although as I worked as a lawyer I frequently encountered victims' tearful accusations of barbaric and callous acts by authorities, referred to as "peaked caps" (due to their uniforms), I believed that the government would be foolish to harm others in a way that brought no benefit to itself. I never considered these phenomena at the systemic level. It was my personal experience of the authorities' unambiguous brutality that educated me.

This first abduction was carried out by the secret police in Shaanxi Province. The pretext was my involvement in a peaceful demonstration by workers who had been laid off from the Northwestern No. 1 National Cotton Mill, but I had not previously had any contact with those workers before my abduction. A friend had merely told me of the persecution of laid-off workers who had staged a peaceful demonstration outside the cotton mill and hoped I could go there and help them out.

As I stepped out of Xianyang Airport, a vehicle drove up soliciting a fare, and when I climbed in, I was surprised to see there was already one person sitting in the front passenger seat and one person sitting in the back seat. The driver smiled at me and said he hoped I would not mind sharing the ride to the city so he could earn a little extra cash. As the car went on its way, I noticed it taking side roads and driving without its headlights on. When I started to ask what was going on, the other two passengers pounced on me. One of them held my arms and the other one covered my head with a hood, while the car came to a sudden halt. Someone pressed my head down between my knees while my arms were pulled behind my back. Immobilized and suffocating, I panted for breath as I heard the others rifling through my bag. I later learned that they were verifying my identity.

After a few minutes, the car started moving forward again. The man pressing my head down relaxed his grip enough for me to straighten my back slightly, and I asked, "My bandit brothers, do you want my money or my life?"

The car became strangely quiet, and then a voice used a local obscenity to tell me to shut up.

As the car moved forward, sweeps of light suggested that we were in an urban area, after which I sensed the car entering a dark place. Then it stopped, and someone got out and pulled me out. As I straightened my back, my hood was yanked off and I was kicked forward from behind. The car sped off and I found that my bag had been tossed to the ground.

I thought I had encountered a band of highway robbers, never thinking that these outlaws were actually with the government. I found myself standing along a dark lane between two major roadways, and calming myself, I picked up my bag and began walking toward the nearest lighted area. After I took a few steps, several men dressed in black barred my way and said, "Gao Zhisheng, you are suspected of disturbing public order. We now declare you placed under compulsory measures, and you need to come with us."

Suddenly I understood the identity of the "bandits" in the car. "Since you are public servants, according to procedure you should show me your identification," I reminded them.

"Keep running your mouth and I will pound you, you prick! When you're in Shaanxi, you play by Shaanxi rules. A lawyer's nothing but a prick here," shouted one of the men in black.

Realizing that discussing the law with them would be like playing piano for a buffalo, I could only continue to proceed forward, while constantly pressed between them. My abductors took me into an old building, steering me through a dark corridor. Then one of them grabbed my hair and shoved me against the wall, and I heard someone around ten yards away from me make a telephone call and say, "We've got the shipment." Then I heard him walk over, and I was turned around. "Head down. Press the prick's head down," the man ordered. Two of the others forced me to bend over at a ninety-degree angle. "Take the belt off and use it to bind the prick's hands." The blood rushed to my head and my eyeballs swelled painfully as someone came over, unbuckled my belt, and used it to bind my hands.

At that point, I heard a group of people entering the corridor, and someone said, "Put it on and take him to Business Class." A black hood was pulled over my head, and I was taken back out and loaded into a car with my head once again pushed between my knees.

After about half an hour's drive, I was pulled out of the car, propelled into a room, and made to stand in place. The room was very quiet, and I could sense that someone else was expected. About twenty minutes later, I heard several people walk in and someone walk out.

My hood was pulled off, and as I swept my eyes around the room, I saw several men standing in front of me gazing at me with a somber imperturbability that suggested they were officials. I seemed to be in the room of a guesthouse that had been emptied of all of its furnishings. A short, fat man approached me with his hands behind his back, who then abruptly grabbed my necktie and yanked hard on it. The only sound in the room was of our frantic footsteps as he rabidly strangled me and tossed me around the room. After both of us were dripping with sweat, he stopped jumping around, and the only sound left in the room was the sound of the two of us panting. At that point, the short, fat man yelled, "Bring a chair in here!" The door opened and someone placed a chair in the corner. The fat man pulled me over to the chair by my tie and ordered, "Stand on the chair!" By then I was exhausted, and even more I was distressed, angry, and shocked. I still did not know why they were inflicting this brutality on me, so I ignored his rants. The short, fat man then punched me below the chin with a fierce uppercut and kneed me hard in the groin.

At that moment, the door opened and four more men came in. The man who led the way was clearly the highest-ranking person at the scene. He stood there with his hands behind his back and lifted his chin, while the short, fat man immediately stood to one side.

The leader gazed expressionlessly into my eyes, and the room became strangely quiet. I discovered that, at some point, the other men who had come in with the short, fat man had left the room. After staring at me for half a minute, the leader broke his silence and said, "Lawyer Gao is an educated man and our guest in Xianyang, and we can't treat our guests this way. Tonight I will play the host and invite Lawyer Gao to our community to eat Shaanxi food." Still perspiring heavily and panting, I ignored him. "Why aren't you saying anything? We'll have dinner together, and I'll arrange for someone from your native northern Shaanxi to accompany you tonight." I felt it would be shameful to say anything.

The leader began to ask me why I had come to Xianyang, and I asked, "If you don't know what I came for, why did you arrest me and inflict violence on me? What does a person have to do to be treated this way? What difference is there between your methods and those of bandits?"

"I don't agree with treating an educated man this way," the leader continued glibly. "I feel we can talk things over and take your circumstances into consideration. Isn't the elderly lady in your family near death? You wouldn't want the old lady to die without seeing you one last time, would you? The higher-ups just wanted us to have a chat with you and arrange a course that benefits all of us. Tonight someone from higher-up will come and chat with you, but we'll have dinner first. It is already late."

I refused to have dinner with them, so they took me to a different room that contained two beds, a table, and stools. I was brought a bowl of egg noodle soup, the man who brought it saying, "We hear you like noodles." I went ahead and ate while I had the chance, not knowing what complications I would have to face afterward.

After I finished eating, I was taken to the inner room of a suite, and my escort had me sit in a chair facing the doorway. After a few minutes a big man came in and taped a white cloth over the doorway to serve as a temporary curtain between my room and the rest of the suite. Then someone else entered the outer room and placed two chairs side by side, and another person placed a glass of hot tea on the chair on the left. I figured some VIP must be making an appearance and did not want to be seen.

About two minutes after the tea was placed on the chair, five or six men entered the suite, but I could only see them from the knees downward. Their leather shoes were highly polished. One of them sat in the chair and sipped some tea, and soon an exquisite thermos cup was placed on the chair next to the cup of tea. There was an unusual silence inside and outside the room, and when the big shot finally spoke, he revealed himself to be a native product, his speech caked with the gritty local Shaanxi accent. "Gao Zhisheng, would you like some tea?" he asked.

I replied, "Just come out and tell me what you have to say."

A few seconds of silence followed. "How is your mother doing? I hear she is in the terminal stage of cancer," he said casually.

"I don't think you are a doctor, besides which you already know the answer. Would you be willing to talk about your mother's health with unidentified people whose faces are concealed?"

There was another silence, and after about half a minute, he said, "It looks like you don't know how to be civil. How are we going to continue when you take that attitude?"

In measured tones I replied, "Before you arrived, brutality occurred that is incompatible with good manners. Besides which, I didn't ask for this conversation, and how can it be considered civil in any way?"

The atmosphere became strained, and after about a minute of deathly silence, he said with obvious displeasure, "Don't fail to appreciate the favor you are being shown."

"I didn't request the honor," I shot back.

"Are you finished with your bullshitting? You are powerless against us!"

"Aren't you also powerless against me? If not, do you dare to pull down the curtain between our rooms?"

The atmosphere became more strained. Finally, he spoke again, "We're acting in good faith, so I invited you for a chat. How can we keep talking when you are so hostile?"

I reminded him, "It is not a problem for me if this conversation can't continue."

That native product gave a huff, stood and paused, and then left the room, the leather shoes behind his chair following after him. That ended the ridiculous conversation, but not the situation.

I remained in my chair under guard for more than an hour, and then someone came in, lifted the temporary curtain, and said, "Come with me." I was taken back to the room with the beds. It appeared that the worst was over for that night, and I decided to focus on getting some rest, not knowing what difficulties I would face the next day.

Soon after I entered that room, a tall, handsome, middle-aged man walked in and immediately introduced himself as being from my native Suide. I nodded and smiled at him. "Why don't you wash up?" he suggested. "You can relax around me. I hear you served in the army. I'm also in the army. I am a political commissar in the People's Armed Police. My assignment at this time is to accompany you while you sleep."

I quickly washed up and went to bed, drawing the shade on my mental process. Eventually, my ability to rapidly fall into a deep sleep—even during breaks in torture sessions—later became legendary within the CCP's secret police force.

Someone shook me awake, and I found it was the political commissar. "Hurry and give yourself a quick wash. Something's happening," he said.

Just as I had finished washing, a group of men came in led by the short, fat man who had so rabidly tormented me the day before. Two men patted me down and then they steered me out the door. Once we were outside, I realized that it was still night.

I was escorted into a vehicle that already had two policemen sitting in the driver's seat and front passenger's seat. The vehicle pulled out into the road with another police vehicle in front and an ordinary sedan in back. Once again, I pulled the shade on my mental processes to protect myself from the mental harm of what was clearly meant to be a war of nerves.

By the time the vehicle stopped, dawn had broken, and I saw a sign inscribed with the words "Shaanxi Province Qian County Detention Center." Apart from the two men holding me on my right and left, everyone else climbed out their vehicles and bustled around between the detention center and the vehicles. Even operating at its most basic level, my brain could comprehend that they were carrying out some kind of formalities. After around twenty minutes or so, all of them climbed back into their vehicles, and the short, fat man said, "It is all set, he'll spend a few days with us first. There are still some things we need him for."

The motorcade turned around, and after a short time, the short, fat man telephoned the local Public Security Bureau (PSB) and said that an official from the Central Political and Legal Affairs Commission had come to Qian County to visit the Tang Imperial Mausoleum, and it was hoped that the local PSB could facilitate things. After hanging up, he said to me, "Old Gao, you are now a leader from the Central Political and Legal Affairs Commission, and they are sure to send some low-ranking officials to accompany us. If you don't say anything, they won't dare take the initiative to talk to you. There's a lot of stuff worth seeing here, and the admission tickets are really expensive. I've arranged it so we don't have to pay for tickets and we'll have a guide accompanying us all day and telling you about the place, and they'll arrange a very nice lunch for us. Just don't say anything. In China there is nothing better than to be a senior official."

Soon after that, the deputy head of the local PSB and the deputy director of the local cultural center rushed over, and I toured the Tang Imperial

Mausoleum grounds accompanied by an entourage of secret police. I found it interesting that some of the secret police officers occasionally made a point of lingering near me, and cautiously spoke to me while others were not paying attention. One of them told me about an inspection tour by Party Secretary Li Jianguo,[1] who demanded to see the destruction of the homes of families that had violated the family planning policies. The policeman said the leaders of Xianyang City were unwilling to commit this kind of evil, so they had several decoy homes built and filled them with the usual furnishings, and when Secretary Li came for his inspection, they arranged for people to pose as residents who had violated the family planning policies as Secretary Li personally witnessed the burning of their homes. I thanked the policeman and quietly expressed my appreciation, understanding that he was telling me that local grassroots officials are sometimes forced to engage in acts of violence against their will.

When the reception by the local officials ended at noon that day, I was escorted back to Xianyang City and formally handed over to Deputy Director Gao, who was responsible for "domestic security" in the Xianyang Municipal PSB. For the next two days, I was held in an unknown location that looked like a guesthouse, but the entire second floor was occupied by me and the two policemen who guarded me around the clock. During that time, new faces constantly came to talk with me, including one long-faced official who was apparently Deputy Director Gao's superior. I was told not to get involved with laid-off workers, Falun Gong, forced relocations, or petitioners. The third day I spent with Deputy Director Gao, who constantly praised the Party's graciousness, using himself as an example. He said his father had died when he was young, and the Party had raised him like a father, covering his living and educational expenses and allowing him to become a state cadre. He had to be either ignorant or unscrupulous to attribute this generosity to the Party when it was the ordinary taxpayer who actually footed the bill. I later learned that Gao was largely responsible for the use of violence against me. When the Beijing authorities abducted me sometime around July 2007, the deputy director of the Beijing Public Security Bureau (PSB),[2] Yu Hongyuan, told me, "Comrade Gao in

---

1. Translator's note (TN): Li Jianguo (b. 1946) was Party secretary of Shaanxi Province from 1997 to 2007. He has been vice chairman of the National People's Congress since 2008, and is a member of the 18th Central Committee and the 18th Politburo of the Chinese Communist Party (2012–2017).

2. TN: Under the Public Security apparatus, Domestic Security (*guobao*) deals with perceived threats to domestic security, while State Security (*guo'an*) deals with security matters relating to foreign countries. Gao Zhisheng refers to Yu Hongyuan and his underlings Sun Di and Zhang Xue as being responsible for Domestic Security.

Shaanxi said it best: Use the Shaanxi methods on Old Gao. There isn't anything that can be done in Shaanxi that can't be done in the Beijing office."

After three days of secret detention, the Xianyang PSB acting on behalf of Shaanxi Province released me on a legal pretext and flew me back to Beijing at my own expense. All this happened as my mother was passing through the last stage of her life, and in order to spare her further pain, I did not tell anyone of this dark experience until a long time after I had returned to Beijing.

Deputy Director Gao continued to visit me in the year that followed, especially while my mother was critically ill and at the time of her funeral, and he was always accompanied by Beijing's secret police. Deputy Director Gao's brutal acts had consequences he would never have expected. A little more than a month after my release, I wrote an open letter to the authorities challenging the CCP's political persecution of Falun Gong practitioners.[3] According to what I was told privately, President Jiang Zemin was absolutely furious, because someone had dared to challenge the government's "core concern" on Chinese soil. For a period of time, teams of the CCP's civilian and armed henchmen were sent to talk with me. On one of these occasions they came three times in a single afternoon, but Deputy Director Gao did not say another word about the Falun Gong issue during his visits. A little more than a year after my abduction by the Shaanxi PSB, the prohibited issues of Falun Gong persecution, laid-off workers, forced relocations, and petitioners had become the focus of all of my work. That should have allowed the relevant authorities to reach their own conclusions about the effect that torture would actually have on me.

2. Abductions after August 15, 2006

The first of these abductions became widely known to the outside world, but there are some further details that must be recorded, because the abduction from my elder sister's home in Shandong served as a prototype for subsequent abductions. All of the abductions were carried out by the Beijing police except for the one that was carried out by the authorities in Yulin, Shaanxi Province, and the one carried out by the secret police in Urumqi. This first abduction and the incidents that followed continued until December 22, 2006. The abduction policy was devised by the "leading comrade" Zhou

---

3. TN: Gao Zhisheng wrote an open letter to the National People's Congress on December 31, 2004, detailing persecution of Falun Gong practitioners. An English translation of the letter can be read at http://gaoworks.wordpress.com/2015/10/07/gao-zhishengs-open -letter-to-chinas-national-peoples-congress (accessed April 12, 2016).

Yongkang; organized by the head of the Beijing Domestic Security apparatus, Yu Hongyuan; and actually carried out by a number of individuals, among whom the most noteworthy is Zhang Xue. As for the other 200 odd participants in my abductions, their faces have become indistinguishable in my memory.

This abduction included an evaluation of the possible consequences, with a particular emphasis on international factors. As Yu Hongyuan put it, "I'm not afraid of anything inside China—we're prepared for that." The chief objective was to avoid using "crimes against state security," no matter how strained the interpretation, so three special groups were organized to investigating whether I had engaged in tax evasion, received unauthorized payments, or been involved in any sex scandals at my former law firm. All three committees failed to produce results, however, leading Yu Hongyuan to joke, "Just our luck to run into a paragon of virtue like you!"

I later learned that the authorities inquired into all of my personal contacts over the previous thirty years, including my time serving in the army's Eighteenth Regiment, and interviewed the head of the Kashgar Brushing Factory in Xinjiang, where I had worked more than twenty years ago, along with some former colleagues. (When I was forced to take a "vacation" in Kashgar in April 2007, one of these old colleagues joked, "Who would have guessed that working with you for a short time all those years ago would cause us so much trouble now!") Other friends and colleagues from the time I lived and worked in Urumqi were likewise interrogated by the secret police.

Most unlucky of all were my colleagues at my former legal firm, especially the head of the firm, Gao Ying, who was put under house arrest by the Xinjiang police for four days. Lawyers Zhang Liang and Wang Huimin, accountant Young Xinjuan, and others were all subpoenaed, and the topic was always the same: Tell us everything about Gao Zhisheng's tax evasion at the law firm. If they did not have such information, they had to think of a way to find it, even if it meant making something up. One of the investigators promised the law firm's leaders that if they agreed to testify to Gao Zhisheng's tax evasion, the law firm would be amply rewarded for fulfilling its solemn political duty by never being penalized for subsequent errors. I am grateful to these former colleagues of mine at the law firm, especially Mr. Gao Ying, who, while facing the threat of house arrest of uncertain duration, never went against his conscience. In today's China, this is immeasurably precious.

After eight or nine months of unsuccessful effort at enormous cost, the Party's dark forces ultimately resorted to abducting me on allegations that I had endangered state security. It was not a decision they made lightly, as indicated by a comment that Yu Hongyuan made on a subsequent occasion. "I started smoking because of you," he said. "The Beijing Domestic Secretary

(DomSec for short) couldn't find anything on you, and the higher-ups left it to us to decide whether or not to arrest you. Another guy and I stayed up all night on August 14th. Neither of us was a smoker, but that night we both went through several packs. So don't think that arresting you was all that easy; it was more damned exhausting than three months of labor."

Early in the morning on August 15th, a waiting motorcade received the order to go to Dongying, Shandong Province, to carry out the abduction, and upon reaching Dongying, the officers met up with the secret police who had been handling surveillance to work out the best opportunity. At that time, my brother-in-law was in the last stage of a terminal illness, and I had rushed over to Dongying with my daughter to help my elder sister get through this most difficult of times. The dark forces had sent two cars with no license plates to follow me all the way to Dongying and then took turns with the Dongying police standing guard outside my sister's home.

Surveillance by the secret police typically involves twelve officers working in shifts, but during sensitive periods it can involve twenty or thirty officers. When I drove anywhere, they would follow me in their cars, and if I rode a bicycle, so would they, and if I walked, they walked behind me. My habit wherever I am is to form a pattern in my daily activities and never depart from it; that keeps me from slacking off. The officers tailing me easily gained a firm grasp of my living patterns, and abducting me could hardly have been easier. For more than a week, I had set off every morning at 9:10, stayed at the hospital from 9:30 to 11:30, and then returned to my sister's home punctually at 11:50. Apart from that, I spent all my time reading in my sister's home.

On that particular morning, as I went to close the windows before setting out, I noticed that the surveillance team was much larger than usual. As I was about to head downstairs, I suddenly experienced a stomach ache, and the pain became so intense that I had to hurry to the bathroom. After two bouts of diarrhea within twenty minutes, I telephoned my sister and told her I could not go to the hospital that day.

Since I could not go to the hospital, I just stayed in and read. My sister came home at noon to make lunch for me, and when she reached the door of her building, she noticed many new faces among the people keeping watch outside. Dozens of people, men and women, were crowded into the stairways and hallways from the first to fifth floor. As soon as she put her key in the door, secret agents sprang on her, one of them covering her mouth while others kicked the door open. Hearing the crashing sound from the bedroom where I was reading, I put down my book just as a group of people burst into the room as if chasing down a fugitive bandit. There followed a ridiculous scene in which the first three people became jammed in the doorway, one of them the aforementioned Zhang Xue. Finally, someone gave them a hard push from outside, and the three of them tumbled into the room and flung themselves at me as I sat on my bed watching it all like a disinterested bystander. Zhang Xue leaped on the bed and clamped a hand over my mouth while others flipped me face-down on the bed, one pressing my face into the mattress while gripping my hair and the other pressing down on the base of my neck.

Someone ordered, "Drag him to the floor, hold him tight!" and several of them forced me to kneel on the floor, one man pulling my hair so I could only see the floor, while another stepped on my legs and yet another cuffed my hands behind my back. Two others covered my mouth with yellow adhesive tape and then wound the tape around my head and my eyes, after which my head was covered with a hood. Others seemed to be searching my sister's home. Because I was inside, I was only wearing shorts, and my bare knees on the floor tiles were in such pain that when I was finally lifted up, I could not walk without others supporting me. I was led downstairs and into what seemed to be a mini passenger van, where my head was pressed between my knees. I heard the roaring of other vehicles around it.

It took eight or nine hours to drive less than 500 km, and I was completely immobilized the entire time. The only thing I heard anyone say was, "If he moves, beat him to death." This time when I was taken to a room and my hood was removed, I found myself in the parlor of the Beijing Municipal Detention Center facing a stretch of black-peaked caps led by a man who was well over six-feet tall. At least five or six cameras were fiercely "firing" at me along with several video cameras to capture me in all my glory, wearing shorts, a T-shirt, and a pair of flip-flops they had stuck on my bare feet. I felt like a panda in the zoo. I was led to a room and stripped bare, and then taken to a prison cell. I had not slept for a minute before there was the ear-piercing slamming of the metal door and a voice yelling, "815 to interrogation!" From that day onward, my name was "815," and I was confined for long periods to a specially manufactured iron chair.

I described my experience in the detention center in a letter to Hu Jia, on April 6, 2007.[4] Regarding what I said in that letter about the disguised torture of being confined for long periods to a special iron chair under strong light, Sun Di later told me in July 2007, "That doesn't qualify as torture, because all prisoners are treated like that." He also said something quite significant: "Old

---

4. TN: An English translation of Gao Zhisheng's letter to the activist Hu Jia (which Gao read over the telephone to Hu when he was not able to get it to him by mail) is provided on the website of *Epoch Times*: http://www.theepochtimes.com/n3/1728746-gao-zhishengs -letter-to-fellow-rights-activist (accessed March 15, 2016).

Gao, no one believes what you wrote. Who would believe that the government could do something like this? Haven't your own confederates publicly stated that they don't believe these things?" (He was referring to an article by Yu Jie.[5])

At the detention center, I learned that the authorities had looted almost all of our property and that my wife, Geng He, had been left with only 300 *yuan* to live on. At that point I realized that I had completely underestimated the fathomless evil of my opponents, and I decided to compromise. I could not bear the thought of what my wife and children were going through, and besides that, I felt I should endorse the value of compromise; even if it was only nominal on the part of the authorities, I felt I should encourage their wish to end the conflict. But then they tried to gain credit in the eyes of their superiors by adding a lot of complications. I finally agreed to technical compromises such as repeating the procedures to show me admitting my guilt from the start, writing a letter of repentance, and promising not to criticize the Party or the government anymore. In return, I demanded that they immediately give my family 5,000 *yuan* in living expenses from the funds the authorities had confiscated.

In starting the process over again, they made me watch numerous videos with brainwashing content, some of which made me weep over the sufferings of our people. The authorities claimed these were the tears of my repentance, as a result of which many were rewarded for rendering meritorious service (in the words of Yu Hongyuan).

Once the formalities were completed, the authorities "released" me on the afternoon of December 22, 2006. In fact, I was handed over to the Beijing secret police, with Sun Di and Fatty Wang taking charge of me. On the way home, Sun Di announced a string of prohibitions that made me realize that my release was just a change in my place of detention. Sun Di also announced that the higher-ups had ordered my entire family to leave Beijing for a period of time, but he could not say exactly where we were to go. I pointed out that our children were still in school, so how could they leave the city? He said, "You have to submit to the big picture. We'll deal with Gege's [my daughter's] schooling. I need to emphasize that starting from now, you have to completely submit to our arrangements. You absolutely must not contact anyone, especially Hu Jia. Furthermore, I need to tell you very clearly that during this month, Geng He and Gege have been somewhat inconvenienced, and they're sure to complain to you when you get home. But don't start bouncing around again. Those people [referring to the secret police] outside your building and at your door are

---

5. TN: The dissident writer Yu Jie sought political asylum in the United States in January 2012 after being repeatedly harassed and tortured.

following the arrangements made by the higher-ups, so don't get into conflicts with them. The situation can only be changed through your cooperation with the government, and lashing out against it is useless."

I immediately responded, "I can leave Beijing in a week's time, but only me. Don't force me to choose to go to prison again." Sun Di did not say anything more. After I changed clothes I was taken to the Xiaoguan police station, where another group of people was waiting for me, along with another string of mind-boggling prohibitions—not only could I not see anyone, but I even had to report to the police station what books I read. Sun Di said, "Go on home. The leader has decided that the police officers will be withdrawn from inside your home, but cadres will continue to keep watch at your doorway, in the corridors and in the small room downstairs, and you are not to get into conflicts with them."

When I returned home, the horrible reality exceeded what any normal person could imagine. Although the secret police had withdrawn from our home, they had really moved only about six inches, from inside to outside of the door. We had to squeeze past a spring bed at the entrance to our home whenever we went in or out, and another bed was placed on the landing halfway up to the next floor of our building, with two "cadres" spending all day sitting on each bed. After many intense representations, they finally agreed to move the bed from our doorway to the landing halfway down the stairway so we could leave and enter our home normally again, but we were still obstructed when going downstairs.

After returning home I learned that while I was being abducted in Shandong, Sun Di had led a troop of "cadres" to our home. One large group [surrounded] my building to establish control over the area. A second group knocked at the door of our neighbor across the hall, and as soon as they gained entry, they pushed the man of the house onto the sofa with a hand clamped over his mouth while two others pushed his wife down on the floor. Several unidentified individuals then stayed in their home for three days and prevented anyone in the family from setting foot outside their home for any reason. I regret that being my neighbor turned out to be such a misfortune to them. Finally, these good people could not bear the constant harassment anymore, and in 2007 they sold their home at a loss and moved away.

Sun Di had led a third group of male and female secret police officers into my home for round-the-clock surveillance. In retrospect, their attention to detail was quite awe-inspiring. They spent several days and nights searching my home. Among the items that attracted their interest were letters from Falun Gong victims of persecution and their families, as well as stacks of letters from petitioners. There were also my books, which they took pains to examine for key evidence of "endangering state security" among the pages and between the lines. Many good books thus fell into the hands of these thugs like pearls cast before swine, and over the past ten years, books valued at more than 10,000 *yuan* have sunken into the eternal darkness of their possession. Several hundred volumes that Guo Feixiong[6] left with my law office met with a similar fate. The actual purpose of this "search" was to deprive my family of everything of value. This included a dozen or so antique Chinese coins, more than US$10,000 in cash, several notebook computers and another eight or nine desktop computers, and all of our savings deposit books and negotiable securities. All of this property remains in their hands to this day except for the bank books and a small portion of the securities, which I was able to demand back.

What I find most unforgivable during this time is the physical violence these thugs repeatedly inflicted on my wife, Geng He, and my daughter, Gege. They could impose whatever abuse they wanted on me, since I was the source of their wrath and unease, but what had Geng He or my daughter ever done? It was only because of their relationship to me that they were subjected to this despicable brutality. Those monsters injured one of Geng He's fingers so badly that it will never be straight again. My wife never told me about it, but I noticed her injuries and received the details from Gege, who herself was beaten on a regular basis because her temperament was similar to mine. At least six male and female agents harassed this child daily, even posting themselves on stools outside her classroom door and following her when she went to the bathroom. Likewise my son, Gao Tianyu, who was only three years old at the time, was trailed by four to six agents whenever he left our home. Geng He had eight to ten male and female agents clinging to her side whenever she went out, and black-coated agents conspicuously followed her to pick up our son at the nursery. After I was abducted, my mother-in-law rushed over from Urumqi, but she was barred from our home until granted official permission. She also was tailed by six agents. Geng He told me that one time they decided to have a meal at a small restaurant nearby, only to have the usual troop of agents insist on following them into the small eatery, filling it to the point of bursting. The proprietor asked Geng He to consider the restaurant's difficulties, as a result of which Geng He and her mother felt obliged to abandon their meal.

One Sunday after my return, outside the Xiaolin Restaurant near my home, the most vicious of the agents, whom I named "Sissy," because of his mannerisms, followed us so closely that he actually stepped on Geng He's heel.

---

6. TN: Born Young Maodong in 1966, Guo Feixiong is a human rights defender from Guangdong Province who has been repeatedly arrested and imprisoned.

Thoroughly fed up, Geng He asked Sissy to stop doing this, at which point Sissy threw a fit and launched himself at Geng He as if to strike her. The other agents immediately grabbed hold of me, while a bystander quickly stood in front of Geng He. This set Sissy into a raving fury. Protected by bystanders, we abandoned our outing and returned home.

After learning through a report by Hu Jia posted on the Internet that the authorities had backed down on forcing my entire family to leave Beijing, I left Beijing on my own to visit my sister in Shandong. Fatty Wang, Sun Di, and some others escorted me out of Beijing in two vehicles, one a minibus full of male and female agents in full battle array. Upon reaching Dongying, Fatty and Sun Di followed me into my sister's home, where my sister gripped my hand and wept. After my escorts withdrew downstairs, my sister told me that my brother-in-law had passed away about two weeks after my abduction. On the day of my abduction, those thugs had forced their way into my sister's home, covered her mouth, and pushed her onto the sofa, and had searched her home for more than two hours, although my sister had no idea what they were looking for. Officers from the Dongying Public Security Bureau (PSB) had then taken her to an unknown location for two days, during which time she was not even allowed to use the toilet without someone watching her, and when she slept at night, a police officer had sat at the head of her bed keeping an eye on her.

The first day she was held, the head of the Dongying PSB had asked her, "Why do you want to be with your brother?"

Answer: "You have your answer—he's my brother."

Q: "Your brother has committed a serious violation of state security, so why do you still want to be with him?"

A: "If an unarmed man can seriously threaten state security, all that proves is that your regime is made of plaster. As to why I want to be with him, my answer is that it is because he is my brother. You are afraid that he is a threat to state security, but I'm not afraid of him."

Q: "We're not wasting any more time with you."

A: "You are the ones who wanted to talk to me. I've never had the slightest interest in going to you."

After my sister recounted this conversation, we both laughed through our tears.

The director of the Dongying PSB is a villainous fellow who sometimes acts as if demon-possessed. Normally, the public security organs do not take the initiative to persecute or harass my family without special arrangements from higher-ups, but the Dongying PSB has been an exception. An informed source in the PSB told us that prior to August 15, 2006, the PSB head tried to engineer a traffic accident to kill me, saying, "It is easy to kill him—just another traffic accident. The upper-level leaders are a bunch of cowards." Around holidays or politically sensitive dates, the Dongying PSB invariably puts my sister under surveillance and orders her not to visit me, and she has to report it to them if she wants to leave Dongying. Around the time of my release in August 2014, the Dongying PSB repeatedly went to see my sister and warned her not to visit me. I reported the wicked conduct of the Dongying PSB to the head of the Ministry of Public Security's First Bureau when he came to see me before my release, and he said this had not been authorized by the higher levels and that he would make it stop.

During the several days I spent at my sister's home, surveillance agents from Beijing kept an eye on me as always. The third morning after I arrived in Dongying, I discovered a note slipped under my car's windshield wiper, like those ads for buying second-hand cars (the authorities naturally also discovered this note). The note expressed concern for me as well as a willingness to help me, especially financially, and told me a signal to use if I needed help. Events later bore out that a network had existed alongside me for a long time, and it made repeat appearances in April 2007 and September 2009, giving my family enormous spiritual comfort. Although we did not want to receive money in this fashion, the value of the offer was inestimable. This same network later became involved in the issue of Gege's schooling and eventually in helping my family leave China.

After my stay in Dongying, my sister and I went to northern Shaanxi under the "protection" of a large contingent of secret police, visiting another sister in Taiyuan, Shanxi Province, on the way. When we reached our home village in northern Shaanxi, my eldest brother choked back sobs and described the hellish experience he had been subjected to: "We were surrounded for months by people from the province [the Shaanxi PSB], Yulin and Jia County, who did whatever they wanted and cursed at whomever they wanted, and they took me off to the county seat several times and even detained my three sons. They were completely lawless! What law have we broken?" he said, weeping. After that, my brother invited the secret police who were with me to come into his cave dwelling for some mutton noodles, which all of them, including Sun Di, Fatty Wang, and Zhang Xue, praised so extravagantly.

Since I could not stay in Beijing for the time being without posing a threat to "state security," after my trip to northern Shaanxi, I had Geng He and the children come to my sister's home in Shandong for the Spring Festival, and Sun Di, Fatty Wang, Zhang Xue, and another dozen or so secret police stayed with us the whole time. After I took Geng He and the children back to Beijing, the state authorities made me quickly leave again. Because the previous abduction scandal had also involved my family in Xinjiang, with even my elderly father-in-law put under twenty-four-hour watch by two red-armband-wearing officers downstairs, I went back to Urumqi, where I listened to my family's tearful complaints and comforted them.

On the way to Xinjiang, one of the secret policemen repeatedly suggested that I stop off in Kashgar, "Because all of us want to see Kashgar, and the only way we will get there is with you." I really did not relish the prospect of visiting Kashgar with the Party's police clustered around me the whole time, especially after I had just shed my ropes, but it was impossible to dissuade them. I said that since it was not my idea to go to Kashgar, they would have to cover the costs, but that was nothing to them. There was nothing I could do but go along with them.

We were allowed to return to Beijing at the end of March. Our family continued to be subjected to tight surveillance, but the main source of conflict was the gradual exhaustion of my family's financial resources. The authorities suggested a solution that I was unwilling to accept: "Just ask us for money—the government doesn't lack it." They were always negotiating with me this way. What I wanted was to be allowed to find work on my own without the government's interference, but they could not agree to that, because during this time I found another note on my windshield like the one in Dongying from someone who was willing to hire me at a salary of 500,000 *yuan* per year. The note also said that if I needed money, I should lower the right rear window of my car about two inches. The authorities learned of this and would not allow me to accept work through such channels, so the only avenue left open was accepting work or money from them. The clear reality presented to me was that I could starve or accept their arrangements. The only way to shake them off was to expose them, which usually forced them to make a technical compromise for appearance's sake.

My attempt to expose them is the background to the letter I sent to Hu Jia on April 6, 2007. Of course I paid a considerable price for this. The dark forces abducted me that same night and took me to the police station. The next day I was handed over to Yu Hongyuan's most intrepid warriors, Sun Di and Zhang Xue. Late at night I was taken to a woodland area in the mountains of Miyun District. Along the way they played their usual mind games, the leading police vehicle changing several times, waiting for a period of mysterious silence each time. It was after midnight when we reached the destination. Yu Hongyuan came to see me that night, saying that he had been attending a meeting in Xi'an. "When we learned that Boss Gao was flipping out again [referring to my letter to Hu Jia], the big leader [Zhou Yongkang] got very impatient and ordered me to hurry back to Beijing to deal with it. There were not any plane tickets available, so I had to drive 13 hours to get here."

My stay in this mountain area was relatively tolerable, and after six days of tangling, both sides yielded ground. They kept nagging at me to write how good the government was to me, and how I had misunderstood the government's good intentions and that is why I had impulsively written that letter to Hu Jia. They said that if I wrote this, my detention would end, and they would let me go out and find work, as long as it was for a private enterprise within China that they had recommended. I knew that Geng He and my other family members must be extremely anxious, and I needed to make a living, so continuing to wrangle over details seemed pointless. I accepted their conditions, and my detention this time ended on the night of April 12.

I eventually found a job with a private company in Beijing, and three vehicles and 12 officers accompanied me to work every day. Secret police outside the first-floor lobby watched me go upstairs to work. My attempts to establish contact with the outside world were soon discovered, which indicated that at least one or two secret police were also posing as staff in the lobby outside my office. Even so, as long as I could go to work, there were ways to make contact with friends outside, because people took special pains to see me. For example, one time when I entered the elevator, two female petitioners were waiting inside and asked if there was anything they could do to help me. That was the background to my September 12, 2007, "Open Letter to the US Congress."[7]

I always suspected that the Chinese Communist Party (CCP) was behind the annual salary of 480,000 *yuan* that the company paid me. One time when the company's boss was chatting with me, he said something that made me even more suspicious: "It is no loss to me to have you here. No one dares to cause problems for us, and you can also help us deal with a lot of legal matters."

I was abducted again about two weeks after this conversation, so I had no opportunity to clarify the point with him. But I believe that without their constraints, I might well have earned one million per year. In 2003, a lawyer in Beiqu, Hebei Province, was willing to pay me 20,000 *yuan* to write a "representation agreement." Although I did not accept that work, it made me realize that I could provide these kinds of services to colleagues all over China. But the Communist authorities absolutely refused to let me maintain contact with individual lawyers or law firms. Their absurd explanation was, "As soon as you see an injustice, you'll do something impulsive."

---

7. TN: An English translation of this letter can be read at http://www.david-kilgour .com/2007/Sep_23_2007_03.htm (accessed March 15, 2016).

In any case, the "Open Letter to the US Congress" made my conflict with the CCP's dark forces public once more.

On the evening of September 21, 2007, Fatty Wang told me that Yu Hongyuan wanted to talk with me, but what ended up happening was that I was violently abducted and tortured again until October 12. I have been tortured three times since September 21, 2007 (not counting the time I spent in the iron chair at the Beijing Detention Center). The torture session from September 21 to October 12, 2007, was a prime example, so I will record the details here while only narrating relevant portions of the other two sessions.

This time I was abducted outside, which took a different pattern from indoor abductions. First someone pounced on me and struck me hard on the back of my neck, and while others overpowered me, someone used my belt to tie my arms behind my back, after which I was hooded and shoved into a waiting vehicle. What followed was identical in every abduction—men on either side of me pressed my head between my legs and did not allow me to move an inch, and the black hood over my head produced sauna conditions that made me feel I was on the verge of suffocation. This demobilization invariably made me go numb from the waist down, so that when we reached our destination my legs were completely useless. I would tumble to the ground after they pulled me out of the vehicle, and they would accuse me of being uncooperative, kicking and punching me as I lay helpless on the ground before lifting me up and dragging me to my place of detention.

I could write an entire book about this particular twenty-day torture session, but that is not my aim. The beginning of the first torture was in fact quite horrifying, and it was almost inconceivable that people calling themselves government employees were capable of such brutality against an ordinary and peaceful citizen. Furthermore, the torture team hired out an entire guesthouse and mobilized vehicles and manpower at an expense almost as remarkable as the level of violence, and all the while using taxpayer funds.

This torture chamber left me with indelible memories from which I was unable to shield myself for years afterward; they replayed before my eyes as soon as the lights went out, no matter where I went or when I went to bed. We always hear how strong and stalwart a hero is in the face of torture, how he refused to utter a sound, but in my judgment this is utterly bogus and impossible. I am sure that my screams were absolutely hair-raising and audible for five or six floors in either direction. I myself had never before heard the kind of noises I made, which emerged from me of their own volition and outside of my control. In the course of these three torture sessions, I learned that typically on the third day one hears a kind of moaning sound that undoubtedly is being uttered by oneself. I tried to control these moans during the second and third torture sessions, but it was a futile effort. I could sense them issuing from every pore in my body as if they were coming from someone else. Likewise, the pain seemed to exist in every part of your body, and you could not tell exactly which part hurt.

I do not know how long I was tortured on the night of September 21st, but it seemed to last all night and all the next day. At night they played mind games with unknown individuals shuttling back and forth, sometimes whispering to one another, sometimes greeting another, purposely creating a mysterious atmosphere. I was exhausted, but sitting was difficult, and I was not allowed to rest for a long time. I was given just one bowl of ice-cold corn mush to eat all day. That night I became so mentally exhausted that I could not sit up. Stripped naked, I was loaded onto a hard, backless stool by two men who then stood behind me, one of them gripping my hair and forcing my face toward the ceiling. Finally, they lifted me up again, and I began to feel removed from the whole process. I heard someone say, "Damn it, lower your head!" and one of the men pressed my head downward, bending me at the waist so my face was parallel with the floor. "Everything's ready, take him to the car," that voice said again. Two feet appeared in front of me, a black hood was pulled over my head, and I was led forward by the two men, still bent at the waist.

I heard someone say, "On the double! Don't let him stall." We began jogging, and I heard the rumbling of a fleet of vehicles as I was loaded into one of them. This was the least painful of all of my midnight transfers, because I became dazed and only sensed that we were on the road for a long time and that we passed through toll booths going onto and off of a highway. When I was unloaded from the vehicle, my numb legs prompted accusations of malingering, and I was kicked and punched while kneeling on the ground. Half a month later, my body was still so bruised that it looked like a coal bed.

Finally, two men dragged me through a doorway and into a room, and someone said, "Make him squat along the wall." By then I had gotten some feeling back in my legs, but they hurt so much that I could not squat, so the two men forced me down with my head touching the wall. After that I do not know for how long I was dragged around and forced to kneel. "Take the hood off!" Someone grabbed the hood, and I saw that two tables had been placed in front of me, and four men were seated behind the tables, staring at me without speaking. On the table was a cardboard box with three electric cattle prods inside; I knew they were about to "go to work."

One of the four was a handsome young man with elegant features and wearing delicate eyeglasses that made him look like a college student. The startling contrast between his appearance and his brutality astounded and distressed me. During this time, I often looked at him and thought how complex people are, allowing something so fine and something so evil to inhabit a single person without apparent conflict. One Sunday, it appeared that he was going out; he had changed into a black suit, his shoes highly polished and his hair varnished. Just before he left, he punched me in the eye and mouth until I bled, and it took a couple of weeks for my eyesight to return to normal. The next day when he saw me, he asked abruptly, "How did you hurt your eye?" When the same group of people tortured me again on Yu Hongyuan's orders from April 28 to May 1, 2010, he was not among them. I can only hope that he had mustered enough human awareness to give up this "work" and was not simply working at the scene of another torture.

Yu Hongyuan and the others had a preconceived objective for the torture session starting in September 2007, which was to force me into complete submission and make me part of their "interest community," and for more than 20 days, the points were all on their side.

I was never as heroic as people outside praised me for being, but neither was I afraid of my own shadow. In negotiating with the Party's dark forces all these years, I was always willing to compromise on technicalities, but on certain fine points I was immovable. As long as my physical shell could support my spirit, I would take an obstructive stance that the forces of evil could not budge. This was something I taught the authorities in countless dealings over the past ten years. At these technical junctures, the authorities would sometimes entertain the foolish misconception that I was weak, failing to see that beneath the softness I held fast to an indestructible bottom line.

These torture sessions over the years actually gave me a wonderful gift, which is my faith in God. I was not a believer previously. Although handling the case of Pastor Cai Zhuohua[8] had given me access to the Bible, it did not move me at the time. But once the Beijing authorities began persecuting me, I came to know God and became part of the brotherhood of Christians. I am especially grateful to brother Fan Yafeng[9] for helping me come to know and receive God. This greatly enhanced the quality of my life as well as my psychological strength in these difficult years. Furthermore, God began to give me visions, the first one coming after I was abducted in August 2006. In that vision, God reassured me that my detention would not be prolonged. Later, in visions that came to

---

8. TN: Gao Zhisheng was the defense counsel for Beijing house church pastor Cai Zhuohua, who on November 8, 2005, was sentenced to three years in jail on charges relating to "illegal business practices" and fined 150,000 *yuan* (18,500 USD) in connection with the possession of Bibles. His wife and brother-in-law were also jailed and fined.

9. TN: Fan Yafeng is a renowned Christian and Chinese legal scholar who specializes in Chinese constitutional law. He has been subjected to constant surveillance and house arrest.

me in 2012, I became convinced that the CCP would collapse in the year 2017, and that the government's leaders and my persecutors would be brought to justice for their crimes against humanity. This was a great and sustaining comfort in my time of suffering.

It is impossible for outsiders to conceive of the complexity of my encounters with the authorities over the past ten years. For example, I was forced to take countless "vacations," each of them following an instance of being secretly abducted and imprisoned. These trips were actually a means of rewarding the secret police who had looked after me all that time. It was an excuse to spend money, which they did with breathtaking gusto. We always stayed in the best hotels and ate the best food, and after being sated with tasty delicacies they would plunge into the nightlife with one person staying behind to watch me. I myself did not have a penny on me and could only spend their money.

For example, on June 28, 2009, my fourth younger brother, who was not easily moved to weeping, started sobbing when he saw me still dressed in the winter clothes I had been wearing when abducted months earlier. Unwilling to inflict this distress on my in-laws when we reached Urumqi, I was obliged to use my captors' money to buy summer clothes, and I never had a chance to pay them back. One time when I was unbearably hot and asked them to spend 80 *yuan* to buy me a T-shirt, they went ahead and bought enough shirts for all seven of them without thinking twice, and this was put to my account. I will not go into other instances, not wishing to harm individuals among them, but their wining and dining and squandering of public funds showed not the least awareness of their obligations to taxpayers.

To outsiders, many practices of the Party's forces of evil seemed no different from practices under a civilized system. For example, the technical function of the black hood in judicial culture is to protect the suspect, defendant, or criminal from public view for the sake of personal dignity and privacy and to meet the needs of preserving confidentiality in the criminal prosecution process. But among the CCP's political and legal cadres, its function is purely to torment people. Its form takes no consideration of your line of vision, having no eye holes and being very thick, and you have to wear it throughout the escorting process, when switching vehicles, at night, when using the restroom, and even in the hallways of Shaya Prison.

Then there are the shackles, which should be purely for restraint, but in China these are a tool of torture. I was apathetic to the humanitarian considerations of the Communist regime's use of shackles until I had to wear them and learned how unutterably painful they are. The shackles in Beijing are about one-third lighter than those in Xinjiang but are still impressively agonizing, and while one is under escort, that pain becomes unbearable. The thickness of the black hood and the heaviness of the shackles contrast with the flimsiness and lightness of humanity, human rights, and basic human feeling among the members of this regime.

In 2008, the authorities declared that they would change me at any cost. "We can't keep leaving things hanging," Yu Hongyuan said solemnly during one conversation. He had repeatedly said that if we cooperated, he would rise in the ranks, and we would have a lot of resources to work with. Several specific benefits were proposed: One was that they would arrange a job for my elder brother's son in the public security apparatus. Another was that they would give us a coal mine (at that time, my cousin was interested in this line of business). A third was that my children could attend Beijing's best schools, and that they would eventually have jobs arranged for them by the government, and my entire family's residency permits would immediately be transferred to Beijing. (Yu repeatedly said, "These are all minor matters for our apparatus.")

But the prerequisite was accepting, as Sun Di put it, "filling a new status on the form." When Sun said this he would often add, "If you are willing to become an official, your rank will be much higher than Yu and me." Each time I reminded him, "I don't think everyone in the Communist apparatus is shameless or dishonorable, but there is no way I can join them, at least as the person I am today."

Yu Hongyuan was keen to rack up official accomplishments, however, and he compelled me to make an all-or-nothing choice that was set before me in terms of my daughter's admission to high school. I finally backed down because my children had to receive a decent education; this was my ultimate bottom line. Yet, Zhou Yongkang and his hatchet men, Yu Hongyuan and Sun Di, thought this was how they could force me into submission. They once ridiculed me to my face: "Old Gao has his soft spots. Before it was the old lady [meaning my mother], and now it is his kids."

I repeatedly told them, "If you don't get in the way, I'm in a position to deal with the problem of my children's schooling, in spite of the difficulties." They said I was not allowed to solve these problems myself; the government would solve them along with all my other problems. In plain language, they were forcing me to join their gang and become part of their "interest community." They kept saying, "Old Gao, the government's paperwork is ready. If you say the word, your kids go to school near you and will also be provided with government jobs in the future."

On July 28, 2008, our entire family was escorted onto a train for Urumqi, and while my wife and children returned to Beijing at the end of August, Gege was not allowed to go to school. That crossed my bottom line, and I immediately took off for Beijing. (The Xinjiang police always said they would turn a blind eye to my leaving Xinjiang as long as I returned to Beijing and did not try to leave the country.)

Even so, what could I do? There were no independent judicial channels for appeal and redress as in a civilized society. I broke all prohibitions to seek a solution to my children's schooling issues as quickly as possible. In order to avoid major conflict, I contacted schools in other parts of China where we had family or connections, but then Sun Di telephoned and told me to come back and stop causing trouble, and that they would make sure the matter was dealt with.

Their dreams of studying elsewhere shattered, the children were even unhappier, and the dissatisfaction of the authorities also increased. But many kind eyes were watching with concern, and one night when I went to make a telephone call from a public phone booth (our telephones were all being tapped), a motorcycle suddenly pulled up in front of me, and I recognized a Beijing resident I had helped before. The people on the motorcycle quickly told me that they knew about Gege not being allowed to go to school, and said that everyone was thinking of a way to deal with the problem. In particular, many Falun Gong practitioners were prepared to sponsor Gege for study abroad, and they told us to be prepared to move as soon as they telephoned me. When the secret police noticed them and began to walk over, the motorcycle disappeared in a puff of smoke. Seeing this as the will of God, I put my faith in their help, and as part of a secret agreement, I started going on walks after dinner.

Only a few of the officers tailing me were dead set on their work; the rest just treated it as a job, and a handful actually did what they could to help our family. I knew their work patterns like the palm of my hand, and I had a pretty good feel for when I could go out and how much space I could utilize. One time when I went to the nursery to pick up Tianyu, one of the young secret policemen took advantage of the crowd of parents at the doorway to come over and tell me, "Old Gao, some of us respect you, and when we're on duty, we will keep our distance, even though that goes against orders." When Geng He and the children eventually fled China, it was because someone turned a blind eye. One of them said to my face, "We knew in advance that Big Sister and the kids were going to leave."

Eventually, news reached me that Gege could leave, and with help she threw off her shadows and secretly left Beijing for a specified location. But she ended up coming home the next night. It turned out that she would have been using the identity of the child of a Falun Gong practitioner as a cover, and this would have had disastrous consequences for that young girl and her family. These kind people who did not even know us had been willing to risk so much to help us, but we could not accept it, so that was the end of that attempt to leave China.

Finally, on January 7, 2009, we were told that Geng He and the children should board a train for Kunming on January 9th, and on the way someone would tell them what to do. This is how my wife and children finally fled China and became refugees. Under the arrangements, I was to leave home on the morning of January 9, 2009, and lure away the "eyes" downstairs. Before I left, we all embraced for a final farewell. I cannot bear to think of the pain Geng He must have felt at finally leaving. I could not see them off; they were to go to a big furniture store, evade their trackers, and then take the subway to the train station. I cannot imagine how Geng He dealt with all this when she was so distressed—and the worst was yet to come. She endured countless hardships from the time she crossed the Chinese border into Thailand to her early days in America, but she never told me about them. Our daughter secretly told only me a little of it, fearing that knowing all they had been through would affect my state of mind.

A Falun Gong practitioner came up with the plan for my family to leave China. Once they crossed the border and needed more extensive assistance, the China Aid Association took over, the head of that organization immediately flying to Thailand to help them. The Party's dark forces frequently told me about the hardships Geng He and the children experienced outside, intending to shake my resolve. At the end of 2010, Yu Hongyuan came to where the army was secretly imprisoning me and told me, "According to reliable military intelligence, Geng He and the kids are having a tough time outside. They are short on cash and they have had to move at least three times. We have people all around your wife. As long as the Communist Party exists, don't think you can get out alive! You are so damned despicable—if all you wanted was money, we have plenty of that." Another time Yu said, "Tell Geng He and the kids to go to the Chinese Embassy in the US. We will give them a large settlement, and I will personally go over to receive them." He said, "She is on her last legs—don't keep doing this to them, tell your wife and kids to come home."

After Geng He and the children left, I went home and was overcome with a feeling of desolation as soon as I opened the door. I did not eat anything that night, and I could not bear to go into the bedroom, spending the whole night on the sofa. In the days that followed, the officer responsible for tailing them, Fatty Wang, telephoned every day asking where they were and whether something had happened. I said we were busy preparing to renovate our apartment. When the questions became more pressing, I said, "I lied to you before. That day they dropped their shadows and went on a trip with an old army buddy of mine." Once they reached Thailand, I knew I would soon be arrested, so early the next morning I drove back to my hometown, where I continued to lie by saying that Geng He and the children were about to arrive in northern Shaanxi to spend the Lunar New Year with me. Finally, they stopped believing me.

3. The Abduction on February 3, 2009

Before February 3, 2009, after I returned to my native Jia County, the Beijing authorities handed my surveillance over to the local Public Security Bureau (PSB). The local surveillance process included taking photos of me at different times in convenient locations. According to a reliable source, they had to report my whereabouts to the Shaanxi Province PSB at specified times and provide photos taken of me that day. When they discovered after a few days that Geng He and the children had not come to Shaanxi as I had said, they probably reported it to Beijing. Around 9:00 p.m. on the night of February 3rd, police officers from the Yulin City and Jia County PSBs burst into my cave dwelling and asked where Geng He and the children were. I said this was our personal business, and what did it have to do with the authorities? Someone from the Jia County PSB shouted at my younger brother, "Zhengyi, where are your sister-in-law and her children?" My brother said they had gone to Xinjiang. Several policemen walked out, and a few minutes later burst back in and said I was being arrested on orders from Beijing.

They drove me to the county seat, where they took me to a cave guesthouse and settled into a game of mahjong while others watched TV. Eight or nine of them were smoking in a room of roughly 150 square feet, and after half an hour, there was so much smoke that you could barely distinguish their outlines. Their living habits were truly alarming, everyone smoking and hollering and drinking out of the same filthy cup. The noise did not affect my sleep, but I had to cover my head with my coat against the noxious smoky atmosphere.

I was shaken awake before dawn; Sun Di, Zhang Xue, and three secret police officers had rushed over from that best of all possible worlds, Beijing. They pushed me down on the sofa and patted me down from head to foot. Then they lifted me to my feet and forced me to stand barefoot on the ice-cold floor while they pretended to carefully search my shoes and socks. Then they pushed me down again and pulled a pair of thick insulated underwear over my head as a hood. Sun Di began talking: "Old Gao, you sent Geng He and the kids out of the country, which was a really stupid move, because you have forced us to reach out to you again. We will go back to Beijing and take our time solving this problem."

I later learned that while I was talking with Sun Di, another gang was at my eldest brother's house turning it inside out. My brothers had rushed to the county seat before dawn looking for me, finally locating the PSB at dawn but they were denied an opportunity to see me. They waited outside the main door, hoping to be able to see me when I was taken away and not realizing that the vehicles transporting me would have blackened windows covered with curtains. Someone from the Jia County PSB later said that when the car drove me away, my brothers were standing next to the entrance weeping in despair.

After the car drove for some time, we stopped at a service station for a short break and my hood was removed. Once we reached the Hebei border, Sun Di pulled the insulated underwear over my head again. Reaching the secret lockup in the mountain areas meant another three hours' drive after passing through Beijing, and after five or six hours of suffocation, my head was throbbing and my eyes felt ready to explode. I reminded myself, "Old Rabbit (I was born in the Year of the Rabbit, so my children gave me the nickname, 'Old Rabbit'), a difficult process has started, but since it is a process, that means it will end. You should thank God that He is giving you a hard process rather than a disastrous end."

Finally, we reached our destination, and as usual the lower half of my body was numb and incapacitated. This time, however, they did not beat me up for it. I was lifted and felt like I was being taken up three floors. Then I was carried into the room where I would spend the next three months. I was pushed down onto a stool, and after about twenty minutes of deathly stillness, I heard the door open and the sound of a table and chairs being moved around, after which point silence returned. "Take the hood off," I finally heard someone say.

My hood was pulled off, and I saw a new group led by a man I came to call, "the Immortal." The torture formula went something like this: Zhou Yongkang pointed them in the desired direction while the specifics were decided by Yu Hongyuan; the technical planning was carried out by Sun Di, Zhang Xue, and the Immortal; while the main hatchet man was Section Chief Wang. The men directing the torture on-site behind the scenes were the Immortal and Sun Di. Sun Di never put in an appearance at the actual torture, but the Immortal would appear at intervals to interrogate me when the goons needed to rest. That is what I learned after several rounds of this persecution. The Immortal was smiling with his legs crossed in one of the chairs, a file gripped under his arm as he stared at me. I swept my eyes over the room and found that it was around seventy-five square feet, with a thick carpet on the floor and a twin bed on either side of my chair. The eastern wall had a round window around two feet in diameter covered by cushion about four inches thick, clearly put there for the purpose of dealing with me.

The room was in the villa's attic and must have been used for storage or as a servant's quarters, because the peaked ceiling was very low at each extremity.

As I looked at the Immortal, he said, "Hero, great hero, when is Obama coming for you?" When I did not answer, he resumed, "Great hero, why aren't you saying anything? According to our intelligence, your American master is sure to come for you on his aircraft carrier." When he stopped speaking, the room returned to its deathly stillness. "Those Americans are damned strange—what is it they like so much about Chinese traitors? Old Gao, you have read some books; how many times in history have traitors met a good end? Is betraying your country addictive? Why else won't you wake up? I'm telling you, the Party and the government have never slacked off when it comes to defending the country's paramount interests. They're willing to use any means necessary against traitors. If you were an American, you'd have been executed many times over by now. The CIA secretly takes out people who endanger America's state security—you must have seen that in the movies and on TV, and those were produced by Americans themselves, so how can they be fake?" His tone was harsh and his expression severe.

Of course, admiring American values and respecting the American people has little to do with being a traitor to China, but I said nothing. After a while, a man I had nicknamed "Big Eyes" (they never gave their names or identities) came into the room. This was the second time I had seen him, and he was one of those people whose attractive exterior masks a rotten core. He spoke to me one-on-one, which according to the rules was not allowed and showed the degree to which Yu Hongyuan trusted him. The so-called conversation actually consisted of them talking and me being forced to listen.

Once Big Eyes arrived, the Immortal stood up and left. Big Eyes began exuberantly threatening me through my children, saying I should not think they had been fortunate to get out. "You've greatly underestimated the Communist Party. No matter where you run, we can find you. There is no place our fist cannot reach. When you're in China, you're in the palm of our hand, but in the US they're in the palm of our hand just the same. While your children were in China, we wouldn't threaten their lives, but now that they're in the US, we cannot rule out further considerations." He rambled on for more than an hour, his main point being that it would be a piece of cake for them to hurt my children, and that the only way to avert this disaster was to "become one of us, or one of our friends." When I did not respond, he asked, "Why won't you say anything? How can you consider yourself a human being if you do not even care about your children?"

Finally, I felt compelled to respond: "You don't need me to declare a stand on your carrying out the mighty feat of harming my children. According to you, it's a piece of cake, which means you don't need any technical support. You have spent half a day telling me that if my children being alive is a hindrance to your regime's happiness, you'll eliminate them and say it's because of their father. No matter how elegantly you package it, it is contemptible."

What I said seemed to surprise him, because he stared at me with an astonished look on his face for a full two minutes. In any event, my new round of secret incarceration had effectively begun.

In accordance with normal practice, two other people were locked up with me—sentries or secret police—in four-hour shifts. In normal life, a doorbell button is installed outside the door, but here it was inside, because after the guards came in, the door was bolted from the outside. If one of the guards wanted to use the bathroom or had some other urgent situation, he would have to press the button and have a guard outside come in and temporarily relieve him.

The main duty of the guards was to ensure that the "target" (I was not allowed to reveal my name) sat in the required posture and did not move or fall asleep. The idea was to make this incarceration seem endless and agonizing. The two of them would be standing in front of you, side-by-side, less than a yard away, and when the atmosphere was strained, they would crowd into your space.

It was slightly better if they were soldiers, but the secret police would sit one in front of you and the other behind, the one in front with his legs interlocking with the "target's" to make the situation as miserable and undignified as possible. With two sides breathing so close to each other, it was extremely unsanitary and neglected the most basic respect for the individual. The breath of the person in front of you rhythmically blew against your chin, while the breath of the person behind made the back of your head hot and humid. The worst was their constant smoking. In Beijing and Xinjiang, the guards were allowed to take a pack of cigarettes with them into the room, and they seemed to feel that they would be losing out if they did not smoke the entire pack during their shift. Some particularly nasty ones would make a point of blowing their cigarette smoke in your face, and if you flinched, they said you were breaking the rules and would cause you no endless trouble. The worst was their coughing and sneezing, which was sometimes so unrestrained that it sprayed on your face.

If you want to go to the bathroom, you had to report it to them, and with scowls on their faces they would take you to the bathroom sandwiched between them. While you were sitting on the toilet, they would stand next to you and light up a cigarette, the ashes falling on you as you defecated. Some particularly inhumane individuals refused to let you defecate on their watch. I once reported this to the relevant leading cadre, who responded, "The sentries have absolute power over how to manage things." But the natural movements and patterns of life could not be negotiated with the sentries, and under these circumstances, a person felt miserable and helpless.

Over the years I have been repeatedly detained in unofficial prisons in Beijing, Shanxi, Shaanxi, Xinjiang, and the People's Armed Police (PAP), and Beijing has to be ranked the worst in terms of inhumane treatment of prisoners. They say this kind of incarceration method has spread all over the country, but nowhere else can hold a candle to Beijing. The least vile lock-up conditions were in Yulin, Shaanxi Province, where at least the guards maintained a basic distance. The secret prisons of Xinjiang, Shanxi, and Shaanxi had bathrooms that they allowed you to use, but the nastiness of Beijing in this respect is hard to imagine. If there was a bathroom, they would not let you use it, but instead would give you a shabby old plastic bucket, which they would never let you wash.

My lockup this time had a bathroom I could use, but at least half of the policemen did not flush after using the toilet, and this became intolerable over the course of those five months. I have always set store by cleanliness, but they would not let you clean the bathroom, nor would they clean it themselves. The worst were those who did not flush after defecating, and only when the whole room reeked would they allow me to go in and do some cleaning.

This time in the secret prison, it was Zhang Xue who never flushed, and the other police officers curled their lips whenever this was mentioned. One of the policemen was a good man, and I could talk to him when he was on duty and even stand up and exercise. (After he allowed me to move around, other shifts did as well, with the exception of Zhang Xue, another surnamed Jia, and a big fellow who claimed to have stayed in my home after August 15, 2008.) While some of the secret police guarding me would spit or flick their cigarette ashes on the carpet, or blow their noses against the wall or wiped their snot on it, not to mention those who did not flush the toilet, this policeman was the only one I saw in more than ten years who did not smoke and was very tidy. He was also bothered by the behavior I described and would frown and shake his head whenever I mentioned it. One time when we were chatting he said, "You see things clearly; of those dozen guys, who do you think is the most likely to be promoted to a leadership position in the next year or two?" I said Zhang Xue, and he laughed and asked me why I thought so. I said, "If there was another person here who didn't bother to flush, I wouldn't be so sure. But he is by far the worst of this lot, and that seems to be the Party's criteria for promoting leading cadres."

He said I was being too extreme, so I made a bet with him, and ultimately I won. When Yu Hongyuan came to a secret prison in the desert of northern Shaanxi to talk to me a year later, he was accompanied by Zhang Xue as always. As soon as he came into my room, Yu Hongyuan said, "Zhang is a leader now, too. He's the deputy commander of the Fengtai Police Station. He was promoted half a year ago. I couldn't bear to lose him, so after he was promoted I had him transferred temporarily to keep working with me."

In fact, only a month after I made my bet with the kindhearted policeman, Zhang Xue was made head of my "location," as the secret prisons were called. For me, his promotion was not a bad thing, because it meant that he no longer came in to guard me, but it made him even more high-handed and bossy. He was just over thirty years old, so his arrogance occasioned much hand-wringing among his colleagues, some of whom were a good twenty years older. I twice witnessed him berating and humiliating colleagues, including once at this location, when a former naval officer more than ten years older than Zhang Xue furtively cracked opened the door to disperse the cigarette smoke a little. The fact was that even if the door was opened all the way, the only people outside were other secret police officers, but Zhang Xue's reprimand was distressing even to me as an onlooker.

The oppressiveness of my situation was exacerbated by my initially not being allowed to bathe in spite of repeated requests. On the eighteenth day, I received a visit from two upper-level "leading comrades" with impressive and westernized bearings who looked capable and open-minded. The younger of them said respectfully, "Old Gao, regarding your wish to bathe, the upper-level leaders take it very seriously, and they specially sent the two of us to give you a response. Your request is currently being channeled upward and is likely to bounce around for a while yet." It is hard to believe that a minor matter like turning on a water faucet could take eighteen days to deal with, and that two people would have to be sent from Beijing to give this ludicrous answer.

Another unforgettable hardship was the boiled cabbage I was fed for several months. That green cabbage was remarkable for its fibrous texture and the fact that it did not change color when cooked. It was served to me twice a day without fail, despite my complaints.

Another infamous hardship was having to sit nonstop eighteen hours a day for several months. I was awakened at 5:30 every morning and made to sit until 10:50 at night, when I was allowed to go to bed. Every day I looked forward to the 10:50 shift change, but sometimes the new guards would just sit down and launch into a video game, and if they did not order you to sleep, you could not move. Fortunately, most of the guards were reasonable, and as soon as they came in they would say, "Go to sleep, Old Gao, hurry up and sleep."

Eventually, they realized that sending me home debilitated from nonstop sitting would be bad for the Party's image, so they agreed to let me move around for fifteen minutes every morning and afternoon. Some would let me exercise even longer by keeping their heads lowered and not saying anything. This kind of environment made me truly recognize the value of exercise for physical health (I would not recommend the experience of secret imprisonment to my countrymen merely as a means of gaining this awareness, however).

Whenever I went to these unofficial jails, my greatest wish was to be transferred to a proper prison as soon as possible, and this in fact reflected the psychological acuity of the people who designed and implemented this kind of imprisonment. One "leader" (whom the guards privately referred to as "Beanpole") responded to my request for transfer to a proper prison by saying, "You want to go to prison? Dream on! As long as the Communist Party exists, you'll never enjoy the advantage of going to prison! Besides, if you went to prison, our people would just follow you there and punish you in the same way." One year later, in the army's secret prison, an official I nicknamed "the Ultimate" said something very similar to me, and Yu Hongyuan, who came to talk to me not long after Beanpole, also said, "Don't think you'll be lucky enough to be transferred to a prison. Prison is too good for you. Little by little, we'll make you think dying would be better than living!"

On the morning of April 28, 2009, Sun Di suddenly entered the room and asked, "Old Gao, have these months of hardship changed you at all? The departments relevant to your interests have talked about it quite a lot. A man has to know when he has lost, and if you go along with the arrangements I'm suggesting, everyone will be happy. After all, the police officers locked up with you also have families, and they haven't been able to go home for months. Doesn't that make you feel mean? If you keep wringing it out, you're only hurting yourself. So go along with my arrangements, will you?"

I replied, "Haven't you been the one responsible for the arrangements over these last few months? Why are you suddenly interested in my views?"

Sun Di stood up and tossed out, "Okay, move him." Then he walked out.

As soon as Sun left, Zhang Xue came in with a black hood, followed by three men. Zhang pulled the hood over my head and said, "Pull on a pillowcase, too." After a pillowcase was pulled on top of the hood, Zhang said, "Add another one." I felt something being pulled over my head again, and then I was carried out of the room where I had been imprisoned for several months.

All that was involved at this point was a change of location, however, and the person in charge of the new location was still Zhang Xue. Here the guards enjoyed more humane management like being allowed to order their own meals and being supplied with not only cigarettes but also various kinds of fruit, drinks and snacks, cotton swabs for their ears, and mosquito repellent. The villa was in a luxury villa compound that had basketball and tennis courts and other such facilities.

After a few days at the new location, Yu Hongyuan came over to "give me another opportunity," and he was very excited. There was nothing objectionable in Yu's outward appearance; he was more than six feet tall, with bright eyes and white teeth. But once he opened his mouth, you would never mistake him for anything but a mediocrity. I always defeated him in our matches of wits, not because I was so able, but because he was so incompetent. After each defeat he inevitably said something like, "It is too damn weird. If anyone says I'm less intelligent than you, you can beat me to death and I won't believe it. Thirty-two years old and I'm a damned department head—the only one that young in the whole country."

This time when he talked with me he was at his most complacent and stupid and was obviously very wound up, laughing as soon as he came in the door: "Last time I saw you I said that sending Geng He and the children overseas was a stupid move against the Party and the government. Yes, oppressive imprisonment is terrible and hard to take, but you created it yourself. Who told you to send your family overseas? You're given a way out and you're unwilling to take it. The Communist Party isn't like before; if you're part of their interest community, they'll give you a very good way out. We're willing to give you conditions that even those who have rendered extraordinary service to the Party wouldn't dare dream of. Put plainly, it's always a question of interests, and ultimately, of money. Even in the global sphere, the Communist Party doesn't have anything it cannot handle. How about America? Haven't we taken care of them, too? When Hillary came this time, what did she want? As soon as we meet they want human rights and discuss your problem, but they also want a billion. With a flick of the hand we give her 800 billion, and once that woman has money in her hands, there's no more mention of human rights or Gao Zhisheng!" (At this point, he became so agitated that he slapped his thigh, leaped to his feet, and began pacing back and forth in front of me while continuing to babble on.)

"We have all that money, and who made us so rich? Secretary of State Hillary Clinton said right out in public that differences of opinion will not affect relations between the US and China. They even told the Chinese side the result they are looking for—800 billion makes the human rights problem and the Gao Zhisheng problem go away. Give up, Old Gao—what good is that human rights bullshit? We know what the Americans want, and they know what we want, and you don't even enter into it. Even if America really cared about China's human rights, so what? If we stomp on you, what can they do about it?

"We're always willing to reach out to you, and you can always grip that hand. We're not worried about the cost. We have plenty of money, and it's worth our while to settle things with you. You just need to get your head around it. This year is the 60th Anniversary [of the founding of the PRC], a major occasion, and you'll have to leave Beijing. We have two possible destinations in mind for you. One is Chengdu, where we'll give you work and a reasonable income, but you have to live with our people in a place we rent for you, and you'll have to tell outsiders that you are free and that no one's controlling you. The other way is to go back to Urumqi, where you'd also have to live with our people, but you would have to handle the rent by yourself. We have to be around whenever you see anyone, even if it is your in-laws. And you will have to find work and tell others that you're free and that no one is controlling you, and the only person you can contact is Geng He. You don't have to answer me today, but don't drag it out too long."

I immediately told him I would go to Xinjiang. I knew that anything was better than being imprisoned, and at least it would give my family some peace of mind. But I raised two points: One was that I had to visit my in-laws once every week, and the police could not enter their home. Second, when I found a job, my shadows could not go to my workplace. Yu said there could be flexi-bility on the second point. For example, if I went to work upstairs, the shad-ows would wait for me downstairs, or if I worked downstairs, they could maintain a set distance. "But visiting your in-laws requires permission from the government, and government personnel have to accompany you the whole time. This is what the higher-ups say, and if the higher-ups won't back down, I cannot back down, either. But this is still an opportunity for you, and isn't it a lot better than staying locked up? Grab the opportunity while you can."

Because we could not reach agreement on the first issue, we were not able to come to terms at that time, but then on June 21st, Sun Di and Fatty Wang came again, and Sun said, "Good news! You're going back to Xinjiang tomor-row, just as you wanted."

I said, "These few years, cracking Hell's door open a little is considered good news." I had one more demand, which was that as soon as I got out I wanted to visit my mother's grave in northern Shaanxi. Sun said, "We'll come for you tomorrow if the higher-ups agree to that. If they don't agree, we won't be able to leave tomorrow."

Around five o'clock in the morning on the next day, June 28, 2009, two people came in with a black hood, so I knew that I would be leaving this place. They had also brought along clothes I had brought from home to change into, but I was discouraged to see that these nice clothes were now shabby and reeked of mildew. I had to remind myself, "Old Rabbit, don't be sad; you've had a tough time, but the damage is only on the outside."

4. The Abduction on September 25, 2009

During the two months I was in Xinjiang, the situation between me and the government developed into an imminent crisis because I refused to spread propaganda abroad that I was completely free, and also because my personal funds were frozen and I discovered that people were secretly following my family members. Another abduction was just a question of time, but I could not share this with my family.

After dinner on the evening of September 25, 2009, I decided to go to the nearby supermarket to purchase some extra goods in preparation for the October 1st National Day holiday, when I expected to have more time to read books. When I went downstairs, I felt there was something odd going on; the special agents who tailed me were always in plain clothes, but on that day they were wearing uniforms, and uniformed officers were posted about every fifty yards along the route they knew I always took when I went to the supermarket after dinner.

I never lingered at the supermarket, and that day I quickly purchased enough items so that I would not have to go again over the next ten days. Carrying my bags full of groceries, I proceeded to walk the 1,000 yards to my home. Just before I reached home, I decided to rest my aching arms and approached one of the iron benches in the square outside my building. Suddenly, the secret policemen following me all disappeared from my line of sight, and I heard the sound of hurried footsteps approaching me. Before I knew it, I was flanked by two husky Uyghurs, who grabbed my shoulders while another person grabbed me by my waist from behind, forcing me to a halt. I struggled against what felt like an attempt to throw me to the ground, but then a black hood was pulled over my head and a dirty hand placed over my mouth. I was forced to bend at the waist, my two bags falling from my hands to the ground. Bent at the waist, I was hustled forward and felt myself being pushed into a vehicle and handcuffed.

Once the vehicle started moving, someone behind me, perhaps the person who had failed to hurl me to the ground, began furiously punching the back of my head. He then started dragging me back into the row of seats with him, only to have me fall on top of him and pin him to his seat. I was tucked between the front and back rows—my feet in the air as I crushed his chest—until others finally pushed me the rest of the way into the back seat while he panted like an ox.

I do not know how long the car drove before it finally stopped. There was an argument outside as guards at the gate refused to allow our car to enter. Someone in the car said they had a "major criminal" who had to be taken to the building in the front. The guard said, "If we let you in, we're already giving you a lot of face." Finally, the driver was forced to park the car outside. I was carried out of the car and propelled forward with great effort until I sensed that we had passed through a door and that we were going up a flight of stairs. Once we reached a room on the third floor, they began ripping off my clothes, but they could not get my jacket off because of the handcuffs. After my shoes and socks were taken off, someone cursed in Uyghur and said that my shoes should be thrown away. My pants were pulled off and I was forced into a chair, and the room took on a deathly stillness as I sat there naked below the waist.

After things quieted down, I became aware of pain where I had been struck, and even more the intolerable pain of the handcuffs, which had tightened during the tussle in the car. I shouted, "The handcuffs are too tight, they're restricting my circulation, please loosen them!" Deadly stillness once again descended. Finally, the pain was so unbearable that I stood up. I heard someone approach from behind me and touch my hands before suddenly walking away. In less than half a minute, I heard someone enter the room and say something in Uyghur that I did not understand. The handcuffs were taken off and then the hood was removed.

I found myself in a room of about hundred square feet with two beds and curtains that covered the window. There were four Uyghurs standing around me. I lowered my head and rubbed my arms and only then understood why they had removed the handcuffs so quickly. My hands and my wrists had turned a purplish black, and the skin where my wrists had been cuffed was shredded, a mixture of water and blood oozing out. At this point, I realized that my pants were in front of my feet, so I withstood the pain and pulled them on. I wanted to search the room for my shoes, but two men stopped me and motioned for me to stay seated.

I recognized their basic techniques and knew that another round of secret imprisonment had begun.

The special difficulties after this kidnapping came one after the other, some of which I understood right away and others that I discovered only later. The first was when they told me to prepare to suffer. One of them "kindly" reminded me, "There is a good way to reduce your suffering: Consider yourself a beast, which means you won't suffer."

In this kind of situation, it was routine to have someone lift his hand to beat you and humiliate you, but there were other hardships as well. First came the two days when I had diarrhea and was given no toilet paper. This was not the first time I had endured such an experience, and in the past I had gotten around the problem by using my socks and then washing them. But this time, I did not even have shoes.

I reminded myself, "Old Rabbit, there is no need to feel anxious; the period when man had no toilet paper far exceeds the days when man had toilet paper. Furthermore, the structural conflict is to defecate, and having toilet paper or not having it is a secondary issue once the primary conflict is resolved."

I thought about setting my shame aside in front of the two beasts who stood beside me in the toilet, and simply taking off my trousers to wipe myself. Then one of the guards spoke up: "What do you normally use to wipe yourself?

"Toilet paper," I replied.

"You idiot, don't you think I know you usually use paper? I'm asking what you normally use in prison."

I replied, "I use my socks."

He turned and walked away as I waited hopefully, and sure enough, he returned and kicked my socks into the room. My problem was once again solved.

When it was finally time to sleep, I cleaned my face and teeth with my hands, as I had learned to do previously, and someone kicked a pair of slippers into my room, solving another problem.

That night, one of the guards secretly asked me why I had been arrested. I said it was because I had written articles criticizing totalitarianism and autocracy. He stared at me for a bit and then said, "They said you are a Falun Gong saboteur."

When he came back on the third day, he said, "We know you're a famous person. How did you get locked up here in Xinjiang?"

I laughed, but did not say anything because by this time, I had already been on a hunger strike for more than forty-eight hours, and I really did not feel like talking. However, I paid a price for going on a hunger strike this time. Beginning on the afternoon of that day, three people were transferred there from other parts of Xinjiang to torture and persecute me. They really made me suffer, and I was forced to give up my hunger strike.

This time the torture and monitoring had a big impact on me, because the people torturing me were so unusual. The authorities made a point of choosing three from different places, but the performance of two of them really exceeded expectations. One of the three, based on what I could see, was a good person.

On September 28th, they came to get me from the place I was imprisoned and took me to a big room and shut the door. As soon as I was inside, a short, dark, dwarf-like man, whom I will refer to as "Niu Er,"[10] turned and punched me hard in the chin. Then he grabbed me by the neck and forced me against the wall as he squeezed. I felt a heavy pressure in my chest and brain, and my eyes swelled as if they were about to explode. My vision began to blur, and I

---

10. TN: Niu Er is a villainous bully in the Chinese classic *The Water Margin*.

felt that my legs could no longer support the weight of my body. Sure enough, as soon as he let go of me, I slid to the ground.

"You beast," he said finally, "playing dumb with me is asking for death." He was expert at beating people. He kicked my left ankle twice, and all the pain I had been feeling moments earlier suddenly migrated to my ankle.

"Beast, are you going to stand up or not?" he demanded. "Do you know who Grandfather is?"

At this point, I was unable to even think, and there was no way I could stand up.

"Beast, I'm talking to you. Do you know who Grandfather is?"

He kicked my left ankle again.

"A beast's grandfather is also an old beast from head to toe," I replied.

Cursing him back ignited a new round of unimaginable persecution, but it was not as if you could lessen your ongoing torment by expressing one less curse. He looked like a madman as he practically leaped and kicked me all over my legs, cursing me and shouting, "Beast, I'm warning you, Grandfather is a counterterrorist!" as he continued his attack.

When he finally got tired of kicking me, he sat down on the sofa, and it was only then that I noticed that the two others who had entered the room with him were gone. But they soon returned, and one of them joined Niu Er in verbally abusing me. This became an ongoing pattern over my two days of torture— Niu Er would inflict his violence and the two others would go out, then they would come back in and one of them would chime in with verbal abuse. But the other never joined in the maltreatment, just looking on with sympathetic eyes. I later discussed this puzzling difference with some of my guards, and their analysis was convincing: The difference was in the three coming from different places and not being subordinate to each other, which meant that they were not in competition and had no need to perform for their leader. Their assignment was to beat people, and in particular to beat people like me, so some would choose to let me off if at all possible, since no one would know the difference.

Niu Er was clearly the meanest of the three, but at least electric shock was not used, unlike Beijing, where shock treatment was the main form of torture right from the first day. When Niu Er arrived on the second day, he ordered me to kneel down on the floor in front of him. "Beast, if you don't bow down in front of me, do you know that I'll kill you?" he growled at me, poking his finger at my head.

Saying he would kill me was layman's talk in a situation in which death was the preferable option. When I failed to respond appropriately, he immediately turned violent, kicking my ankles until my legs trembled and threatened to collapse. This was followed by punches to my head as he continued to demand that I kneel.

Still unable to move me, he pulled out his pistol and aimed it at my forehead. I smiled with effort as he opened his mouth and gasped for breath. I said, "Be strong and let me hear the sound of your gun. Otherwise, you are ultimately nothing but a dwarf."

He dashed into the bedroom and I expected the worst, but he just came back with a pillowcase wrapped around his pistol and began striking my head with it while cursing me nonstop. "Those dicks above me are all damn cowards, but the minute someone dares to give me the order, I'll immediately give this beast a peanut [meaning a bullet]. Does this beast know what counterterrorism is? It means catching Fur Hats [referring to Uyghurs, who wear hats made of animal fur] and killing them. Those dogs higher-up don't dare give the order, but if I have to serve you, I will make sure you never forget me for the rest of your life. I've hated traitors and collaborationists my whole life. I'd choke one of those sons of bitches on sight, along with his mother, wife and kid."

After tormenting me for close to an hour, he sat back down on the sofa and began to curse at me, at which point the other two came back in. It was all very repetitive from then on.

Niu Er gave me his longest lecture during the first break in this second day of torture. Sitting down, he grabbed a pear from the tea table, rubbed it with his hands a few times, and then began eating it. "Beast, are you able to talk? Eh, beast?" he asked me a few times as he reduced the pear to its core and then mashed it in my face.

"Beast, do you know who the Chinese people detest the most? Traitors, people who have betrayed China. Do you realize how seriously your writings have damaged the image of the Party and the state?"

"Let me remind you," I said, "that it is actually the crimes that I've written about that have ruined your image."

"You damned idiot. Aren't you a Chinese? Didn't you grow up in China? You can't wash your dirty linen in public. If your mother sold her body as a whore, would you go around knocking on every door telling everyone? And if you did, would your family call you a hero? You're just an opportunist looking abroad. Doesn't America also have its scandals? Look at those jails in Iraq!" The more he spoke, the angrier he got.

"That's right, there are scandals everywhere," I said. "The essential difference is that America's media and government will, at the first opportunity, make its own scandals known to the world. But how does your government deal with scandals? Kidnappings, electric shock torture, detentions, and creating even bigger scandals to cover up scandals. What you've been doing to me the past two days is already a scandal, and you've done it to cover up other scandals. Maybe you don't see it this way, but isn't that the truth?"

He began to curse me again, using the foulest language. "If a child is disobedient and a parent spanks him, isn't that for everyone's good? Do you know what's been going on outside these past few years? There was a financial crisis, did you know that? The entire world was in recession. Even the Americans fell flat on their faces. It was only China that had no problem. When Americans saw our Chairman Hu, they could only wag their tails. Now the Americans are trying to learn from us, and so is the rest of the world. In ten years the damned Americans won't even be worth our attention. Once China becomes the No. 1 country in the world, we'll deal with garbage like you any way that we like."

I leaned against the base of the wall, half laying down as I listened in silence. No matter what, this was more civilized than being beaten up.

Noticing my silence, he raised his chin and said, "Beast, do you think I'm right? Say something, this is your opportunity."

I remained silent, understanding that anything I said could lead to persecution.

"Beast, answer me! Is what I just said correct or not?"

He kept staring at me, so I said, "I'm a layman regarding the financial crisis, but I can affirm that it's just a technical issue in the development of a free economy. The study of the Chinese economic phenomenon can only be the technical aspects, and there absolutely will be no structural change of the free economic system. Avoiding criticism is the common failing of all totalitarian regimes and the source of their destruction. No political system is perfect; perfection belongs to God. It is exactly this imperfection that is the driving force for human beings and social movements to keep working for goodness and perfection and to grow. Had God given humanity perfection right from the beginning, our lives would have had only one direction, and in the end we would turn into pigs. As you always insist that you're perfect and strive for glory, you can only move toward your destruction. It's the same with all the world's Communist totalitarian governments. You've all lost the chance to examine yourself in the mirror and learn from the experience."

As I spoke, he lost all control and leapt up and began to curse me, stuffing the core of his unfinished pear into my mouth. He said my brain had turned into dog shit and that his attempts to reason with me had been a waste of time. With that, he began another round of persecution, and when that finally wore him out, he began to lecture me again, this time about how foreigners were swarming to China to learn from China's experience. I simply could not believe that the outside world, especially Americans, would suddenly fall uncontrollably in love with a people who are totally corrupt and degenerate, and that they would walk in the footsteps of this suffering people and turn the unnatural deaths of tens of millions of Chinese into a glorious thing. Although Niu Er had worked with his mouth and fists for two days, in the end he still achieved nothing except the physical bruising that plagued me for the next month.

I returned to my imprisonment with no end in sight. It included some unforgettable incidents. The Uyghurs were more careless, for example in not having monitoring devices in my prison cell. This was the main exception in the years that I was detained. This exception provided me with a new angle for understanding the Communist Party's secret police. The vast majority of them are average people just like us. They are kind, decent, and compassionate people who are concerned about the problems of today and who hate injustice. In the other places where I was imprisoned, monitoring and listening devices were all over the place. Because of this the secret police never dared to speak to me, much less express any good will toward me. In the time I spent locked up under the Xinjiang Public Security Bureau (PSB), I experienced the most caring that I had ever been shown, and the highest frequency of face-to-face personal exchanges with the secret police.

I previously always had the impression that China's secret police were cruel and callous, ignorant, and lacking in any regard for others. But this period of imprisonment without video monitoring and listening devices proved that they also had their lucidity, personality, and human touch. The provision of slippers, essential in winter, and the return of my socks were two acts of humanitarianism that satisfied basic needs of life. On the fifth day, Mr. Cao from Kirghiz Prefecture bought two rolls of toilet paper and quietly put them in my room, and this set a precedent that others followed. Within a few days, someone had bought a toothbrush and toothpaste for me, and someone else secretly bought me a face towel. Xiao Yan from Yili bought me five mooncakes and several pounds of pears for the Mid-Autumn Festival. (Two days later he disappeared, and I never saw him again.) Uyghur police officers on several occasions bought snacks and left them on my bed, motioning with their eyes for me to eat them. Eventually, I found myself no longer lacking daily necessities.

They would often share their difficulties with me, telling me about sick children, family problems, their difficulty of living apart from their families, injustices in society, unfair things that happened in their units, and leaders of units who were overbearing. One Uyghur police officer complained to me about the Communist Party's policy on religion and gave me a more realistic and concrete understanding of the issue. He told me that as soon as a child is born, he or she enters this world through Muslim etiquette and rites and is always a Muslim before all else. He told me that not allowing Muslims to practice their faith was absolutely unrealistic, and that regardless of your vows and pledges as a

Communist Party cadre, as soon as you left work, you returned to the Muslim world and a Muslim home with all its attendant rites and customs. He added, "When one retires, so does the Party identity." He said that the Party's policy against religion forced Muslims who became Party cadres to live a lie, because Muslim society requires customs to be observed in order to be buried properly after one dies. Like me, he did not understand the policy and was disgusted by it. He said that the identity of a Party member and a Muslim could absolutely go hand-in-hand. "The whole world is like this," he said. "Why do they have to create so many problems for people? It's completely unnecessary."

Another decent police officer would come to my cell to comfort me after I was tortured or abused and would denounce the savagery. He would say, "Never judge them by what they say to others; they do things that an animal would not do."

After I was locked up for close to a month, these guards were all suddenly transferred, but I will never forget them.

They were replaced by PSB agents from Urumqi and Domestic Secretary (DomSec) agents from Dongcheng District of Beijing, who greatly increased my suffering, not out of malice, but because of their uncivilized habits, especially their nonstop smoking.

Two of them liked to crack melon seeds with their teeth throughout the night, and they tossed the shells all over the table and rug. Some played computer games or mahjong all night. But one thing that was better in Xinjiang than in Beijing was that when they entered the room, they would do their own thing and leave me alone; as long as you did not walk outside, there would be no problem. When you were sleeping, they would allow you to cover your face with a scarf to avoid the cigarette smoke. In Beijing, this was not allowed. The first thing I did every morning when I woke up was to thoroughly sweep the room. I would sweep it during the day as well. Bad breath and smelly feet dominated the room, and although these were small things, they were all part of the inescapable misery of that time. Another unforgettable privation was my lack of garments with additional lining, since I had been abducted in September, when the weather was still warm. My only defense against the cold was to wrap myself up in my quilt.

During several conversations I had during my secret detention, I could tell that the Communist authorities were conflicted and confused about me. During one particular conversation, they used killing me as a threat. When they spoke to me, they never identified themselves or told me their names. One day, two of them came to see me, and without even sitting down, they began to ask me questions.

"Old Gao, how are you?" one asked me.

"You have all the answers," I said, "so there is no need to ask."

"Why don't you tell us your thoughts on the government," the leader asked me.

"I don't feel there is a government," I said. "There are only the developers and managers of Hell. Acknowledging and respecting laws and regulations are the most basic features of all governments. The law is the guarantee and foundation for a state to exercise control, and it is the law that distinguishes a government from a gang. You both know what you have done to me."

"What have we done to you?" he asked. "We haven't treated you like a criminal."

"Don't tell me that you don't know about the savage treatment I've been given. What do you call my imprisonment? The only way for a government to deprive a citizen of his or her freedom is through legal procedures. There are no exceptions."

He said, "I've heard that someone beat you, but it wasn't us that did that. It was probably an outsider who was responsible. We don't allow the use of torture; it is strictly prohibited."

(These were almost the exact words spoken by DomSec head Ren Xiaolin, while in reality, it was Ren who had ordered me beaten.)

"I'm finished talking, I don't really feel like bullshitting with you. Old Gao, do you realize the difficult situation that you're in right now? You're as good as dead. We are just monitoring the reaction from outside of China. As far as the Chinese government is concerned, your death is no longer a question of if; when and how we exterminate you is up to you. You know the current situation in Xinjiang. Every day, a Han Chinese disappears in Urumqi. If others can disappear, so can you. Even your family thinks you were murdered by Uyghurs. Your father- and mother-in-law have been putting up missing person notices all over the city. This helps us by showing the outside world that even your family doesn't think you are in our hands."

He added, "Actually, killing you is no big deal. If you die, the outside world will have to accept this reality. They will complain for a while and then they won't say anything anymore. The Party has executed far more formidable people than you without any repercussions. Those useless people at the top are cowards. If they let us lower levels handle this, there wouldn't be so much trouble."

A few days later, DomSec head Ren Xiaolin came to chat with me, and the content was almost the same. He came back again with several others on November 27, 2009, saying Beijing had decided to send me back to my old home in northern Shaanxi Province. However, someone secretly told me, "Ren is lying to you, you're only being transferred there for detention."

That evening, the number of people guarding me tripled. Since I was wearing summer clothes, I asked if I could get some warmer clothing from my family, but I was told, "The government doesn't acknowledge that you are in our hands. Your family thinks you are dead, and the outside world has accepted this. Just put up with the situation. You are already lucky to be alive, so why are you asking for so much? We're just waiting for the higher-ups to give the word to kill you."

The next morning around five o'clock, a large group of people arrived for what they called a "VIP tour with specifications not below premier." An Air Force deputy brigade commander surnamed Cui handed me a short overcoat when he entered my cell. "I just don't believe that giving you an overcoat will cause a major upheaval," he said with a laugh. Among the people who looked after me this time, he was something like a gentleman, polite and tolerant, and he did not smoke or play video games. The coat he gave me spared me a great deal of misery, and I would like to express my gratitude to him here.

Ren Xiaolin and the others just watched, and then all of us went downstairs, for once without a hood on my head.

It was quite an impressive entourage, with three officers from Beijing, two from Shaanxi, and two from the Xinjiang Public Security Bureau and the Urumqi Municipal PSB, respectively. The plane took off at around seven o'clock that evening and took me to an indeterminate place with a prison. And so my days of clandestine detention in Xinjiang came to an end.

I spent exactly five months in Xinjiang, of which half of that time was under house arrest, while the other half was in secret detention. The experience made me wonder if I was actually alive and in this world, and it was devastatingly painful for my in-laws. Apparently, Gao Zhisheng had been kidnapped and murdered by Uyghurs, but the corpse had not yet been discovered. Although the secret policemen responsible for monitoring me in Beijing had witnessed the abduction with their own eyes, policemen accompanied my father-in-law as he searched for me and posted missing person flyers all over the city and visited mortuaries to identify corpses. Their enthusiasm completely destroyed my family's last shreds of hope, because my relatives knew all of them and that they had been with me twenty-four hours a day, and now even these policemen were looking everywhere for me.

Communist special agents were always following my father-in-law and knew exactly where he was at all times. Once, after reading a notice asking for someone to claim a corpse, he went to a hospital morgue to examine a body. The facial features had been destroyed, but the height and other characteristics closely resembled mine. Unable to reach a definite conclusion, my father-in-law phoned other family members to come and try to identify the body. While he was waiting at the morgue, the authorities put on a grand performance for him—a group of immaculately dressed police officers arriving and informing the people at the morgue that they were "carrying out official business." "They looked very professional and formal, each one equipped with white gloves, surgical masks, a camera and video camera," my father-in-law recalled. They were examining the same body that my father-in-law had just looked at.

After examining the body very carefully for half an hour and taking samples, the policemen stepped out of the morgue for a smoke. Two of the policemen standing near my father-in-law started a conversation. Taking a puff on his cigarette, one said, "We can be certain it's not Gao Zhisheng."

The other one said, "Where did he go off to, making us run around to morgues every day?"

When my father-in-law heard these two "inadvertent" remarks, it was like a booming thunderclap in his ears, because the family was still clinging to the hope that the police had kidnapped me, but it was clear that the police were now searching for my corpse. My father-in-law said that he began to shake uncontrollably from head to toe and propped himself against the wall, forgetting where he was or why he had come there.

Two months later, he no longer had any illusions about my survival, and he began tearfully putting my "remaining possessions" into order. He told his daughters, "I'm afraid the only things Gao Zhisheng has left to us are a pair of socks and a pen. I'll wrap them up for Gege and Tianyu as the only things their father left behind in this mortal world. I'll tell them their father was a good dad."

Writing this, I had to stand up several times and take a break because of my tears. I owe my family so much love, but I have been unable to completely give myself to them. Although I have suffered immensely, their suffering has been far greater than mine.

My father-in-law told me that one morning in early 2010, just before he woke up, he had a dream in which two strange men walked into his bedroom, stood at the foot of the bed, and told him, "Gao Zhisheng is not dead. He is still alive and being detained in Shaanxi, so don't worry about him." He said he woke up before he could ask for more details, but after this dream, hope began to revive within him. "It now appears that this dream was correct," he told me when we finally met again.

After flying for several hours, our group arrived in Shaanxi's Xianyang Airport. I felt I was being constantly stared at on the plane and when we entered the airport because of my appearance. At the time of my abduction, I was overdue for a haircut and had not even bathed in the two months since then. One of my minders had secretly let me shower once on his watch, but the water coming out of the faucet was a saucy red the entire time, so it did not do much good. I had requested a haircut several times, but each time the response was,

"The Xinjiang Public Security Bureau doesn't have the authority to permit you to get a haircut. We have made a request, but there still has been no response." Finally, the officer in charge (a very decent man who had once been a teacher) came up with the idea of giving me scissors so I could cut my own hair. Worried that I would only get that one chance, I cut my hair as short as possible. As I was a layman feeling my way without a mirror, the result was too horrible to look at. It did not matter in the secret prison cell, but it definitely made me stand out in public.

I was taken from the airport to a guesthouse, where the Urumqi police turned me over to Commander Han of the Yulin PAP, accompanied by an officer from Yulin DomSec. I was then transported back to the airport for the flight to Yulin. As it happened, however, a dense fog resulted in all flights being canceled. The airlines offered food and lodging, but because of my special status, I was detained in a guesthouse with a group of people specially transferred from Xi'an. The watchers that night were especially considerate and maintained a quiet atmosphere that allowed me a peaceful night's sleep. Early the next morning, we all flew to Yulin City, where my initial impression was very favorable. As soon as we landed, Shaanxi DomSec provided me a down-filled quilt.

The person in charge of Shaanxi DomSec was an "old acquaintance" of mine who had left an exceedingly odious impression on me in April 2006, when he led a group of hooligans to my eldest brother's home in northern Shaanxi Province. They had turned the house upside down and created a completely unnecessary disturbance, just ten days after the birth of my brother's grandson. They had damaged my car and urinated outside the front door of our cave home, and had aimed their flashlights into the women's bedroom in the middle of the night. This time the situation was much different. When they put the black hood over my head after leaving the airport, they politely explained to me, "We have to do this, please cooperate." And while transporting me, they did not force my head between my knees as they did in Beijing and Xinjiang.

In my cell I found an autumn outfit, insulated underclothes, two cotton outer garments, toilet paper, and a complete set of toiletries for washing my face and brushing my teeth. The cell was quite small, however, only around seventy-five square feet, the two beds taking up forty square feet. The only space where I could exercise was in the thirty-odd square feet between the beds. The cell was fitted out with two very sophisticated video cameras through which my every movement was monitored in a room next door, as well as in Beijing.

Inside the prison cell, one soldier and one police officer were responsible for persecuting me, while another guard on duty at the door prevented anyone from entering and another sentry ensured that the guards did not bring mobile phones or other contraband into the cell. Adding in the soldiers who were on duty around the clock and two others who did the cooking, there were more than twenty-five people assigned to me throughout the day, not counting the monitoring team in Beijing.

Having said that, this was my only "civilized" spell of detention. First of all, the guards did not use the toilet in my cell or smoke, which was a rare and precious thing. They also never spoke, read books, or played with their mobile phones, and they were far more polite than the soldiers and policemen in Beijing. The food was also the best in my experience of being a prisoner, with plenty to eat and meat at every noon meal. I was also given light reading materials, which was unprecedented, although some were books that only an idiot would want read, such as a compilation of documents from the 17th Party Congress. For someone who had gone for years without contact with the written word, it was really meaningful to familiarize myself with some long-forgotten texts. And after two weeks in Yulin, I had my first shower in three months. From then on I was allowed to bathe once every two weeks.

My intuition suggested that I was being held in Hengshan County, which is surrounded by desert on all sides, because when the sentries entered the room every day, they tracked in ashen-colored sand. And it must have been very cold outside, because the soldier standing at the door wore a heavy army overcoat, fur hat, and knee pads. I was saddened at the thought of how much suffering ordinary people have to endure to prop up an evil regime.

At every new phase in my prison life, I always channeled my days into a fixed pattern of thinking, activity, and rest. Although there was no way for me to know what time it was, I was never off by more than five minutes. Wherever I was held, the guards were always astounded by the accuracy of my patterns.

The Spring Festival of 2010 soon arrived, and with it a depressing if trivial experience. We ate quite late that morning, and I was elated to hear the soldier say they were wrapping dumplings. But when it came time to eat, I was brought three cold steamed buns. Since we were all separated from our families at this important festival, I kept silent rather than ruin the mood for the others, and I ate the cold buns while watching the movie *Genghis Khan*. Afterward someone told me, "The provincial authorities didn't dare decide whether to give you dumplings on New Year's Day, and then Beijing made a special call, so there was nothing we could do."

Not long after that, around March 24, someone from the Yulin PSB told me, "Your eldest brother keeps trying to go to Beijing to find out if you are dead or alive. The higher-ups keep telling us to arrest him, but we don't want all that trouble. Write a note to your brother and tell him you are alive and in the hands of the government, but don't give him any details, and we will get the letter to him."

I immediately agreed and gave a letter to the guards. My hope was that my family would be spared the lingering uncertainty of whether I was alive or not, and would not continue to be tormented by the fake "searches" and "autopsies" of the Xinjiang police.

On March 26, I was informed that someone from Beijing wanted to talk with me. Soon after he left, Yu Hongyuan strode into my cell and told the two sentries to leave.

"How are you, Old Gao?" he asked while sitting down.

"I am alive and happy," I replied.

"Well, I have to tell you your happiness will last only a few days," he said. "We won't drag this out indefinitely. We just sentenced Liu Xiaobo to eleven years in prison, and he's been sent to Dalian. A high-level meeting to resolve your issue was just concluded, and I'm here with eleven comrades to deal with you over the next few days. Some people abroad are kicking up a fuss about giving you the Nobel Peace Prize. Don't they know what time it is or what the present-day Communist Party is? Look at what the Communist Party was in the past, and they still didn't give the Nobel Peace Prize to a Chinese, so will they dare to do it now?"

I just quietly stared at him.

"Doesn't what I say make sense?" he demanded, staring at me.

I replied, "The two of us have been having these face-to-face chats for years now, so if you are asking me, I might as well say a few words. Let's start off with Liu Xiaobo. What did he do to be sentenced to eleven years in jail? All he did was say that China should implement democracy and a constitutional government. Your sentencing has made Liu Xiaobo into a powerful person. He didn't start out as an activist; for a whole year he barely left his apartment. Your current thinking is going to result in two Chinese citizens winning the Nobel Peace Prize in the next six years, first Liu Xiaobo and then me. The Party seems impervious to reason. Why would a regime that is armed to the teeth react so strongly to an article by Liu Xiaobo? What is so frightening about him? As for my situation, I don't really think that Hu Jintao wants to reignite my issue and increase my punishment. The most he can do is jail me under my original sentence. You have come here to bullshit with me about that high-level and wide-ranging meeting, but you still haven't said how you're going to deal with me. You should be more realistic about resolving my problem."

He thought for a bit, lit a cigarette, and stared at the ground for three or four minutes. The room was extraordinarily quiet. He took a puff of his cigarette and then put it out with his fingers and said, "You say the Nobel committee will give the Peace Prize to two Chinese within six years, but this is ridiculous. Even if Liu Xiaobo is able to win the award, or even Hu Jia, they haven't had any real successes, and as long as you don't get the Nobel Peace Prize, that will be fine. We'll do whatever is necessary to make sure that won't happen.

"You've already given us enough trouble. On the Cai Zhuohua case, someone once warned me, 'Watch out for Gao Zhisheng and that circle of people working with him,' and damned if I didn't meet the devil himself. It is unfortunate for you that your circle stuck together, but it was also definitely not good for the government. I hear that Xiao Tong [referring to Tong Zhonghua, who interrogated me in the period after August 15, 2006] also told you we were not afraid of you and Guo Feixiong, but we were afraid that you and Fan Youfeng would team up. People within the system all say Fan Youfeng is a master schemer. And after just a few years the three of you joined together.

"As for Liu Xiaobo being a threat to us, aren't we clearer about that than you? Liu's article posed a threat to the state. If we hadn't crushed him, he may well have overthrown us. As for how exactly we'll deal with you, don't put too much hope in your luck."

When he finished speaking, I picked up the conversation: "Old Yu, the notion that one piece of writing could overthrow your government suggests that the survival of your regime depends entirely on chance. How much luck will be needed to turn you into flying ashes and smoke? Your logic has really boosted my confidence that every second and minute offers the possibility of overturning your regime."

Having gotten nowhere, Yu stood up and left the room. But when it came time for my noon meal, several soldiers carried in a dining table and three chairs, piling the table high with various dishes, dumplings, and red wine. After the soldiers left, Yu returned with a big smile on his face, looking like a completely different person. Behind him was his favorite lackey, the burly Zhang Xue.

As soon as he entered the room, Yu said, "Old Gao, I hear they didn't give you any dumplings at the New Year. What nonsense. I was really upset to hear it, so I have arranged this lunch to especially include some dumplings."

I sat down and ate, but it was clear that Yu's focus was not on this meal. After the failure of that morning's discussion, he had not come back for a casual chat.

After a few bites, Yu began to speak again.

"Old Gao, our discussion this morning didn't reach any conclusion. You can't stay here forever. What's your plan?"

"First, not reaching a conclusion is in itself is a conclusion. Second, I never expected I would stay here forever. And third, I never thought I needed to discuss my plans with you."

"To make a long story short, Old Gao, I have decided to take you back to Beijing with me. Leave everything to me. If you need money, I will give it to you. 'If you want a job, I will give you one. The job and pay are all up to you, no conditions. I will give you your freedom when we get back to Beijing. What do you think?" he said, looking at me as he spoke.

"As far as I'm concerned, setting no conditions is a condition. If I let you handle this, the money and a job are all your conditions. You don't seem to have heard what I just said about not needing to discuss my situation with you. In any case, your coming here is positive, as the dumplings I am now chewing would suggest. After releasing me in Beijing, you will feel like you lost and then you will continue to control me. The Communist Party itself is my prison. As long as it exists, my prison exists. But I don't want to digress too far," I said, continuing to eat.

"If you go back and don't rely on the government, you will just end up back with your old circle of friends, and won't that land you in jail within a few days?" he said, putting on an expression of concern.

"If I end up in prison because I don't depend on the government, what kind of logic is that? I've never asked you to do anything and you don't have to put yourself out," I told him.

I stopped trying to figure out his real meaning, and we parted on bad terms. But I ate my fill—and it was dumplings.   .

After lunch, Yu came back to talk with me again, saying my eldest brother kept creating a disturbance because he did not know if I was alive or not. Yu said the local police wanted to deal with my brother by force, but the government did not want to see this happen.

"Old Gao, we can't be too self-absorbed. You have to do something to let your family know you are still alive. This is more important than any of your bullshit principles. I'll make a concession to let you go back to Beijing and get your freedom. You can decide whether you want living expenses or a job, but you also have to give the government some room to maneuver. You can cooperate by saying that your disappearance on September 25 had nothing to do with the government, and you just went to Wutai Mountain in Shanxi Province to meditate for a couple of months.

"Think of it this way: Your situation is in a deadlock, and the ones suffering the most are you and your family members. I hear the old man [referring to my father-in-law] has become confused, and your brother cries like a child. I've often said that I don't believe you have a higher IQ than me, but I will admit that whatever I can think of, you can too. I'm sure you agree that it is important for your family to know you are alive. There are some things that are not convenient for me to say straight out, but why not take a step back and gain some space?"

I immediately caught his meaning. "I agree with your suggestion, but no tricks!"

"Okay, Old Gao. One arrangement is for you to write to your brother and tell him you needed to think over the bitter experiences of these past few years, so you took off for Wutai Shan on September 25, and after mediating there for several months, everything is fine, and the family shouldn't worry now.

"Another option is to make the show more realistic. We could return to Beijing on the 28th, which is the 15th day of the first month of the lunar year, and invite your family to come and see you. I can find a Buddhist monk to accompany you, one we have dealt with in the past. With a monk beside you, your relatives are more likely to believe that you just got back from Wutai Mountain," Yu said.

"If my family comes here to play their part in your show, you have to pay for their expenses," I reminded him.

Yu agreed that they would cover all expenses.

After dinner on the evening of the 27th, Yu came back and said that he and the friends who had come with him would take a flight back to Beijing the next day, and that cars from Beijing would pick me up in Yulin before sunrise and take me back to Beijing. He looked somber, and I joked that he looked depressed. This made him blow off some steam. "It's all because of your goddamned situation. Everything's turned upside down. For good or ill, we represent the ministry, and we brought the leaders of the local department two cases of Erguotou, a liquor that the national leaders serve to foreign heads of state and that costs 10,000 *yuan* a case. But no one has showed up to fetch it, not even a low-ranking soldier. We pretended it was nothing, but now Xiao Zhang [Zhang Xue] has been running around all day reserving two tables for dinner at the best hotel in the area, and not a single local official showed up! It is damned disgusting! Who are the people in this little backwater? Isn't this the goddamned world of the Communist Party? Now, the comrades in Xinjiang are really good. They receive you and send you off in style, and go out eating and drinking with you every day."

I said, "You came as representatives of the Ministry of Public Security, but the Ministry can't decide a single thing that benefits people in Yulin. If the Shaanxi PSB had come here, that would have been a different story. The fact that the comrades in Xinjiang treat you right is proof that they are either ignorant or not cunning enough. You described my detention as a big deal, but all the funds remain in your hands in Beijing. Aside from Xinjiang, no place in China wants to be responsible for me. Everyone knows what you are doing."

"When it comes to safeguarding national security, whoever's in charge would do the same thing," Yu huffed, changing the subject.

After breakfast on the morning of February 28, 2010, Sun Di and Zhang Xue entered my cell with two police officers. I was hooded and loaded into a car, and as we drove, I could hear police vehicles in front and behind ordering civilian vehicles to make way and stay clear of the motorcade. Once we reached the highway, my hood was removed, and I saw to my horror that Zhang Xue was driving.

Zhang Xue would drive fast like a demon and then suddenly slow down. In less than an hour we almost crashed into a pedicab. Then as he was driving furiously to overtake a truck, there was an explosive sound and we were enveloped in a cloud of dust. The truck's tire had blown, and it was wobbling in front of us like a drunk. Zhang Xue pulled the car over to the side of the road and said he did not dare to drive anymore. That saved me further terror during the rest of the journey.

It was dark by the time we reached Beijing, and when I noticed that the car was not heading in the direction of my home, I asked why. Sun Di said we would rest first and then I could go home. I did not say anything, thinking that what he said made sense, although they often went back on their word. I spent that night in a guesthouse in the hills with several policemen watching over me. Early the next morning, Sun Di came in and said someone wanted to have a chat with me. He led me to a small conference room, where a chubby monk was sitting on a sofa next to Yu Hongyuan.

After I sat down, Yu said, "This is one of the masters from Wutai Mountain, and he will accompany you from now on. Your younger brother will be on a plane this afternoon [Sun Di had had me call him the day before], and we'll take you to the airport to meet him. I'll send my people to the place where he is staying tonight to take care of the expenses for the trip. You can tell him they are your friends. After you pick him up, you can have a simple meal with him and the master and some people I have assigned to pose as friends of yours. Once the meal is over, explain that you have an urgent business and have to leave. Then you'll come back here, and my people will take care of your brother's lodging and food."

I realized that the show they were putting on was for outsiders rather than for my family, but the most important thing was for my family to see that I was alive. A little after five o'clock that evening, we met my fourth brother at the airport and went straight to a restaurant that provided food to people who had been making offerings to the Buddha. I had a hasty meal with my brother, but with Yu Hongyuan's people glued to me, we could only convey our feelings with our eyes. After we finished eating, I rushed off.

Our car drove through Beijing, the first time in more than a year that I had seen a night view. I felt as if I were in a dream, and doubted I was on this earth. I knew I was just passing through on my way to the world of secret imprisonment, the actual destination my car was racing to. I was prepared, but I was afraid they had put on another false show. Their aim was to make the outside world believe I was not actually being detained, while my aim was to let my family know I was still alive. Successfully achieving my objective caused new tension between the two sides.

The next morning after breakfast, Yu Hongyuan came to chat with me again, and he looked as if his evil and possessed mind had been kicked by a donkey. As soon as he began talking, the atmosphere became tense.

"According to the promise you made face-to-face with me in Yulin, I was supposed to go home yesterday without conditions. What is there left to talk about?" I started.

Yu replied, "Your return home is still completely in my hands. Stay here a few more days and take a rest first."

"There's no better place to rest than home," I replied. "Don't beat around the bush. What exactly are you trying to do?"

"Old Gao, you can't beat us. Over the next few days, I am going to be directing a big play with you in the starring role. You'll act like you haven't been in our hands in the past or now. Your family has seen that you are not being detained by us, and you wrote a letter to your family members saying you went to Wutai Mountain on your own. Your fate now has nothing to do with the government, so I hope you will seriously consider your situation and not lose everything in the end. What do you say, Old Gao?"

"The objective situation is exactly as you say it is, but what can I do about it?" I asked him.

"Old Gao, it is not hard to communicate with you; you are direct and not at all stupid. Don't struggle, just change your status. It will be a secret, and after you do that, you will have two choices. One is to remain in China and continue to play the hero and raise a fuss, cursing the Communist Party and remaining in the same old circles. My men will contact you at various times, and we will give you a bank account, either in China or abroad, so you have enough to live on.

"The other way is for you to go abroad. We will use the pretext of expelling you, and you will go to Thailand and make your way to the United States. We will open an account for you abroad and deposit money at fixed dates. We can come up with a concrete figure for solving your problem. The higher-ups have authorized me to approve a limit of tens of thousands of dollars a month. For a larger amount, I'll have to go back to them, but money isn't a problem, because you are a big shot, and worth spending a lot of money on. My people over there will be in contact with you. Old Gao, be realistic: Right now a lot of people are working for us—I mean overseas. Only the two of us will know about the change in your status. I won't even tell my parents. Old Gao, these are the only options for you at this time, and even I don't have any other way out—I've given the top leaders my guarantee." Yu spoke nonstop for more than forty minutes, staring at me the whole time, even when he lit a cigarette.

I told him, "Old Yu, you always act like my heart is in your hands, and it has made you complacent. Even at this late hour you still think you're dealing with a fool and that you have sent your enemies scurrying. But you're wrong. I don't imagine being the winner in this kind of process, but I will cling to some things; for example, that I will once again return to Beijing alive. You cannot change this and neither can the regime that you rely on. After all these years, you have failed every time you have created problems for me. Remember when you abducted me in July or August 2007 and took me to Changping? You said at the time that you would 'use the techniques used by Shaanxi comrades,' and that this would make me give in to you. And what happened?"

He suddenly became violently angry and banged the tea table with the palm of his hand, shouting, "Shut up! Stop going off on a goddamned tangent! Did I lie when I said I'd use Shaanxi methods to mess you up? Didn't you beg for mercy? Am I not still messing with your useless life? If you refuse to comply, we'll screw you over and kill you. I'll do it myself!"

"Old Yu, don't get so upset. That's not a strength, and it is not scaring anyone. I don't want to die, but I will never abandon anything just to avoid death, and I have never believed that my life will end in your hands. Dying is not a matter of chance, and someday you will understand this," I said. "And I need to tell you that although you think you fooled the world with your farce, after dinner I found a couple of minutes to tell my brother that I had been detained by you all along and that we were surrounded by Communist Party agents. And I told him to tell the rest of the family."

"You son of a bitch, you went back on your word! I have already given my guarantee to the top leaders. Now you either change your status and make everyone happy, or else find yourself in a life and death struggle. I've been goddamned covered in dirt. No more Mr. Nice Guy from now on! I'll give you a few days to think this over."

Then Yu stood up and left, and Sun Di and Zhang Xue came in and took me to a room of about seventy square feet with two beds. Policemen watched me in shifts around the clock, and the air in room was filthy with their cigarette smoke.

After I had been locked up for a week, Sun Di came to speak with me. "Director Yu gave you time to think things over, so what have you decided? Do you plan to spend your whole life here? We keep offering you a way out, but you insist on taking the road to ruin. It is time to start thinking of yourself and your family. Speak up, and we'll find a way out together."

I replied, "You seem to assume that I am not thinking of myself, but I'm just an ordinary person and I think about myself every moment. I am just not thinking in the same way you are. The process I am going through will come to an end, and that time is not far off. I don't doubt for a minute that I'll outlive the Chinese Communist Party."

"Old Gao, have you lost your damned mind after your years in detention? What are you talking about? No more airy-fairy shit—it is time for you to think about how you are going to get home. Director Yu has given you several days to think things over. We don't have time to bullshit with you. Just give us a clear answer." Sun Di seemed a bit impatient, but I said nothing further in spite of his repeated insistence, and he finally left panting with rage, slamming the door behind him.

He walked in again about a week later. "Let's go. Secretary Yu wants to have a word with you."

When we entered the conference room, Yu Hongyuan and Beanpole were sitting on a sofa, Yu's face beaming with a smile. "Hey, Old Gao, you seem to have good color, how are things going?" he asked me.

"Color is the actual color of the heart, and the outer representation of one's mood. Your face is one big smile, but your color is ashen, so you're definitely not in a good mood," I said as I sat down.

"Uncle Gao, these days I get more nervous meeting you than I do meeting senior leaders. You're right. Your case is still unresolved, so how can I be happy? I'm worried about you. Let's have a chat today. We have to move forward. I'll give you a more comfortable environment, and you give me a bit more room to maneuver. We'll both give a little, in your words, a technical compromise. What do you think Old Gao?" he said, still beaming.

"I have never been opposed to talking, although talking itself doesn't resolve anything, but talking is just a ruse to you, and it never brings any substantive benefit. Please forgive me for being blunt, but you have traveled a long way to see me, so why don't you tell me what is really on your mind."

"Hey, Gao, no wonder you are called a great lawyer! You lay down your fundamentals and you leave a possible way out. I realize that the initiative on whether or not to cooperate is actually with the weaker party, but now we are in a deadlock, and we need to talk about how to change the present situation. What do you say, Old Gao?" Yu said with ease and confidence.

"Old Yu, what you have just said proves that you have not yet thought out the relative and changing connection between power and weakness. After fighting with me for five years and completely exhausting your means, what has been the result? I hope you can draw some lessons from this. As for being in a deadlock, the deadlock has never been my fault. Why don't you explain your thinking to me?" I said.

"Okay, it's like this. We have told the outside world that you disappeared on your own and that you came back from Wutai Mountain. But you have been silent since your return and the outside world has a lot of questions, and the government is under pressure. This time you suffered a bit during your detention, and when you leave here we know you will write something again. When you write that stuff, you make life difficult for all of us. Speaking frankly, we need something to hold onto, so we want you to write about how well the government has treated you over the past few months, and how grateful you are, and that now that you have returned to society, you want to do some beneficial work within the embrace of the government. Give us something we can show to the top leaders. Putting it simply, we want to put a rope around your neck to lead you, otherwise I know that once you get out you will write things again and be detained. If you won't give in on this, then we will continue to detain you indefinitely, and this next time will make you feel that what you suffered in Xinjiang was kid stuff. If you want, we can let you go within a month, but if you don't answer us, we'll turn you over to the supervision of the Army. We don't want to mess with you anymore. To be frank, if it was up to me personally, I'd send you straight off for a long spell locked up with the military, because once we release you, won't you just start everything all over again?

"Geng He and the kids are no longer in China, the old lady's dead, so who can control you now? Besides, over the past five years, we have spent an ocean of money dealing with you, and releasing you would be like wasting all our effort. Enough, Old Gao, you should have a normal life. The thing to do now is to write something for the government, the more over-the-top the better. Letting us off the hook will be good for everyone. Otherwise, we'll send you off to realize your mighty aspirations with the military. Xiao Sun will be back in a couple of days to get your letter. For today, we will end here. Starting today, we will give you books to read, and you can watch TV. But the guards will hold onto the remote control."

After Yu Hongyuan and Beanpole left, Sun Di took me back to my cell, where he immediately gave me a stack of lined paper and a pen. "Remember, the more over-the-top it is, the better," he said.

When I did not respond, he looked dumbstruck. "Didn't we just agree on this?"

"Who agreed to anything? Speaking amicably isn't the same as agreeing," I replied.

"If you didn't agree, why didn't you say so while Director Yu was here? If you act like this now, the leaders will accuse me of being incompetent!" Sun Di stood there hollering at me, but I remained silent, and finally he stormed off.

I had never opposed a compromise, but Yu's request was more like an order. My previous compromises had proven to be mistakes, because my opponents only knew tricks and not how to compromise, and all I got out of it was suffering.

I once discussed this phenomenon with an older policeman, who said a key issue in my torture was the Falun Gong problem. "The Falun Gong issue is absolutely high voltage, and whoever touches it dies," he said, adding that another reason was that I always gave in under a bit of torture. "They see this as your weakness and believe that torturing you is useful. If you don't give in right at the beginning, they usually won't use torture against you. They say they don't torture Liu Xiaobo because he never yields."

Finally, for the sake of my family, I wrote an article saying that they had treated me well in detention and that I was ready to return to a "normal" life. I also wrote a few pages praising the economic successes they had achieved. But Sun Di was not satisfied, saying it was not anywhere near sappy enough and that I would have to rewrite it. But I simply could not write anything more disgusting than I had already done, so this effort had to be abandoned.

After a month in the mountains of the Miyun District of Beijing, early on March 28, Sun Di and Zhang Xue took me to the interrogation room, where Yu Hongyuan was sitting and staring morosely at the floor. "How's it going, Old Gao?" he said.

"Just come out with it. I'm being illegally detained. What are you going to do?"

Yu looked at me. "So you are not happy? Well, I'm running all over the damn place trying to find somewhere in Shanxi for you to stay for a while according to the plan by the relevant leaders, but those assholes won't get back to me. I told them to find you a one-family courtyard in Wutai Mountain and get back to me before midnight or they would bear the consequences, but those assholes are just ignoring your situation. Now I'm screwed and have to go along to deal with it myself. I am not in the mood to bullshit with you. We are relocating you today, so don't ask any questions. We're all just chess pieces on the board. I originally wanted to discuss some issues with you, but since you're acting like this, forget it." He told Sun Di and Zhang Xue, "Take him back. We will head out after we eat. I will leave first, and if you can make it by dark, that will be fine."

We set off for Shanxi at noon that day and arrived by nightfall. Yu Hongyuan had been unable to arrange for a one-family courtyard or for the local PSB to take over responsibility for me, so they had to take over an entire guesthouse at enormous expense.

On my first day in Wutai Mountain, Yu came into my room and handed me a phone. "We just released the news that you are in Wutai Mountain, and we have posted your phone number on the Internet. Just tell outsiders that you spent several months at Wutai Mountain and that you'll return to Beijing in a few days. Say you came to Wutai Mountain on your own initiative last year, and that you are now free. Once you've communicated with the outside world for a few days, we'll let you go. In any case, your family knows your real situation, and you have nothing to fear."

That is the actual story of how the outside world discovered "my phone number" online and resumed telephone communications with me. But this situation terrified the authorities. Yu repeatedly came to my room and said I was getting way too many phone calls. He said they thought locking me up for such a long time would make the world forget me, but "we miscalculated."

Several special agents were assigned to monitor my calls, and after I had a conversation with Dr. Fan Yafeng, Yu barged into my room and started cursing me.

On the third morning, before dawn, I was put in a car and driven away from Wutai Mountain, apparently due to intelligence they had received. After hours of driving through winding hills and deep gullies, we reached Qizhou and found a family guesthouse in a rural village. The place was really luxurious. That night after dinner, Zhang Xue and a young police officer surnamed Jing drove me to a local luxury hotel, where we stayed for three days. During that time, they relaxed their surveillance over me, and I was allowed to walk outside for an hour after breakfast and dinner, accompanied by guards, of course. It was the first time in half a year that I was able to stroll in the sunlight without a hood over my head.

Before dawn on the fourth day, we set off for Datong, and at that point I understood that the real goal of moving me from place to place was for sightseeing while pulling the wool over the eyes of the higher-ups. That afternoon, they took me to the Hanging Monastery. Among the people who emerged from a vast array of military and police vehicles were several families of women, children, and doddering old people. I pointed out that this was an illegal use of public vehicles for tourism, but the police officer watching me said I should mind my own business. In order to prevent me from further observation of their misuse of public resources, they left me behind with a guard when the rest of the group visited Yungang Grotto that afternoon.

After enjoying themselves in Datong, they suggested letting me return to my native home for a visit. I would have to wear monk robes and be accompanied by a police officer surnamed Jing, also disguised as a monk. I refused point-blank to do this, as immensely appealing as it was for me to go home to see my family and sweep the tombs of my father and mother. After a deadlock, we reached a compromise: I would not wear monk robes, but Xiao Jing would accompany me around the clock, disguised as a monk.

On the evening of April 3, 2010, I returned home accompanied by that "monk." My family wept with happiness, my eldest brother sobbing like a child. Clutching my hand, he said, "Third Brother, please don't go anywhere again. China is too dangerous and they are inhuman. You cannot take someone's pig or goat or even a newborn puppy without telling the owner, but they can take away a member of our family without even a word and refuse to admit it for months. Is there any other government in the world like this? Your eldest brother is begging you, please stay here in the village. We'll take care of you. Don't endure any more hardship."

My heart ached for the suffering of my family, but every time I had compromised for their sake, it had resulted in failure. I had to continue speaking out against the evil I saw. People continued to commit crimes in broad daylight because victims and witnesses remained silent. The refusal to speak out was a crime.

While my brother and I were shedding tears, the "monk" held up his palm, his fingers rubbing his prayer beads, his eyes shut tightly while he muttered incantations with knitted brow. This was not brought on by my brother's distress, but by something my brother said when his son telephoned and he said I was back: "He came with a fake monk." The "monk" was stunned when he heard this, but my brother said to him, "Don't be surprised. Can the Communist Party actually understand you better than your own family? How could someone like my brother disappear on his own without calling his family for a half year? Why would he bring a 'monk' home with him? You couldn't even fool our three-year-old." With this, the monk dropped his Buddhist ritual and lowered his head in silence.

I had returned in time for the Qingming tomb-sweeping festival, and my whole family, with the "monk" accompanying us, went to sweep the tombs of my father and mother. I stayed home for less than two days. On the afternoon of April 5th, the "monk" and I drove to the Yulin Guesthouse, where we met up with the leaders of the group. At nightfall on April 6th, we returned to the home I had left fourteen months before. That home had never seemed so dreary as now, with my wife and children gone, turning the apartment into an empty shell.

I had no lack of companionship and attention, however. There were people posted outside my door, and I was given a digital audio recorder-pen to carry in my pocket and place beside my pillow at night. I was not to turn it off. Early the next morning, Sun Di and Zhang Xue came to see me, and Su Di asked me for the pen so he could check the recording quality. I fetched it from the kitchen and handed it to him, and he was very unhappy to see that I had turned it off.

I had an appointment later that day with several Associated Press (AP) journalists, and Sun Di said I had to turn the pen on or else the meeting would be canceled. I immediately agreed, knowing that when the time came, it would be up to me whether to turn the device on. After breakfast, I met the four AP reporters at a tea house. Special agents hovered around me under Sun Di's direction as I talked with Charles Hutzler, an old acquaintance of mine, and the others. This was the first time in five years that I had met with friends from the media. I turned off the recorder and told them the true situation of the past few years, and then I turned the recorder on and began the "interview."

I am deeply grateful to them and to other media friends who followed my situation over the years. Their dedication guaranteed my safety, and they are an integral part of China's movement toward freedom and democratic constitutionalism.

5. My Abduction on April 8, 2010, and Subsequent Torture and Imprisonment

Right after I parted with my friends from Associated Press (AP) and was returning home, Sun Di and Zhang Xue came up behind me and asked for the recording device, saying that Director Yu wanted to listen to the recording. I handed them the pen, and then Sun took a phone call and walked away.

As soon as Sun was gone, several foreign friends came to see me. During those two days, almost all of the people who came to see me were friends from America, Britain, Germany, and Canada. Some were so happy to see me that they cried. The number and frequency of the visits aroused anxiety among the authorities, however. The next afternoon, shortly after a group of friends left, Sun Di and Zhang Xue came to talk with me. "If you insist on maintaining contact with the outside world, you will be arrested again in less than three days," Sun said. "If someone knocks on your door, don't open it."

I refused his demand, and as a result, I was abducted again within forty-eight hours.

The last group of people who visited me included four Beijing lawyers. We talked for a long time, and after they left, someone knocked on my door. Thinking it was more visitors, I opened the door, only to have Sun Di and Zhang

Xue squeeze their way in, saying they had urgent business and needed me to come outside. I said there really could not be anything urgent connected to me at that late hour, and that if we were going to be gone for a while, I would like to tidy up a bit first. When they refused, I asked if I could get a change of clothes, but they still said no.

The situation could not be more obvious. I was detained once again. Once we were outside, the door of a vehicle opened, and as I bent to enter it, a hand covered my mouth and something was thrown over my head. After a drive of about two hours, I resumed my life in detention in a room of less than a hundred square feet, most of it taken up by two beds, two chairs, and a table. Just as I finished breakfast the next morning, Sun Di and Zhang Xue came in and asked the guard to leave the room. Sun Di said he had never expected me to end up back in detention so soon. I replied that this was not necessarily a bad thing, as I had slept well the night before after sleeping poorly at home. Sun Di asked me why I had not slept well at home. I told him that in detention, it is possible to adjust to a sage-like mindset and remove all worry, but back at home, reality imposes its mundane concerns. On the night that I returned home, I had made a list of more than a dozen expenses I needed to pay and errands that would take ten days to complete. Being detained had solved all of these problems.

Sun Di said my way of thinking was abnormal and that the government sent me into this kind of environment so I could reflect on the error of my ways, but apparently this was a wasted effort. I said it was not a waste for me, because everyone needs time for reflection, but I had no intention of reflecting in the way they hoped.

Sun Di said that my two-day return home had made the top leaders incredibly anxious, and that my constantly meeting foreigners showed a lack of concern for the government's feelings and compelled the government to take action. He added that a large group of people had been surrounding me for more than a year without being able to go home for a few days' rest. "Is this how a person should act?" he demanded.

I told him this was exactly the kind of absurd logic that spurred the authorities to carry out so many inconceivable actions that drew the censure of civilized people.

"Are you saying that everyone in China is absurd and muddle-headed except you, Old Gao?" he asked. Getting back on topic, Sun Di said that the government wanted me to take a break in the suburbs for a while and not tell anyone I had been detained again. I could read and watch TV, take a walk outside every morning and afternoon, and they promised to let me visit my father-in-law and mother-in-law in Xinjiang before the end of the month. I agreed, because my sudden disappearance the previous year had been devastating to my in-laws, and it was my greatest desire to see them and comfort them face-to-face.

Our group landed in Urumqi on April 14, and my detention during that time was much more relaxed than in the past. Even the food was quite good. Compared to my previous secret detentions, this could be considered a few days in a good Hell.

But this evil regime is incapable of any genuine kindness. It was only after I returned to Urumqi that I learned that this so-called family visit was just a publicity stunt to reduce pressure on the local authorities. A group of people had been sent in advance to make careful "security" arrangements. When Sun Di, Zhang Xue, and others took me to the front gate of the Kaziwan Cement Factory, I was surrounded by a group of soldiers. Anyone who did not know better would think they were welcoming a long-lost friend. The unfettered hooliganism of the police utterly terrified my elderly in-laws, who were the kind of people who always follow the rules. After I went upstairs, the police parked a vehicle to block the entrance to the residential unit and stationed soldiers there, inconveniencing everyone entering and leaving the building and attracting a crowd of curious onlookers. I could clearly sense my family's tension and discomfort.

The Communist special agents knew very well that soft punches did not have much impact on me, but that my affection and concern for my family was my "weak spot." Seeing the hardship my visit was causing them, I told my relatives that I could only stay a short time. The whole family wept while accepting this reality.

My father-in-law was not at home when I arrived, but when he heard I was back, he trotted the whole way home. When he reached the door, he cried out, "Zhisheng is back, how wonderful! As long as you are still alive, everything is fine. Mysterious things have happened to you all your life, Zhisheng, but you have never been defeated. Your present situation is not a consequence but a process. You are alive and so is the faith of our family."

The whole family spent that afternoon talking. My father-in-law, occasionally brushing tears from his eyes, recounted his search for me, including at the morgues. He told me that each time he examined a corpse he would kneel on the floor and touch his head to the floor three times to kowtow. He said he did this because he had disturbed the dead man's tranquility, but also because he could relate to the family's misfortune of being unable to reunite with their loved one. He said that each time he would say in his heart, "Your family and Zhisheng's family both share the same suffering. Please take me as your relative. I have bowed to you in hopes that you will rest in peace." He would also leave grapes as an offering to comfort the deceased until his family could find him.

As we parted, I hugged my father-in-law with emotion, patting his back and saying, "Thank you, my father. You said I have never been defeated, and this must be true because we have faith. I ask the whole family to firmly believe that my life will not be extinguished by some random process."

After getting into the taxi, I wept at the unhappy way my visit had ended, and at the obvious pain of my family.

My early return did not seem to surprise Sun Di, who said calmly, "I know what happened. Rest here for a while. The return air ticket is booked for the 20th." (That day was the 15th.) My family visit that was supposed to last a week had ended in just one day.

The police left one person behind to guard me while the rest went sightseeing in Turfan and other places over the next few days. My father-in-law came to see me every day at the guesthouse, and he brought my elder sister-in-law along with him on April 19th. I could not bear to tell them the real situation, but said that if they did not receive a phone call from me within twelve hours of my plane taking off, it meant that I had been detained. Sun Di had come by earlier that day to tell me that the authorities hoped to find a place in Shanxi to hold me during the next phase. After about a month or two, I would be allowed to return to Beijing and maintain phone contact with my family. He said I could not divulge to foreigners that I was still being held by the government. I had immediately rejected his proposal, and Sun Di had said, "You know the consequences of taking a hard stand against the government. Isn't this for your own good? When the time comes, no one will be able to save you." I did not let my family see me off at the airport because I did not want them exposed to the shameless people surrounding me. Instead, I said goodbye to my father-in-law and sister-in-law in the freezing rain.

As soon as our plane landed in Beijing on the afternoon of April 20, 2010, Sun Di told me to telephone my family and tell them I had arrived home safely, but I refused, because I had not arrived home.

"If you don't cooperate, you will be responsible for the consequences," said Sun Di, his face clouded over. "You are a smart guy, you don't need me to say it again."

As we boarded a vehicle outside the airport, Su Di told me again to telephone my family, but again I refused. The vehicle headed toward the lockup in the mountains of Miyun District, and upon our arrival, I was taken to the room where I had been held so many times before, with two men guarding it.

Around an hour later, Sun Di and Zhang Xue came in and motioned for the guards to withdraw. Then they sat down and Sun Di said, "Old Gao, let's get to the point. We will give you a few more days, but once that is over we will be sending a different group of people to look after you." (They were referring to the people who carried out torture.) "There is nothing wrong with your brain, you understand what I'm saying."

There was no point in responding, and the room became deathly silent. Sun Di sat for a few more minutes, but when I still said nothing, he finally got up and left. We had wrangled enough over the years to know what to expect of each other. This time, there seemed little doubt that torture would be inflicted in the next few days, and both sides also knew that the torture would change nothing, and that it had no meaning outside its own cruel logic of venting a primitive and retributive fury.

All day on April 28th, my right eye kept twitching. I knew the torture process would begin that day, because the authorities had completed their battle preparations (as Yu Hongyuan put it). The truth was, thank God, that my opponents no longer had the capacity to make me afraid, and their cruelty just showed they had run out of options.

Because torture was always carried out at night in Beijing, after dinner on April 28th, I quickly gathered up the things I had brought with me from Urumqi. I had just finished packing when four men burst into my room. They were the same team who had tortured me on September 21, 2007. The one in the lead was the cruelest of them, a big fellow about 6'2" tall, whom I had nicknamed Zhu Zhongba.[11] Grabbing my hair from his advantageous height, he pressed my head down, saying, "Hey kid, Daddy's here." As "Zhu Zhongba" forced me to bend at the waist, another of them pulled a black hood over my head while yet another handcuffed my hands behind me. Still pressing my head down with all his strength, Zhu Zhongba yelled, "Add a couple of pillowcases— we have to give him the VIP treatment!"

Two pillowcases were pulled over the hood, and with my body bent into a ninety-degree angle, I was propelled downstairs and outside into a gale-force wind. In their haste they failed in two attempts to load me into a vehicle. "You damned idiot! Don't you know how to lift your leg?" A hand gripped me fiercely at the back of my neck, and then I was inside between two of them, my head pressed between my knees. I suspect that they purposely took a roundabout route to prolong that unendurable pain and the suffocation that made my eyeballs feel ready to explode. My lower body went numb, which temporarily relieved it of pain, but brought on another round of beating when I was taken from the vehicle and tumbled helplessly to the ground. Completely irrational,

---

11. TN: The original name of Zhu Yuanzhang, first emperor of the Ming dynasty, a ruthless and cunning man who rose to power after being born an impoverished peasant.

the men shouted at me and joined in beating me for a while. I was still unable to stand after the beating, so someone yelled, "Pull him up!"

I was propelled into a building and down a long staircase and then shoved onto the ground. I heard several people walk over, and then someone said, "Pull the hood off!" A hand roughly pulled the hood and pillowcases off my head, and lying on my side, I saw three pairs of feet in front of me. As my eyes swept over my surroundings, I found I was in a dimly lit corridor with no end in sight. I did not try to look at the faces of the people in front of me. A voice from above me said, "Look at that damned dog's face! You animal, look at who's standing in front of you! You're in our hands again, and isn't that your lousy luck!" When I did not look up at them, a pair of large feet in suede shoes kicked fiercely at my belly. The owner of the shoes stooped over and grabbed me by the hair, pulled me into a half-seated position, and yanked my face upward. "Have a look at your dads." Standing before me was the group of men who had tortured me on September 21th, including the main torturer and leader of the group, Section Chief Wang (as he introduced himself during the torture process). I saw he was holding an electric cattle prod about two feet long, and his other hand lifted a cigarette to his lips. "Look at your traitor's face, you animal! Your dads will be giving you an unforgettable experience over the next few weeks."

He released my hair, and when I tumbled to the floor, Wang walked over and trod on my face, saying, "You are a dead dog, and to tell the truth, you are not even as good as a dead dog!" As he yelled, he ground his shoe into my face harder and harder, then lifted his foot, and kicked me in the mouth (I later found that several of my teeth were loose). "Let's give you a taste first," he said, and at his shout, the three others joined in kicking me. I could not avoid them, and they were completely out of control. This outburst continued for around twenty minutes and then gradually stopped as they stood there panting. Strangely, I did not feel intense pain, but when the attack let up, I found I was trembling uncontrollably. I had learned through experience that this trembling was purely physiological, because I felt no fear. The three of them stood there panting almost in unison, then each of them lit a cigarette and silence descended.

Finally, Section Chief Wang said, "How do you feel, dog shit? Did you enjoy that first taste? Don't worry, we've got lots of time, and you've been unlucky enough to fall into our hands again. But your dads think you've got guts—we have been doing this for a long time without running into anyone who wrote about it before. So you wanna write? It is not like no one's died in here, and if you die, it's all for nothing, we'll just bury you in secret. It happened before. So go ahead and write—it won't do any good. We'll be wearing big red badges at the end of the year." As Wang spoke, another one I had nicknamed "Giant" (he was only about five feet tall, creating a comical impression as he constantly shadowed the 6'2" Zhu Zhongba) pulled me over against the wall, then calmly lit five cigarettes he held in his mouth. I knew what was coming next from the last time I was tortured, and sure enough, he slowly bent down, grabbed my hair with his left hand, and pressed my head down, then held the five cigarettes in his right hand below my face so the smoke blew into my eyes.

Off to the side, Section Chief Wang kept haranguing me, and I cannot remember much more than the general outlines: "We're gonna keep you here tonight and we're gonna serve you right and wipe out the stuff that was written last time. You're gonna write something else to send up, and as to how to write it, we'll leave that to you, but don't think of not writing. The guys upstairs had their reasons for sending us to serve you this time."

I just vaguely listened, shutting down my thought process and putting all my effort into disassociating with the pain at the biological level.

"Stand up, you stinking dog shit! Are you gonna write or not?"

Giant pulled me into a standing position while Zhu Zhongba walked over to my right side and fiercely grabbed my clothes at the shoulders so I was bent at the waist and asked if I was going to write. When I did not answer, he gave me a hard knee to the chest, then asked me and kneed me, asked me and kneed me, and finally did not bother asking any more but just kept kneeing me in the chest. I heard a strange screaming sound that I would have sworn had nothing to do with my consciousness. My eyes were too blurred to see anything. Although my thought process had almost completely shut down, I could still hear, and I was certain that anyone could hear those screams from at least ten floors away. Gradually, I lost the strength to stand, but Zhu Zhongba's strength was immense, and eventually he was the only thing holding me up. Later still, I no longer heard the screaming but rather a sound like exaggerated vomiting. Finally, he seemed to run out of steam and let me go, and I crashed to the floor, my forehead slamming to the ground. I kept vomiting, but there was nothing left but a sticky liquid by then. Half of my face lay against the tiles, and with my hands cuffed behind me the whole time, I was unable to adjust my position. The beating had made me nearly black out, and as I slowly regained consciousness, I felt the ice-cold floor and sticky substance beneath my face. They began lighting up cigarettes again as I lay there gasping. After they finished smoking, Wang walked near my shoulder and said, "You two go take a break."

Then he stepped on my shoulder, and his electric cattle prod emitted a buzzing sound. He stuck the prod under my chin, and I shut my eyes tight and heard another strange sound, which undoubtedly came from me. The best way I can describe that sound is like the howling of a dog when its master steps on its tail, or like a puppy when its tail gets pinched. That sound rang through the corridor along with the buzzing of the electric cattle prod, but there was no way to control it; it just came out, and you could hear it but you had no way of stopping it. I felt my muscles separate from my bones; it was a physiological pain that an ordinary person cannot clearly describe with words. But this time with the electric prod was child's play compared with September 2007. It lasted less than half an hour and was carried out only by Wang, and he did not shock my genitals.

After Wang stopped the electric shock treatment, I heard him enter a room behind me and what sounded like the electric prod being tossed onto a table. In less than a minute, two more people came in, and I heard the sound of the door closing, and there was deathly silence in the corridors again. I heard a faint moaning sound, and I began to feel how cold the floor was. I reminded myself not to think and just to go along with whatever happened: "You're walking down a road of extreme hardship, and no matter what, you have to keep going; turning back or off to the side is the road to death. They'll carry you along, you don't have to worry about it." I suddenly saw the faces of Geng He and the children before my eyes, and I became very alert and thought about how distressed they would be to watch all this happening to me, but then I quickly shut off that activity in my mind.

They must have been discussing something in the room, because then the door opened and I heard them walk out. "Pull him up!" ordered Wang's voice. Someone pulled me upright, and I felt that my legs and back were strong enough to stand up straight, but that appeared to offend Section Head Wang: "You dog traitor, you think you deserve to stand all high and mighty in front of your dads?" Then Zhu Zhongba leaped at me and slapped me on both sides of my face, but I stood there like a wooden post and did not dodge him, because they would only laugh at my attempt and would not stop attacking me. After twenty or thirty slaps, he switched to a fist and punched me on the chin. There was no more pain, just the feeling of concussion in my brain. After hitting me for a while he stopped, probably because his fist was starting to hurt.

Off to one side, Wang picked up the electric prod and touched it against my chin, pressing the switch at intervals. As before, I did not evade it, because I had learned what to do after repeatedly being subjected to this treatment. This infuriated Section Chief Wang: "Damn your high and mighty pose! Do you have water on the brain, you dog traitor?" Two others leaped at me and began pummeling me, and I do not even remember how I fell to the floor, just that I felt a blunt object strike my head and became aware of falling. After a brief dream-like state, there was another round of frenzied kicking, and again I heard screaming. By the time they took a break and lit up their cigarettes, I was in a peculiar sensory condition, but eventually I realized that I was prostrate on the floor and that the people around me were my persecutors. The pain was vague and unidentifiable, and as sweat poured from me from head to toe, my strength began to ebb as if flowing away with my sweat.

They moved some chairs from the room and sat down and continued smoking, and I kept sweating, and after about half an hour, Section Chief Wang spoke again, "How are you doing, you beast? Have you cooled off? We have just gotten started. You see these three dads? A lot of dads have come this time to play with you nice and slow. You know why you got that just now? 'Cause I can't stand looking at a damned traitor putting on airs like you're in the right. What pills are you on? You think you have the right? I'm telling you, don't bring trouble on yourself. Tuck your tail between your legs in front of these dads. These dads are tired, too, so there is no need to waste words. You don't need to write anything, just say in front of these dads that what you wrote about being tortured in 2007 is fake. There is no recording, no video, so saying it or not doesn't matter, but these dads are in a bad mood that you can end with a word."

When he said that, my mind became completely clear, because based on past experience, they were looking for a way to back off. They were in fact also tired. But still I said nothing. "I'll ask you again: Will you talk or not?" In my heart I thought, "It is starting again." The three of them seemed to leap from their chairs at once, and again I heard the sound of screaming and of kicking and hitting, their yells echoing in the hallway as they cursed me as a beast. Finally, the corridor became quieter, with just the sound of groaning, but not very loud, and the corridor was lit up for a while as they smoked. I again felt the coolness of the tiles against my face.

Someone stood up and grabbed me by the shoulders, and I was lifted into a seated position. A black hood was pulled over my head, and I was taken into a room. After my hood was removed, I found myself in what looked like an ordinary hotel room, but with the bed removed and just a table holding a stiff plastic garment bag from which the ends of two electric cattle prods extended. This made it clear that they would torture me again. Again, my upright posture and unafraid attitude seemed to violate some taboo of theirs, and again Section Chief Wang shouted abuse about a dog traitor striking a righteous pose against these dads, and another round of hysterical violence ensued. The room was much more spacious than the hallway, so this beating was even more hair-raising than the previous rounds.

I felt a violent urge to resist, and if my hands had not been cuffed, I would have grabbed one of those villains by the throat, and unless someone broke my hands, I would have strangled him to death. Of course, this impulse toward self-defense was directed at the violence as it occurred, and once they stopped their violence, I no longer had that impulse.

I did not hate them, and while I cannot say I had compassion for them, I often felt distressed for their misfortune in taking on such an ignominious role. In today's China, the truly despicable criminals are the autocratic authorities, and these men are just the henchmen; even the occasional individual among them knows this deep inside.

Of the three of them, Giant was different from the other two. Throughout that time from 2007 to April 2010, he never let our eyes meet, and his beatings were so different from those of Zhu Zhongba that I could tell them apart even with my eyes closed. During my torture in 2007, Zhu Zhongba, Section Chief Wang, and the handsome youth were savage, callous, and practical, but Giant was clearly more restrained.

The aim now was to get me to kneel down in submission, and they repeatedly attacked me from behind and knocked me almost flat on my face. "Thinking people" may laugh and accuse me of being superstitious, but in all these times that I fell to the floor, my head was not even slightly injured, which shows that God was protecting me. And the way they kneed me so fiercely in the chest, in purely biological terms, should have injured or even destroyed my cardio-pulmonary organs, but miraculously, my internal organs were not injured at all. When I talked about this with the secret police head, Big Eyes, on the night of November 15, 2011, he said, "Old Gao, your physique is something else! You are a damned god!"

Since they were unable to accept a righteous stance from someone they considered a dog traitor, Zhu Zhongba once again savagely kneed me in the chest. I heard that strange scream and spit out a viscous liquid, my eyes too blurred to see anything but the rough outlines of my attackers. An interesting interlude emerged in which Zhu Zhongba clearly lost all rationality and became fiercer with each blow, and then Section Chief Wang rushed over and pushed me away with his electric cattle prod and held Zhu Zhongba off to one side. I read this as: (1) the upper levels having bottom line instructions not to beat me to death; (2) Section Chief Wang seeing that Zhu Zhongba was out of control.

The conflict over whether to kneel never really ended, because kneeling brought about through the use of violence was a sham, and as soon as they loosened their grip I would stand up again unless I had lost all ability to do so. I should remind readers not to regard this process as an instance of courage. I feel it is inconsistent with human nature to show heroism or courage in such bleak circumstances. Rather, I feel it was a matter of either descending into the basest cowardice or becoming almost completely unyielding. Both should be understood as consistent with human nature, and I fell into the latter category.

Some may think that the price of resistance was too great (as quite a few of my guards felt), but the price of cowardice would have been infinitely greater.

From 2006 to the present, the Chinese Communist Party (CCP) has tortured me several times for the purpose of making me change my status, even nominally, or obliterating all I had written about being tortured. Now they wanted to force me to kneel, and should I give them what they wanted on this last point? Reliance on an electric prod and cruelty was in itself a kind of self-negation. My strength was evidenced by the number of personnel deployed to surround me day and night. Now this was the final torture session, and the report to the upper levels depicting me kneeling down would be marred by the fact that Zhu Zhongba was pressing down on my shoulders, and Giant was stepping on my lower legs. Unless the "leading comrades" were complete idiots, they would know at a glance how bogus this kneeling was.

After returning me to my room, Section Chief Wang brought up the old issue of verbally retracting my narrative of the 2007 torture, but although he exerted his barbarous skills to this end, huffing and puffing amidst my screams, the results were unsatisfactory. Section Chief Wang and the others were tired. It was already late at night, and the torture had not attained its objective. One of them ran out and soon came back with two new faces, after which Section Chief Wang went outside, and Zhu Zhongba said, "My boy, your dads are tired and we're going back to rest, so some others are coming to play with you." Then he also left.

I was lying on the bed at that time, and did not raise my head to look at the new arrivals. The main advantage of cutting off my thought processes was that whenever there was a break, sleep would overcome me. I heard someone move a chair and sit next to my head, and when I opened my eyes, a leather-clad foot was in front of my nose. Apparently, I had been snoring in an unseemly fashion, drawing a couple of kicks in the head. It was not a hard kick, and was accompanied by a scolding: "Damn your eyes, how can you fall asleep so fast in this environment?" That unmistakable voice had to belong to my old nemesis, Sissy. I intend no gender bias here: A female voice is an indispensable component of womanly beauty, but it sounds odd coming from a man. In less than two minutes, I was sound asleep again and was again kicked awake, and Sissy cursed me, "Gao Zhisheng, you dumb shit, how can you sleep after what went on today?"

I had developed the ability to fall asleep in an instant during my years as a lawyer, fitting in a short nap whenever the court recessed. Likewise, shutting down my emotions allowed me to immediately fall asleep when my torturers took a break. Back in 2007, I had been kept awake for nights on end, and I knew this could happen again at any time; when my opponents were unable to break my will, they would target my physical health by depriving me of food and sleep. Especially during my twenty-one months in the hands of the People's Armed

Police (PAP) and three years in Shaya Prison, the authorities racked their brains to torment me through the details of my imprisonment and diet, but apart from taking thirty pounds off my weight, they had come up empty-handed (and I regained that thirty pounds a little more than a month after being released from Shaya Prison).

Now sleep arrived fast and deep in spite of Sissy's interference. As I had anticipated, in the days that followed, the physical violence was replaced with softer methods aimed at exhausting and depleting my body. I was overseen by pairs of guards working in eight-hour shifts. The lead guard on each shift had clearly been selected for his willingness to engage in evil acts on his own initiative, and this caused me real suffering. I became groggy and confused and shut down my brain to disperse my attention and contain the suffering to my physical being. I spent my days in a state of unconsciousness or semi-consciousness, even when I was forced to stand. Each time I fell asleep, the guards struck my knee caps and kicked me violently, but they were unable to obstruct that overwhelming sleepiness, which was aided by the black hood placed over my head. The three lead guards were all vile, depraved, and cruel. Two of them were big and fat, with swarthy skin, necks as thick as their heads and no clear demarcation between the waist and buttocks. They also wore the same clothes—black suits with white socks and white sneakers. I called them "Demon No. 1" and "Demon No. 2." Demon No. 1 once made me stand facing the wall for three full hours without moving, which was very hard, especially since I was exhausted from lack of sleep. The third bad egg was Sissy, who would point his finger at me and say, "Gao Zhisheng, on my shift, don't even consider yourself human or I'll make you suffer for it." He cursed and spit at me all day long, but I simply ignored him, since the foul language could not hurt me, but I eventually learned the extent of his evil intentions toward me. The day after the physical torture ended, when it was time for my regular visit to the latrine, Sissy had just arrived on his shift. When I told him that I needed to go to the toilet, he stared and cursed at me: "You heard what I said about considering yourself human. Humans shit. You think you're human?"

"I've never been prohibited from going to the toilet," I protested. "Even domestic animals have to empty their bowels. It has nothing to do with politics."

He cursed me with the foulest language possible and said, "You son of a bitch, are you trying to teach me? I'm telling you one last time, no shitting on my shift! Just hold it!"

It was useless to argue with him; he had lost his soul. Ordinarily, going to the toilet is a small thing, but when it cannot be properly dealt with, it becomes an extremely big deal. During this period, I was tortured by this trifling matter as never before. My "toilet" was nothing more than an old plastic bucket placed outside the door of my cell, and the guards on all three shifts were very reluctant to let me use it. When I needed to, they would move my handcuffs from behind my back to in front of me, put the black hood over my head, and take me to the latrine on the second floor, where I used my feet as my "eyes" to find the right place and achieve my objective while the guards stood by cursing and telling me to hurry up. The whole process was absurd. The excretory function and its process are basic components of human life, and according to the rules of civilization, it is a private process. Unless a person is disabled and requires assistance, to conduct this procedure in the view of others is unbearable and nauseating. But the Chinese regime has included it among its filthy tricks, and designed the whole procedure with the objective of humiliating its opponents, but it ends up also harming the people assigned to its supervision.

Sissy had countless other ways of punishing you, which he painstakingly refined and improved every day. When he gave me my meals, he always found a way to make it unpleasant, for instance by "forgetting to move my handcuffs from back to front for more than an hour after the food was delivered." Once I was surprised to see that he had given me three meal boxes. With great difficulty, I opened the first box with my handcuffed hands. It was empty. I opened the second box: empty. I did not even bother to open the third box. He laughed until he almost choked. His conduct made you feel sorry for him. When a person's actions have sunk this low, it is he himself, more than anyone else, who is truly unfortunate.

The bottom line for human conduct should be an unconditional respect for the individual. When this bottom line is crossed, the world we live in is transformed from a beautiful place to a dangerous prison. There is no greater misfortune than a life without kindness, and his misery was apparent at first sight. But a system like this one has a lot of people like him, and there is no hope of any kind of rational, reason-based exchange with such a person.

The teammates of these three villains were of three very different types. The assistant of Demon No. 2 liked to show who was boss. Once when my legs were completely numb, I asked for permission to move in place for a few minutes, and Demon No. 2 agreed. But after I had been moving for less than a minute, his assistant, who had not spoken a word in days, said, "You've moved enough. Just pretend you're a spring onion." The assistant guard of Sissy, on the other hand, was the common face of today's Chinese. He could not care less if the person beside him was alive or dead. He would not spare you a glance, but neither would he take the initiative to hurt you. He just pretended you were not there. I originally did not want to write about the assistant of Demon No. 1, for fear that his kindness would get him into trouble, but I have decided to mention him because there is nothing more precious than an act of human kindness, especially when it takes place in the midst of the worst kind of brutality. During periods of torture, I was fed nothing but cold rice and vege- tables and cold water. Although I was shivering with cold at the end of April, I needed to drink that cold water. Then, on the second day, the assistant guard of Demon No. 1 gave me a bottle of water that he had somehow managed to heat. When I felt the bottle's warmth, my eyes lit up, and he gave me a kind glance. From then on, he always found a way to quietly let me have hot water when the others were not paying attention. He took pains to ensure that he was always the one to bring me my food, and it was only during his shift that I received hot food and enough to fill my stomach. He carefully tended the fire of human kindness in that netherworld, and I will always remember him as a shining light in that dark madness.

On the afternoon of my fourth day of torture, I was hooded and taken to another room and made to sit on a backless wooden stool for several hours. I could hear people turning on the two beds beside me. I had been standing all morning, so I took the opportunity to sleep. Then I was led into a basement room, where my hood was removed. The room was full of people dressed in black, and dirty carpets had been laid on the floor with two mattresses on top of them. The window had been sealed and covered with thick rubber boards, just like the walls.

The next morning, a large group of people dressed in black entered the room, and the torturers left. Demon No. 2 walked in and said, "The handover has been completed." Completely naked, I was handed over to the custody of some leaders of the PAP. I later learned that this unit is under the direct command of the CCP's Central Disciplinary Commission (CDC) and used for "double- designation"[12] procedures such as arrests, secret confinement, and detentions, mainly targeting corrupt officials. They initially thought I was another corrupt official and therefore assumed an extremely vicious attitude. This was the begin- ning of my twenty-one months in the hands of the PAP.

Section Chief Wang and the others remained on-site as the PAP's "honored guests," but Sissy and the others were no longer responsible for guarding me. One of the cadres I was handed over to was a brigade leader over six feet tall with a restless expression on his face and resolute movements. The brigade leader read out the PAP's assignment to guard me and the rules: I must obey the guards' directions and orders without any questions. If I violated the rules,

---

12. "Double designation" (also translated as "dual designation") refers to an internal investigation practice that requires an accused official to be held at a designated time and place.

the guards would have the right to adopt drastic punishment measures. Second, every day, I was allowed to stand up in my original position four times to exercise for ten to fifteen minutes each time. "This means that most of the day, all you can do is sit," he added. Third, except for communicating a need to go to the toilet and other necessary matters, I was not allowed to speak.

From then on, the PAP assumed responsibility for my secret confinement. A surveillance camera and three listening devices were installed in my cell. I was not allowed to speak to the guards and the guards were prohibited from speaking with each other. I was long accustomed to the first prohibition, but the second prohibition was never effectively enforced in spite of harsh and frequent punishment.

In just a few days, I managed to gather a lot of information regarding my transfer to the PAP, and my confinement there gave me the opportunity to observe two of the darkest aspects of the CCP system at close range: first, the CDC's utter contempt for the law and its disastrous effect on human rights and the rule of law in China, and second, the unbelievable depravity and corruption of the PAP on both the material and spiritual levels. During those twenty-one months, I met around two hundred personnel from two PAP units and was allowed to see behind the meticulously embellished facade of strength and earnestness.

In this memoir, I have tried to use the guards' real names as much as possible, in the belief that recording them as real, living people will make it possible for future generations to know the truth about this historical period. In any case, it was very hard to learn their real names, and most went under nicknames or false names. A number of the guards quickly learned my identity. Quite a few of them were good with the Internet, and could penetrate the Great Firewall and access outside news, which they relayed to me through their teeth. Some were caught and beaten because of this. Their branch unit came from the Fifth Squadron of the Second Battalion of Seventeenth Detachment of Third Division of the Beijing PAP (one year later, they were replaced by the Sixth Squadron of the Second Battalion).

Some of the soldiers who had been serving as guards for a long time said they had never experienced this level of secrecy before, even though some had taken part in arresting and guarding former Shanghai Party Secretary Chen Liangyu and other senior officials. In the previous year, they had guarded Liu Xiaobo. The guards told me they rarely saw the leaders of the Beijing PAP, but this time they had seen several PAP lieutenant generals from the Beijing headquarters, and two lieutenant general deputy commanders had come here to inspect their work.

The original purpose of the secretive atmosphere created by the CCP was to conjure a sense of sacred mission among the guards, but it naturally also tickled their curiosity. They were usually informed of their assignment and sent directly to their destination, but this time they had been blindfolded and put on a train for one day and one night. Only upon arriving here had they learned that they were in a mountainous area of Beijing's Changping District, which can be reached in two hours from their garrison in Beijing's Haidian District.

The guards told me how their work was organized. An ordinary PAP unit is made up of twenty-seven soldiers. Of these, ten were assigned as guards in my cell, working in pairs in five shifts. Five officers were assigned to the adjacent monitoring room, working alone on the same five shifts. There was also a "self-defense" group and an emergency group, each made up of five soldiers working in shifts. In addition, there were two on-duty cadres, one battalion leader and one squadron leader. The Public Security Bureau (PSB) also provided a police dog, which was a bit lame and therefore called "Little Limpy." After listening to it bark for twenty-one months, I can still hear the sound in my ears to this day.

The security arrangement had a pyramid shape with me at the bottom. The PAP soldiers guarding me were monitored from a central control room staffed by three old PSB officers working in shifts. Although the PAP and PSB are separate entities, the PAP had to submit a "daily target control situation report form" to the PSB, with the "target" being me. Later, the PSB set up an "interrogation group" comprising three men and one woman, which only assembled when some leader came to make an inspection. As for the nine mysterious persons known as the "honored guests," these people were simply my torturers, and their position was never explicitly stated, even in their internal organization. In this manner, at least thirty-nine people were assigned to duties relating to me.

The assistant guard in my cell held a "daily target monitoring log" in his hand. When I was not moving, an entry was made every fifteen minutes, and when I was doing something, my actions were recorded. This log was kept around the clock, and some 1,400 log books were filled during my imprisonment here. On the basis of these daily logs, a "copy report" had to be filled in for the PSB system every evening, along with a "report to the superior level" for the PAP battalion. On the basis of this report, the battalion reported to the detachment, the detachment reported to the division, the division reported to the general command, and the general command reported to the headquarters. A "summary report" was then issued once a week, with a copy submitted to the PSB. Every week, the PSB's central control room submitted a video and audio report with an attached CD to the higher authorities.

The guards told me that I was imprisoned in a village called Yihu Mountain in Beijing's Changping District. (On April 28, 2009, I was transferred to another secret detention place, also located in Yihu Mountain. I knew this, because I had found two napkins used by the guards with the characters "Yihu Mountain Village welcomes you" written on them.) The guards said the place was owned and operated by the Beijing PSB, which held almost all of its important meetings in the village, and was responsible for its security. I learned that the office building used for my imprisonment had been erected on the site of Ming dynasty grave, and that it had finally been abandoned because of ghosts. Now the Beijing PSB was renting the office building for more than 100,000 RMB per month for holding major dissidents.

My cell was in the basement, which was two-thirds below ground. The cadre duty room and the PAP's monitoring room were also in the basement, while the toilet was on the second floor, where the guards lived. That basement cell had two unforgettable characteristics. First, it was incredibly humid. A paper box placed in that cell for two weeks looked as if it had been soaked in a water basin. Second, it was freezing cold in the winter and extremely hot in the summer. I was transferred there as summer was approaching, and the heat was getting hard to bear. The PAP unit decided to install air conditioners, and at the end of May, the Beijing PSB paid for the installation of air conditioners in all of the rooms except for my cell.

After the PAP assumed responsibility for guarding me, even my right to empty my bowels in a proper toilet was taken away, and I could only use an old plastic bucket left in the corridor outside my door. When I needed to relieve myself, I had to shout "report" to the guards, who would press the call button in the cell for the personnel in the monitoring room to open the door. The process of me going to the toilet required increased security. Regardless of whether I was urinating or defecating, I was surrounded by three guards who formed a triangle at a distance of less than a yard from me, ready to handle any kind of emergency situation. It was an unbelievable and revolting process. Some people say that you get used to it, but I never did, even after ten years.

The PAP clearly objected to the arrangements as well, because on the night of my transfer to the custody of the PAP, I heard someone I assume was an important person in that organization shout, "Watch him shit! Our people won't be able to eat for two days. And when he's finished, we have to empty his bucket! We won't be able to eat for two weeks! We won't empty the bucket!" It seems that the two sides negotiated some kind of solution, because my latrine bucket was emptied by the PSB's janitors. In any case, the routine never worked well, and sometimes the bucket was not emptied for two weeks. I apologize to my readers for recording these unpalatable memories, but it was part of the meticulous planning aimed at humiliating me over an extended period of time. One of the guards, a university graduate from Henan, said, "Even the Japanese installed water toilets in the prisons in Manchuria where Chinese prisoners were held eighty or ninety years ago. Today, the CCP has water toilets, but they won't let Chinese people use them. I just can't believe it."

Sometimes the main source of my problems was the unreasonableness of certain guards. Although I never experienced anything as bad as when Sissy prohibited me outright from using the toilet on his watch, some guards pressured me to avoid it, and others were clearly trying to give me a hard time. For example, there was a guard from Hubei nicknamed the "Artist," a university graduate who had become a soldier after failing to find other work. He told me not to defecate on his shift, and one morning when I did, he retaliated by refusing to give me any water to drink. Others also gave me trouble for this toilet matter, but under these extraordinary circumstances, I tried to understand their feelings and did my best to change my routine. After six months, I was defecating only once every four days. This ultimately resulted in my becoming constipated.

There was a guard named Liu Wei whose mother was Mongolian. He was over six feet tall, a graduate of Tianjin University, interesting and humorous, with a kind heart. One time during his shift, I was having great difficulties defecating. Since there was video but no audio surveillance during the defecation process, I told him about my problems with regard to this matter. He told me, "Go during my shift, as many times as you want. I really understand your situation." Hearing these words almost made me cry. Later, the other guards who had joined the PAP the same year as Liu Wei—Xia Zhicheng, Zheng Zhizhong, and Guo Tong—all said the same thing to me. These young men had one thing in common—kind hearts—and treated me like a human being. Naturally, it was very dangerous for them to do this.

Both the cause and the treatment of my affliction displayed Chinese characteristics. Consciously or subconsciously, everybody was splashing around in a dark, bitter swamp from which no one could escape, not even the forces of evil themselves.

The second day after I was handed over to the custody of the PAP, a chat was arranged with four people, ostensibly as a result of the most recent torture session, which focused on the demand that I continue to talk with the government. Pushing his electric prod under my chin, Section Chief Wang had said, "If you won't talk, this time you're a dead man." Their brutality served as no inducement to me, and it was only after more than an hour of frenzied torment, when they began using their linguistic skills in a relaxed atmosphere, that I finally said, "It was never a problem in the first place." Of the four people who came to talk with me, two of them were among the three who had spent more than three months interrogating me after my August 15, 2006, abduction (the leader of those three, Tong Zhonghua, had been promoted in the meantime), and one was a female police officer. The leader of the group was around fifty years old. He sat there saying nothing, his eyes glowing with cunning and experience. He was more than six feet tall, with a radiant bald spot at the top of his head, and I could hear from the way he talked that he had some education. Since like all the others he never introduced himself, I called him "the Ultimate."

The Ultimate and his entourage arrived around noon on May 2, 2010, and he opened the conversation by saying, "Old Gao, we're responsible for talking with you at this next stage, and frankly speaking, we haven't been looking forward to it. When I was told I was taking over your case, I began feeling anxious days in advance, and that has never happened to me before. I have been handling cases for decades, most of them major cases involving genuine criminals. Talking with murderers and arsonists doesn't require weighing every word, but it is different with you. Three days ago I began thinking about what should be the first thing I said to you. I've handled cases involving senior officials and even university professors, so it is not that I lack the capability, but I still feel anxious about dealing with you. We're going to be spending some time together from now on, so my main objective today is to meet you for the first time, and the specifics of our talks will come later. Old Gao, since taking on your case, I've been in contact with a lot of people who have told me in private that you are a good man, and this is extremely unusual. I am telling you this because a lot of people want to help you, and you need to understand this so you can take the long view. Forget about everything and go back to normal life. A lot of people hope to get you out of the situation as soon as possible so you can rejoin your family and let them stop worrying. What does it matter to you if there is injustice and darkness and abuse in our society? There is nothing any of us can do about it anyway. Getting yourself into this predicament isn't worth it. I hope I can convince you to reach an understanding with the government and let bygones be bygones."

All of what he said sounded very reasonable and humane, but what followed in the subsequent months proved it to be nothing more than a tactic, because the core objective was no different from that of all the conversations that had come before: cooperate with the government or die. He just packaged the message more skillfully.

After he had talked for more than an hour, I said, "You're not going to tell me that you don't know what has been happening to me over the past few days."

He said, "Old Gao, it's not smart of you to bring this up. First of all, as the saying goes, the gentleman shares his joys but not his miseries. Secondly, all that is water under the bridge, and there is no point in revisiting it."

I said, "The people who inflicted that brutality on me were sent by the government, and now the government has sent you to talk with me. It is like you people wear two faces, and which one am I supposed to believe?"

"Ai, Old Gao, just be grateful! The reasoning is very simple: If you see your son is about to be hit by a car, you won't think twice before running over to push him out of harm's way, even if he gets bruised in the process. You certainly won't stand there talking reason with him. You are already in a perilous situation, and if we don't use urgent measures, we are only hurting you." He became increasingly complacent as he went along, his eyes gleaming. I said nothing more, and our first conversation ended there.

I do not remember exactly how many conversations I had with the Ultimate, but they spanned a good eight months, and the objective was always to get me to cooperate with the government, or at least to abandon my resistance and accept the government's help.

Over the course of these eight months, they offered a specific benefit on a matter I had been concerned about for years. My cousin had taken on a contract for one stage of a water diversion project, and the project had passed inspection in 2007, but the authorities were holding back 12 million *yuan* in project fees, of which nearly 10 million was owed in wages to migrant workers. My cousin took out a loan to pay the workers, but it had driven him close to bankruptcy. Given my feelings for my cousin, resolving this was very important, and if we were willing we could have received even greater benefit. But they did not mention any specifics in this regard, because they had come to realize over the years that I could not be moved by personal interests anymore than by the deprivations of solitary confinement.

There was a soldier from Henan called Anjia who described how Chen Shaoji,[13] upon having solitary confinement imposed on him, repeatedly sighed, "I never guessed that the methods I'd devised would be used on me." Anjia deserves further mention, but at this point I will only mention one of his experiences. One day with great animation he described how he and ten other soldiers had beaten a Falun Gong practitioner nearly to death and "ripped off his scalp." Then several days later, other soldiers said Anjia himself was beaten

---

13. TN: In July 2010, Chen Shaoji, former top political advisor of south China's Guangdong Province, was sentenced to death with a two-year reprieve for accepting bribes.

by Chief Fatty. Since this was commonplace, I took no great notice of it at the time, but when he came to stand sentry that afternoon, I was shocked to see that a large patch of skin was missing from his forehead near his hairline, and still seeping blood. When I asked what had happened, he said, "Chief Fatty ripped it off."

Apart from the indignities of the toilet process, another intolerable aspect of my imprisonment here was the lack of circulation in the basement where my cell was located, especially in the heat of summer. It even made the soldiers standing sentry become nauseated, and their vomiting only increased the toxic quality of the air. A Hubei soldier, Li Junliang, and the chief sentry he accompanied, Biggy Lu, had not been on duty for even an hour when I noticed their shirts sticking to their bodies as if they'd been drenched in water. Their faces were deathly pale, and they were unrecognizable as the two men who had walked in at the beginning of their shift. Soon after that, they began frantically punching the doorbell, and as soon as the door opened, they dashed out and began vomiting. The chief sentry tumbled to the floor in a dead faint, and he did not stand guard there again for the next seven days. This was a common occurrence, with one soldier, Jin Yeren, vomiting the most often. I am only grateful that the vast majority of the soldiers did all in their power to vomit outside in the corridor rather than inside the room.

An unfortunate exception was a Henan soldier called "Rugby," who with another Henan soldier suddenly vomited inside, creating a horrendous odor that did not dissipate for days. Jin Yeren once suggested that his lead sentry report the problem to the upper levels so the guards would be allowed to wear oxygen masks in the cell, but he was only berated for his effort. For all the meticulous planning to make my confinement as unpleasant as possible, however, it was of little effect, because the noxious atmosphere never made me vomit or even feel light-headed, which astonished the soldiers. I feel this was because I remained steadfast in my hopeful mentality. Besides that, the soldiers were coming in from the clean mountain air, and it was the difficulty of adapting to the radically inferior air quality that caused them such discomfort.

I did sometimes suffer from fluctuating emotions, especially when I considered what Geng He and the children were going through, but I never reached the point of feeling the need to cooperate with the authorities in spite of their constant and extraordinary exertions. During a conversation in August, the Ultimate began revealing some impatience. I understood his mentality, because he was unable to report any substantive gains to his superiors. The fact was that I had dealing with the government for more than five years by then, and there is no medicine that will revive a dead horse; it was his misfortune that he had become involved.

That day, failing to reach a resolution with me, he said, "The Empress Dowager Ci Xi said to her Finance Minister that no one is immune to good name and wealth, but you don't act the way normal humans do."

I told him, "Your conclusion is based on the standards of brutality. I am not the least bit immune to these things. My refusal to cooperate with the authorities is in fact for the sake of my good name, and the fact that I have four properties is proof that I had had wealth. Your conclusion reflects a narrow and overbearing mentality, like your definition of patriotism: Anyone who doesn't grasp benefit through your methods isn't acting like a human being, and anyone who doesn't destroy our country the way you do is a traitor." We parted on bad terms.

During another conversation in late October, he said, "There have been some changes in external forms, but don't think that means the larger environment has changed. I can tell you it has not. The government wants to see you walk out of this place." After saying this he just looked at me.

I said, "You know perfectly well who has illegally imprisoned me here and who isn't letting me walk out."

"It is easier than ever to get out of here. Let's set aside some of the problems we can't solve for the present—just write a few sentences for the government admitting your error and expressing your gratitude, and you will be out of here before you know it."

But I refused. There is nothing worse than a government that persists in using gangland methods to imprison citizens and inflict inhuman brutality on them, and then asks you to admit your error and thank it as well.

My refusal angered him, and he said, "Old Gao, we have given you a way out, but if you aren't going to take it, you can just stew in here for a while longer." And so this conversation, like all the others, ended with no result.

The Ultimate came to talk with me again in November, and this was his last contact with me. This time he was looking very relaxed as he said, "You don't have to admit your guilt. Just write a thank you to the Director [meaning Yu Hongyuan] and that will do."

I told him, "It is abnormal to thank the person who's persecuting you, and to thank him just because he's taking a rest from his violence is perverse." That was the end of our conversations.

These twenty-months of imprisonment left me with many memories worth recording, some of which would seem utterly trivial in normal life, but which in this unusual environment left one wondering whether to laugh or cry. One example was my first haircut in this prison. By this time my hair had grown very long, and it bothered me all the more in the scorching heat. As in every spell of detention, my request for a haircut had been passed up through multiple layers of bureaucracy and still had not obtained results. Indeed, I was repeat-edly told that a haircut was an earth-shakingly major matter, but that the report had been passed upward and a letter of permission should be imminent, so I should just be patient a little longer.

I said to a police officer surnamed Guo, "Every Sunday I hear people being given haircuts in the outer passageway. Why don't you just open the door and let a soldier give me a quick haircut?"

"That won't do! Anyone who does that will face immediate dismissal," he said.

Finally, coordination across departments achieved results. One day, my cell door opened and Officer Guo came in with a solemn expression on his face and said, "Old Gao, I have good news. You have been given permission for a haircut. Do you know what day it is today? It is Sunday, which should be my day off, but I ran all the way over here to give you a haircut. Once permission was granted, I did not want you to have to wait one day more." And so my hair was finally cut.

Another thing worth mentioning is my daily ablutions. Before the PAP took charge of me, I never had a chance to wash up or brush my teeth because there was no water in the cell and water had to be specially brought in, which seemed beyond the capabilities of the secret police. After I was handed over to the PAP, a soldier would bring me water every morning and evening for washing up, and few of them ever gave me any trouble about this. But what really bothered me was that I was never given the opportunity to wash my hands before eating or after using the toilet. I requested this repeatedly to no avail. When I asked a soldier from the northeast why this was, he replied, "The leaders say that you are not here on a vacation."

Nor could I get permission to wash my soil bucket once a week, even though the lack of cleansing created an unbearable odor. Since there is nothing one can do to avoid excretion, it only makes sense to at least reduce its effects as much as possible, and I was more than happy to do the dirty work myself. A soldier from Sichuan called Big Brother said, "The problem is that you requested washing it. Anything that you request the upper levels are sure to refuse."

Before the PAP took charge of me, bathing was an impossible idea, but after they took charge, the relevant authorities in Beijing handed down authori-zation for me to bathe once every twenty-one days, that is, three weeks. And it was only when you bathed that you could wash your clothes. It was truly intolerable, especially in summer, when after ten days one reeked from being constantly bathed in sweat. The bathing process itself was stupefying to any normal person, and gave the impression that any movement of hand or foot risked sending the entire regime up in a puff of smoke. I had to go to the second floor to bathe where a hot water heater had been installed for the soldiers to use. Embarking on the bathing process first required obtaining permission from the policeman on duty in the monitoring room. Then the loudspeaker announced, "All in place for the target to bathe," after which my cell door would open, and a stern-faced officer would come in and announce to me, "In accordance with permission granted by the upper levels, we have been ordered to arrange a bath for you. We request that you cooperate in accordance with law." He would then turn and order, "Proceed as arranged," and two soldiers standing on each side of me led me out of the cell. As soon as I stepped outside, four soldiers took their places, two in front and two in back, extending their arms as if to protect me. This cluster of seven then proceeded up two flights of stairs, with a soldier stationed about every three yards and one officer directing the proceedings downstairs and another upstairs. During the actual bathing process, I was usually surrounded by at least six soldiers, among whom two stripped down to their shorts and flip-flops to stand near and keep their eyes on me throughout the process. After I finished, it was announced, "The target has finished bathing, all in place!" I was then returned to my cell in the same way that I had left it. One time an officer surnamed Gu, who was standing behind me, said in a low voice, "You must be pretty special. There cannot possibly be bathing arrangements like these anywhere else in the world."

I had suffered from hearing loss following my most recent torture, and instead or returning after two weeks or a month, my hearing continued to deteriorate. For a full four months, I was completely deaf in one ear. This made me uneasy, and I repeatedly requested medical treatment, but I received no response. The PAP worried that they would be held responsible if I lost my hearing, and soldiers told me that a request had been passed up to the Beijing PSB for me to be examined and treated. Finally, the PSB was obliged to send two people to the location to talk with the PAP, and according to a soldier on duty that day, one of them was a doctor. The soldier said, "They didn't come here to look at your ear but to explain operations to the PAP. They seemed to be experienced and said your hearing would return within a year, and then they left."

Another time, long-term sitting without exercise, coupled with my unsanitary environment, resulted in prostate problems that made urination difficult and painful. I did not like to ask for medicine unless absolutely necessary, but when the situation became unbearable I finally requested treatment. The public security authorities refused me flat out, but the PAP worried that if the situation continued I would not be able to urinate at all, so they began allowing me to exercise in my cell within a limited parameter. This may not seem like much, but in that situation it was a hugely positive development that gladdened me for a good long time. I firmly believed that as long as I was allowed to move around without time constraints, within a year I could cure my prostate problems. And indeed, my faith was rewarded, as in less than a year I was completely healed, and my hearing returned as well.

I would like to devote part of this narrative to the pressure the PAP officers and men lived under and the decency they were capable of despite the darkness of their lives.

I was often dumbfounded by what I witnessed of the actual conditions of the PAP. In fact, anyone with the slightest understanding of the situation in China today knows the Communist regime remains in power through the brute force it applies through its military, police, and spies. Without this capacity, the regime would become utterly powerless.

When a human being lacks a wholesome personality and capacity for kindness, he regresses into a purely biological existence. Character and human feeling are what empower people, and that is why the Chinese regime is so harmful to the Chinese people and even to human civilization. Some may counter that lying is one of the traditional pillars of autocracy and provides the environment that empowers such systems. But without violence to back these lies, would anyone give credence to claims that are clearly so contrary to common sense? Of course, some may believe out of ignorance, but for the vast majority, "believing" is just a means of covering up the indignity of cowardice. That is why "public opinion" polls invariably show strong support for totalitarian regimes.

Before I had direct contact with the PAP, I thought that China's evil regime must treasure and pamper the military and police forces that are its lifeblood. The reality, however, is that the government controls the armed forces through coercive force and violence. The violence is combined with brainwashing, but soldiers believe the brainwashing is only for "stability preservation," ensuring that soldiers have no time to create "factors of instability," obtain "harmful information," or indulge in careless talk or thinking about their discontent.

I was amazed to learn that "stability preservation offices" have been established at all levels of the armed forces, from headquarters to the detachments. Lest we underestimate the intelligence of soldiers as a group, it is worth noting that they refer to the ubiquitous "stability preservation" personnel as the "spayed dogs" of their senior officers, who resort to unlawful methods of control because official corruption and popular disenchantment have rendered the normal restraining principles and processes ineffective.

The awareness of college-educated soldiers, in particular, exceeded my expectations. A Jiangsu soldier named Chen Jie told me, "In fact, this is inevitable. They don't treat people like human beings, so ultimately everyone feels insecure. It is only natural, and they reap what they've sown." Liu Wei felt that the army initially had great expectations of brainwashing, but when they discovered that soldiers were resistant to the tactic, brainwashing became purely means of occupying the soldiers' time and keeping them from causing trouble. In fact, however, soldiers regarded the stability protection offices as a main cause of increasing instability within the ranks.

A squad leader surnamed Gu from Jiangsu remarked that wherever there were "spayed dogs," there was sure to be instability because of the anxiety they caused. "It's pure luck that that PAP hasn't experienced any major problems yet. It's only a matter of time, because the relationship between the officers and men is like fire and water; the officers simply don't treat the soldiers like human beings."

Another soldier surnamed Guo, who had graduated with a degree in psychology from Peking University and had been serving for a year and a half, said he had filled forty-three notebooks during mandatory daily study sessions, but that the content was not even remotely useful. When I asked why so much energy was expended on taking useless notes, he said the officers wanted to leave the soldiers no time for independent thinking. Every time a notebook was filled up, it had to be handed over to a higher authority, allegedly out of worries about leaking state secrets, but he said the real worry was of the scandal that would ensue if the public became aware of the useless content, which apart from endless education in loving the Party and the country consisted mainly of speeches by officers. It was a source of unspeakable misery to the soldiers.

The soldiers said the "spayed dogs" were much less ferocious than they appeared and were sometimes actually beaten by the officers and men. In the Seventeenth Detachment, I generally only heard about the "spayed dogs," because they were not supposed to enter the jail cells, but I once had the "honor" of a chance personal encounter with one named Yan Limou, when he suddenly burst into the lockup for a surprise search. His face showed the same misery as other PAP officers, with a pair of unusually small and rat-like eyes. When our eyes met, his expression quickly became complicated, and he quickly turned away.

As the main enforcement tool of the CCP's Commission for Discipline Inspection (CDI), the PAP's pitiful spayed dogs had to spend all day rushing between various locations. Where there is pressure, there will be resistance; this is what physics and human nature have in common. My lockup had what was called a "self-defense whistle" (according to the soldiers, every lockup had one), and one blow of the whistle and the cry "Inspection team has arrived!" would cause the entire building to erupt in a deafening rumble like a great herd of sheep stampeding as a lion bursts in among them.

The purpose of all this fuss was to prevent the soldiers from using cell phones, ostensibly for the sake of "state security." The controllers of the armed forces worry that soldiers will gain access to "negative" information through their cell phones, but another major aspect is that most of the evil acts carried out by the CCP are executed by PAP soldiers, and the worry is that they will divulge secrets that will arouse popular discontent. Given that cell phones are now a part of daily life, these raids proved completely counterproductive; every soldier kept at least two cell phones so that if one was confiscated, he could continue his online activities uninterrupted. Concealing cell phones and guarding against sudden searches for cell phones was a major topic of private conversation among soldiers.

One college-educated soldier made the prescient comment that the officers actually create the factors for instability in the armed forces. He said that when you have a group of people responsible for seeking out factors of instability, they do not want their effort to be in vain, so they will find it even if it does not exist. In particular, it was the soldiers who were most willing to speak the truth who were treated as factors of instability.

A few days after the PAP took over guard duties, the soldier Anjia described an experience he had as a new recruit, which suggests that China has made little progress since the palace eunuch Zhao Gao forced others to call a deer a horse.[14] As a new recruit, Anjia had to attend an inaugural meeting, an old Communist Army practice. After roll call, the squad leader pointed to a soldier next to the classroom's shiny white wall and asked, "What color is that wall?" When the soldier answered that it was white, he was immediately subjected to a horrific thrashing. After five soldiers in a row were beaten like this for giving the same answer, the sixth one replied, "It is whatever color the squad leader says it is." The squad leader immediately praised the soldier, and when he once again asked the soldiers who had been beaten what color the wall was, they all replied, "It is whatever color the squad leader says it is." Not a single soldier acknowledged the color that appeared before their eyes. When I discussed the phenomenon with Liu Wei, he said he would automatically go along with whatever the squad leader said: "If you aren't willing to say black is white, you'll be beaten and humiliated endlessly."

14. TN: Zhao Gao (died 207 BC) was a eunuch who conspired with the Chancellor Li Si to influence the succession to the First Emperor. According to Sima Qian's *Records of the Grand Historian*, Zhao Gao was contemplating treason and wanted to test his support among other officials, so he presented a deer to the emperor and called it a horse. The emperor, thinking this strange, asked those around him what the animal was. Some were silent, others said it was a deer, and yet others, apparently wanting to curry favor with Zhao Gao, said it was a horse. Zhao later secretly arranged for those who said it was a deer to be executed, and from then on, all the officials lived in fear of him. Zhao Gao rose to power as a result.

The newly recruited soldiers had all been beaten at one time or another, except for one, who admitted, "I'm more obedient than a pug dog and am even more attentive to him than a servant, and I give him cartons of cigarettes, so he has never beaten me."

Almost every new soldier I talked to said that he had to take a test right after joining the army. At first no one knew the purpose of this test, but when a group of new soldiers who had been sent back home began talking with each other, they discovered that all had chosen to tell the truth when answering the test questions. The openly stated reason was mental illness or radical inclinations, but in fact, soldiers who had served for a year all understood that the real objective of the test was to eliminate those who had principles.

Even soldiers who were not sent home sometimes got caught in the trap. A Hubei soldier named Chengcheng, over six feet tall and built like a bear, was a very decent and naive man, which proved disastrous to him when he joined the army. One time while he was stationed at the lockup where I was being held, someone from the division came to organize a test. The cadre emphasized that the soldiers absolutely must tell the truth this time and should not be afraid to do so, because the division would resolutely protect them. But in the end, the only person who told the truth was Chengcheng. When the results of the test came in, the cadre asked, "Which one is Xia Zhicheng?" Chengcheng shouted out and stood up. "Good, my brave young fellow, we finally discovered one," said the cadre, and then he read out the answer Chengcheng had written on the test. Chengcheng then took his turn standing sentry, eagerly awaiting his leader's praise. Instead, about half an hour later someone came in to relieve him, and his replacement murmured anxiously to him, "Be prepared. Everyone is squatting on the ground to take their turn being beaten." Chengcheng returned to sentry duty less than half an hour later, and I will never forget the fear in his eyes. It is a look I saw time and time again among those who were pulled out to be beaten, and when I looked at them with a sympathetic expression, they would raise their heads and stare at the ceiling with tears dripping down their faces. On this occasion, Chengcheng kept staring at the ceiling but said to me, "Old man, every day I fantasize about suddenly getting an illness that makes me fall into a coma, and the day I wake up is the day I am due for discharge, and I shave and get a haircut and quickly leave this damned place." After Chengcheng became a bit calmer, he told me that the squad leader, Zhou Xiaosai, had pulled him into a room and beaten him. But that was just the beginning. The person who took over sentry duty at noon told him, "Don't think about eating lunch. There's a big shake-up going on today, and we had to spend all morning squatting without being allowed to stand up. Now it's your turn." Chengcheng went out with an uneasy look on his face.

Someone may ask, why should the whole group be punished because one person told the truth? This is the old system of guilt by association unique to totalitarian China, in which not only an individual is punished, but also all those around him. This compels everyone to hate the person who "committed the error," and everyone monitors everyone else and quickly informs on others. As a result of Chengcheng's "error," everyone at that posting was punished with squatting for half a day and being deprived of their lunch. This "serious incident" was rapidly reported to the battalion and detachment, and ultimately a notice was circulated to the whole division.

One time when a soldier named Li Junliang was chatting in the detention room with chief sentry Zhang Tianya, someone from the PSB who was monitoring those on duty reported them to the PAP. After they were pulled out and beaten, Li Junliang stared at the ceiling for a long time, tears glistening on his face. Zhang Tianya showed no expression on his face, however, and when I asked why he did not seem to mind the beatings, he said, "He [pointing at Li Junliang] won't cry either, after getting beaten tomorrow. It is easier once you get used to it."

The beatings for talking in the detention room never came to an end, but neither did the talking. Once Yao Jiaheng returned from his beating, he immediately began chatting again. Chief Deng, who had seven years of experience in this field, was pulled out by an assistant political instructor and choked against a wall to teach him a lesson. Once he arrived back, he immediately started chatting again. Jin Yeren was also beaten many times for talking. Even the platoon leader and those on his shift continued chatting as if nothing had happened. Superiors treated PAP soldiers talking on duty as a mortal threat, but the only solution that they came up with was violence, and it always failed. Once after being beaten by the division's political commissar, Tian Yangyang asked me, "Why does my right eye keep blinking?" I told him he really needed to stop talking, but he said he would keep talking even if it meant a beating. Less than half an hour later, he was dragged out and given a horrible beating. Once, Liu Wei shouted at the monitors, "The only way to stop us from talking is to cut our heads off." I often wondered why the authorities seemed to never take the time to assess the effectiveness of their reign of terror, which seemed to have become an end in itself.

Equally ineffective was the brainwashing, likewise inflicted through violence. The majority of these young people grew up in families that did not prioritize education. Now they were forced to take careful notes on leaders' remarks and even memorize leaders' speeches. One would be hard pressed to think of any school or other institution characterized by more intensive and endless study, but in my observation, the results could not possibly be further removed from the intentions of its designers. For example, whenever a new soldier was sent to watch over me, he would eventually ask me about June 4, 1989. I would always ask why he was interested in this particular issue, and the responses always had certain points in common: (1) The soldier would express great curiosity, having never heard of the "June 4th Incident" prior to his military training; (2) he learned the government's account of this so-called "incident" during his military training; and (3) he could not believe the government's claim that protesting students had killed a large number of soldiers.

The soldiers all mentioned a video they had been shown during training, which featured tearful testimony from a "hero" who had been promoted to the position of Commander of the Beijing PAP corps after "suppressing the riots," and who claimed that he had personally witnessed students massacring soldiers. He even claimed that only 800 of the more than 10,000 soldiers who had been sent to Beijing had survived. Anjia said he had wondered how many students had been killed if so many trained soldiers had died. His fellow guard added, "Regardless of how many students died, we should know about this." Most of the soldiers who discussed this topic with me said they did not believe the government's version of events: "If we believed them, why would we ask you?" Some soldiers with a better understanding of the Internet had proceeded to the information highway to learn the truth about this massacre, and some soldiers declared, "The Communist Party's specialty is crying wolf while acting like a wolf."

One of the clearest indicators of the complete failure of this brainwashing education was that at the time of year when older soldiers were demobilized, some would ask me the truth about "June 4th" during their last few days. I asked one soldier known as "Big-faced Cat" why he did not believe the stories about 1989 told on the training video. He told me that his grandfather had told him as a young boy, "Whatever the Party tells you, know that the exact opposite is true."

During the final eight months of my detention, detention center heads came and went, but the individual mainly responsible for me was a man the soldiers called, "Glasses." Glasses had an unshakeable authoritarian power complex, exerting pressure and almost perverse control over me and the soldiers watching over me. He was the only officer who ever took away my drinking water during detention, a move that pressed me to take dramatic measures of resistance. But ultimately I do not believe he was a bad person. Being a PAP officer is high-pressure work, as evidenced by the gray hair and prematurely aged look common among the officers, and on top of that, Glasses was consumed by a desire to get ahead. He was young and eager but not yet ready, a situation that inevitably leads to failure. (The one I really believe was a bad person was his predecessor. I could tell what a truly fierce person he was, even though he never had a direct conflict with me and would just smile and laugh when we met. He was eventually awarded second-class honors for watching over me for ten months. A soldier told me he had "trampled without mercy all over you and us soldiers to get there.")

During one education session, while Glasses was discussing the sacred, honorable, and righteous nature of the detention center's work, a soldier asked, "Normally when a person commits a crime, they go to court and then to prison. Isn't the way we detain people a bit abnormal?" He further asked, "Since our responsibilities are so sacred, honorable and righteous, why must everything be kept so top secret, as if our very lives depended upon it? We have been told that if we reveal that so-and-so is being held here, not only will we be imprisoned, but our entire families will also be punished. Where else in the world are people so afraid of letting anyone know about the sacred and honorable work that they're doing?"

Two soldiers told me this story on two separate occasions, and both said that this question left Glasses in stunned silence for a full thirty seconds. But the response Glasses gave revealed three things about him: (1) He is not an evil person, or at least not yet; (2) he understands some of the stark reality surrounding him, even if he keeps that understanding hidden deep inside; and (3) he is an honest man, at least to a certain degree. His response was: "First of all, you shouldn't be asking such questions; if someone else were teaching this training course, it would be very dangerous. Second, I really can't answer your question about the top-secret nature of our work here, because people only do this type of work in countries like ours. In normal countries, things like this don't go on, so we have to keep it secret."

While respecting the honesty and lack of stupidity reflected in this response, I found that Glasses could show utter disregard of conscience just for the sake of promotion. In that respect, it was harder to forgive him than some other officials who seemed simply too stupid to comprehend the evil they were committing. Glasses was not very easy to get along with, but he never permitted even a hint of belligerent attitude among his detainees. He warned me a number of times that I had a "bad attitude" and had forgotten who I was as well as who he was, and he kept feeling the need to "correct" my attitude. This was the basis for him eventually cutting off my drinking water, which led to real conflict between us. He scolded, "I'll use any means necessary to make you know where you stand." I retorted, "You are just an insignificant cog in this machine, so you need to calm down a little. I'm accountable to no one, but you are in a very different situation."

Another area where Glasses famously failed was in his relations with soldiers. The most sensitive time for the Party and its soldiers is when soldiers are demobilized every year—it was already an issue back when I was in the army thirty years ago. Back then, our division leader would be far more reserved and polite and would avoid interactions with soldiers who were about to be demobilized. But nowadays "stability maintenance" seems to have made this process even more of an ordeal than before. During my imprisonment, two rounds of soldiers faced demobilization, and at these times, even I was more nervous than usual, worried that the young men who accompanied me around the clock might act rashly. Such concern was not unfounded. Two soldiers, one from Henan and the other from Anhui, talked obsessively about launching revenge attacks on other soldiers while watching over me in the middle of the night. Back in my day, there was a sense of resentment among regular soldiers toward officers, but today, that resentment has turned into pure hatred. Roughly half of the soldiers watching over me said straight out that they hated their officers.

The rule that was in effect where I was being held dictated that soon-to-be-demobilized soldiers would no longer participate in regular exercises after late September, but in 2011 this shift occurred two months earlier than usual in the Sixth Squadron. Soldiers due for demobilization did not even join in study sessions and did nothing but stand guard. When Liu Fei and the Artist were watching me, I asked why this had happened, and they responded almost simultaneously, "The two sides [soldiers and officers] hate each other too much." "Then why do the soldiers continue to stand guard?" I asked. "The number of people on duty is set well in advance. If we don't stand guard, things will be even harder for the others." Relations between senior and lower-level officers were so tense around this time that I prevented at least five large-scale fights during my imprisonment. The soldiers gave me a nickname "Gaoren," meaning a great man, and some shared their detailed fight plans with me without a second thought. They said, "Gaoren, I have something I need to ask your opinion about." And I always said, "It is best that you talk to me about it."

Zhang Hao alone planned two elaborate revenge attacks in just two months, and was determined to gather a critical mass of accomplices to finally "finish off" his target, "Giraffe." Both times I beseeched him not to go through with it. "Giraffe" was the name I gave to Zhang Longfei, who was around 6'4" and an all-around bad guy. He was sly and skilled, with four years of experience in the ranks, and he was known for dragging soldiers into an empty room to give them a beating. Liu Fei was beaten until he had "panda eyes," and Kuku came in to stand guard with blood dripping from his head. His mental processes seemed to be affected, and I convinced him to ring himself out and go to the hospital for a check-up. Glasses was left covering over a thousand *yuan* in hospital bills on account of this incident. He covered it because Zhang Longfei had been in the army longer than Glasses, and also because Zhang's fists had become the sole guarantor of a certain order within the detention center during his reign.

From start to finish both Zhang and Glasses showed an inexplicable animosity toward me, never imagining how many violent attacks against them I had stopped. Some plans were designed to kill their target immediately, while others were meant to break their target's legs. I argued the soldiers out of these plans because they were all just kids who had seen nothing of the world, and going forward with these revenge attacks would have destroyed their already extremely limited opportunities. Glasses and Giraffe were clearly not wonderful people, but they were also only in their mid-twenties, and I could not help but think that they were not really bad people, just in bad situations. Glasses so longed for promotion that he could no longer control himself, giving him an unpredictable temper made worse by his inexperience. Meanwhile, all of Giraffe's issues seemed to arise from innate intellectual defects. His tragedy was that he struggled daily for what he considered a great and patriotic cause, while in reality his superiors were just taking advantage of his simple mind.

One time I tried talking about this with him in the shower (the only place where there were no listening devices), but it was a complete failure. I asked him whether it was better to show true love to his fellow soldiers who surrounded him every day, or to practice an empty love for "the motherland and the people." He said that of course the only option is to love "the motherland and the people." In so many respects, we were no longer talking about simple differences of opinion; it was like we were living on two different planets. His case showed not only the pointlessness of the never-ending political education that soldiers receive, but even more the complete failure of China's schools and society to produce functioning and thoughtful human beings.

At one point, the young people around me were both excited and anxious: A massive earthquake had rattled Japan, and they were sleepless with joy. More than eight million "patriots" immediately celebrated this disaster in online postings, which then produced the anxiety of delaying expressions of their "patriotism" as the overburdened Internet slowed to a crawl.

My one chance to share in a moment of glory with China's legendary patriotic youth left me deeply pained. The tragedy of contemporary patriotism is due not only to the perverse way in which this patriotism is expressed, but even more in the way that this perversion has become the only "correct" way to love China. This means that patriotic fervor that is a disservice to humanity itself will continue to rage on without anyone being allowed to express doubts or articulate alternative understandings of patriotism.

Once while watching over me, a soldier called Sprout told me how excited all of China's patriots were to celebrate the 2011 earthquake in Japan. When he noticed that I responded with silence, he leaned in to ask my opinion of the earthquake. I had not intended to say anything, having had far too many negative experiences attempting to communicate with such "patriots," but as he continued to ask, I felt compelled to respond. I told him that the loss of life in this earthquake was tragic, and that we should pray for all those who had died, sympathize with Japan in this troubled time, and render all possible assistance. As his face sank, my spirits rose, and I told him that the type of patriotism that he was promoting was a recipe for ruin and showed that contemporary China's patriots were completely lacking in humanity, morality, and basic common sense.

A look of fury came over Sprout's face as he said over and over again, "I won't let you talk bad about my country, I won't let you talk bad about my country!" and shook his head back and forth, as if refusing any input from the outside world. "Our commanders told us that people like you don't love our country. They were not lying." The look of hatred on his face was far too real, so I stopped talking; China's "patriots" are not a group of people with whom one can have a reasonable discussion, even though he had raised the topic himself, and nearly a year after the earthquake.

The only soldier I met who refused to take joy in the earthquake was Zheng Jun, from Beijing. He told me his views were shaped by two unexpected phenomena that he observed at the time of the massive May 12th earthquake in Wenchuan in 2008: No one from Japan celebrated the Wenchuan earthquake or sang its praises online, and whenever the Japanese rescue team discovered a body during their rescue work, the entire team would pause for a moment of silence to honor the deceased. He told me this truly moved him. I noted that such respect for human life should be expected of all of humanity, and that those who were celebrating the earthquake in Japan had greatly harmed our nation's reputation, and he agreed.

When I asked him why he had such a different attitude from his fellow soldiers, he told me that his fiancée had studied in Japan and had exposed him to a completely different understanding of Japanese society and the Japanese people than he had seen in Chinese newspapers. But he told me that he was of course a patriot and cried every time he heard the words to certain patriotic songs. I told him that such "patriotic" behavior could not even begin to compare with the simple act of sparing a few cents for a beggar on the streets.

The most disheartening aspect of discussing these issues with the soldiers standing guard over me was that none of them could even begin to see the relationship between patriotism and caring for animals and plants that one came

across on the road, caring for the people that one passes by every day, and helping all who need it. Patriotism to them was nothing but lofty platitudes and
empty declarations without the slightest application in the real world. I often
thought to myself that they spent almost all of their time engaged in "education," but nothing they studied had even the slightest relationship to ordinary
people's lives.

Would it be possible to take some time out from these impractical studies
to convey a few basic pieces of common sense? For example, based upon my
observations, most soldiers have no grasp of basic etiquette, and when it comes
to matters of respecting, helping, and caring for one another, they seem completely clueless. Soldiers bringing me meals would often hold the plate in such
a way that their thumbs would be sticking into my food. They would cough or
sneeze on my food or on me, and would talk constantly in the middle of the
night when I was trying to sleep.

In contrast to such behavior, soldiers showed an almost ridiculous degree
of care for the military's image. Focusing all their energy on trivial formalities,
they showed no understanding of the intrinsic link between a person's internal cultivation and exterior image. In order to produce a positive image of the
PAP before me, a member of the "enemy forces," all soldiers standing guard over
me were required to remain completely still and straight, except for when they
were taking notes. They were not even allowed to blink. Anyone who failed to
live up to these unrealistic standards would be dragged out and beaten.

Newer soldiers who believed that maintaining the proper stance and posture were necessary to maintain the sacred status of the Party and military usually suffered real damage to their health within a few months. Most of the
soldiers were plagued with streaming eyes, varicose veins, or lumbar muscle
degeneration. A tall and handsome soldier in the Sixth Squadron watched over
me for more than a month before being transferred to another location. Six
months later, he returned and was put in charge of security monitoring, and at
one point took over watching me when another guard became indisposed.
When I recognized him, I asked how he was doing, and tears suddenly poured
down his face as he told me that his back was so bad that he could no longer
stand guard. This was by no means exceptional, and some said that the most
unfortunate are the soldiers standing guard at Tiananmen Square: The "number one guards under heaven," as they are called, reportedly suffer from circulatory issues that render them unable to father a child. Soldiers sent to stand
guard embassies and consulates are not allowed to wear winter jackets, no
matter how cold the weather, as a means of demonstrating the sheer strength
and will of our countrymen.

In their "education sessions," there is no discussion of the concept of a citizen or of citizens' rights or responsibilities to their country, society, and others. I discussed this issue of citizens' rights and the taxpayer's role in society with almost all of the young soldiers who guarded me, as well as with my prison guards at Shaya Prison and elsewhere, and found almost all of them lacking the most basic knowledge that a contributing and active member of a modern society should possess.

One of the first soldiers with whom I discussed the idea that taxpayers should have a say in governance was Lu Kun. His first response was simply, "We are not taxpayers, are we?" Among the college-educated guards, not a single one had a clear understanding of their status as taxpayers. In Shaya Prison, I discussed this issue with six police trainees in college, and not one of them thought of himself as a taxpayer. Even more shockingly, four were unable to respond affirmatively to the straightforward question, "Are you a citizen?" Two responded, "We're public servants, so how can we be citizens?" From the perspective of brainwashing officials, this is a sign of great success, no matter how you look at it, but it crushes all momentum for cultural development and civilizational vitality. When all that is left alive within a society is its totalitarian system, where can anything healthy take root and grow?

The world's two models of taxation, "price including tax" (clandestine taxation) and "price before tax" (open taxation), provide a clear standard for distinguishing a civilized political system from its barbarous counterpart. Open taxation gives people the pride of being taxpayers and makes them pay attention to how their taxes spent. That is why, within a civilized political system, those in power tend to budget precisely and spend taxpayers' money carefully.

The inverse is found in totalitarian and autocratic countries, where the price of every product you buy includes a certain amount of tax that is secretly taken away from you by the state and prevents you from realizing that you, too, are a taxpayer. The result of such a system is the situation that we see in China today, where the CCP relies upon taxpayers for all of its expenses while demanding that taxpayers express their perpetual thanks and gratitude to the CCP. State media rant about the need for loyalty from those who "get their food from the Party" or who "live off the Party," but there cannot be many political parties anywhere in the world as reliant on taxpayers as the CCP, with the possible exception of the Worker's Party of North Korea.

One time, I asked a few of the college-trained soldiers watching over me what kinds of hopes they had for the future of the rule of law in China, and basically everyone gave the same response: "It doesn't matter. So long as I don't break the law, I won't have any problems with the law." This response shows an absence of civic responsibility, but even more an utter lack of conscience: So long as I do not break the law, what does justice have to do with me? In the real world, in modern society, there is no way for you to avoid the law from the minute you leave the womb. From legal relationships with family member to status as citizen and taxpayer, a person takes on a multitude of rights and responsibilities even if he does nothing but sit at home all day. Once a person steps out his door, he enters into legal relations with everyone else on the street; once he boards a bus, he enters into a contractual relationship with the bus operator. And the list goes on. When I shared these insights with a college-trained soldier from Jiangsu, he was shocked and told me that he has never been told this from kindergarten through college or in his daily study sessions as a soldier, adding, "Of course, they don't tell us anything that might be of any use."

This phenomenon stood out for me during my twenty-four months of detention (including the three months with the Yulin PAP). The soldiers working in these detention centers have a pressing need for genuine educational enlightenment: the provision of common sense knowledge for people living in modern society. At the very least, there is a real need to cultivate some of the most basic traits required of human beings, such as morals, a sense of shame, empathy, self-control, honesty, and a basic understanding of rules. Such learning could then be expanded and applied to loving and having a sense of responsibility toward other human beings, and to having a basic understanding of the accomplishments of human civilization. According to what the soldiers told me, almost all of their studies focus on loving the country, the Party, and socialism. Most soldiers have reached the conclusion that such education is complete bullshit. As Liu Wei and Guo Tong said, whether one loves or not, to whom one directs one's love, and how one shows one's love are all very personal choices, and forced love ultimately produces the opposite of what was intended.

The educators' own stupidity was at times so glaring that it left me dumbstruck. Many soldiers told me about officers' corrupt, illogical, and basically inhuman behavior, especially in the Beijing PAP. In all of Beijing, any construction or redevelopment project is inevitably taken on by a commander's daughter-in-law, who in most cases just shows up at the beginning and then does nothing. The wives of unit commanders are all involved in Amway pyramid scheme sales within their units and ensure that soldiers buy whatever they need from Amway at outlandish prices. In the center where I was being held, at least once every two months the wives of senior offices would lower themselves to sell their wares to the soldiers, who all had to buy something. Even soldiers standing guard in the detention center would be given a temporary replacement and called out to make their purchases. Every soldier would curse this forced buying under their breath, but in the end they had no choice. In the interests of maintaining secrecy, soldiers in the detention center were not allowed to wear military uniforms, and a number of soldiers went through years of service without wearing a military uniform for more than a few days. Even so, all of the soldiers' clothes had to be purchased by the wives of group or corps commanders, and the soldiers had to take whatever they purchased.

Soldiers' assessments, promotion to the level of officer, and acceptance into the Party all relied on spending money. Jiang Minzhou spoke with a lisp on account of his cleft lip, which meant he did not meet the standards for recruitment as a soldier, much less for becoming an officer. But this was not a serious problem; he just had to pay three times the standard rate. He told me that in order for him to make the transition from a regular soldier to an officer, his father had to give the unit commander over 80,000 *yuan*. "Big Brother," who grew up in Sichuan and Guiyang, was basically deaf, so he had to spend many times the standard amount in bribes to become a soldier. The head of PAP's Seventeenth Detachment came from Henan, and according to other soldiers from his province, all of his promotions were overseen by his elder sister.

Every year, throngs of people come from Henan, Hebei, Anhui, Hunan, and other such places with bribes for entry and promotion. According to what the soldiers told me, every position has a clearly marked price; promotion from soldier to cadre costs at least 500,000 *yuan*. Soldiers told me that everyone within the bureaucracy had bribed their way into their current positions, so everyone focused on protecting their positions, making money, and most importantly, "maintaining stability."

Some soldiers claimed that the thorough corruption of all military institutions originated with the state's handling of the assassination of the former vice-chairman of the Standing Committee of the National People's Congress, Li Peiyao, in 1996.[15] The Jiang Zemin clique's frenzied employment of revenge and silencing in this case revitalized China's premodern practice of collective punishment. After Zhang Jinrong killed Li, all of Zhang's superiors up to his division commander were punished with dismissal or imprisonment. Even Zhang's former drill instructor, already demobilized, was thrown into prison, as were Zhang's elementary and middle school teachers, the chief of his local police station, and the officer responsible for his original military training. The most unthinkable part of this entire response was that the leaders were about to send the entire Beijing PAP Corps to Tibet and move all of the Tibet-based soldiers to Beijing. Finally, someone pointed out that such a

---

15. TN: Zhang Jinrong was apparently Li Peiyao's bodyguard. A summary of this case is provided in a Google forum: http://groups.google.com/forum/#!topic/talk.politics.china /Lknl4gIkQyE (accessed April 15, 2016).

move was likely to result in chaos, and proposed that only those officials who were to be punished be sent out to Tibet.

Soldiers told me that the handling of this affair left military officials feeling that punishment was unrelated to whether one had actually done anything wrong and instead was dependent on the behavior of others over which one had no control. This led these officials to feel that their futures and their fates were out of their hands. Before this, officials would genuinely assess people's skills, but after the Li Peiyao affair, all they cared about was money, and it was no longer strange to see someone half blind and half deaf being accepted into the army. Another reason military officials were unhappy with the handling of this case was a claim that I had never heard before: They claimed that Zhang had killed Li not because Zhang had been caught stealing something, but because Li had raped Zhang's younger sister. Some Domestic Secretary (Dom-Sec) officers I spoke to made the same claim. The authorities' eagerness to maintain face for the leadership demonstrated a willingness to ignore questions of right and wrong, a readiness to cruelly punish completely innocent people, and a disregard for the basic dignity of Zhang Jinrong and other PAP soldiers and officers. To this day, on the anniversary of the killing, February 2nd, every member of the PAP has to spend the entire day engaged in tedious security training.

Another aspect of life in the PAP that soldiers found highly frustrating was the everyday management of senior leaders, which demonstrated consistently stunning depths of stupidity. One example demonstrates the contradictions created by the presence of "stability maintenance" officers. Officers sent to inspect the Seventeenth Detachment were told they could not return home to celebrate the New Year until they had found a quota of problems. On the other side, the detachment's commander had decreed that any units found to have problems would not be allowed a break to celebrate the New Year. The two sides were thus caught in an unyielding deadlock. Finally, the stability maintenance officers were ecstatic to discover ashes sitting in the office ashtrays of the Second Battalion, as well as garbage in their garbage cans, and the commander of the group was called in to make self-criticism at a cadre meeting. Soldiers, describing this moment as if it had just happened yesterday, said that while the commander made a great show of being earnest, some of the phrases he used became classic jokes that were circulated throughout the corps. For example, he stated, "Our group's serious error was in putting ashes in our ashtrays and garbage in our garbage cans. This has left a dark stain on our entire detachment, so we earnestly promise to correct our errors and will never again put ashes in our ashtrays or garbage in our garbage cans." According to their recounting of this event, this statement brought the meeting to complete silence, and the leaders said nothing. But at the end of the day this self-criticism had real value, as the inspectors were able to eliminate ashes, garbage, and other potential sources of instability before returning home victorious to celebrate the New Year.

Another case of almost satirical stupidity making the rounds illustrated the unrealistic policies implemented by new leaders taking control. According to this story, one new leader tried to distinguish himself from his predecessors through a new "dry workplace" policy. Under this policy, no water was allowed anywhere in the PAP workplace. Those responsible for inspections took this policy to a whole new level of absurdity. No matter how lofty or how holy the PAP are, they are still human beings and cannot live without water, but once unannounced on-site inspections began, something as simple as water in a cooking pot became an indelible blot on one's record. In order to avoid becoming a negative example in the valiant struggle for a completely dry workplace, soldiers stopped cooking rice and instead bought steamed buns and bread, and some who grew tired of steamed buns started eating dry instant noodles. When they needed to drink water, soldiers would gather in an inner room (preferably one that required passing through multiple doors) and guzzle it as quickly as possible. Such vigilance was essential: If a single drop of water was discovered in a cup, bottle, or water dispenser, the sacrifices of all one's fellow soldiers were for naught. Soldiers were pushed close to the brink of a breakdown trying to meet this absurd goal.

The biggest headache for everyone in this situation was the water at the bottom of the toilet. The designers of toilets incorporated this feature in order to arrest unappealing smells, never anticipating the demands of a dry workplace policy. As a result of their lack of foresight, each soldier had to be issued with a towel so he could soak up the offending fluid after using the toilet. But of course the wet towel then had to be hidden to conceal any signs of contact with water. Soldiers told me this policy left them unable to wash their faces or take showers, and they had to furtively wash their clothes as if committing a major offense. If I had not had the chance to talk face-to-face with people who had experienced the implementation of this policy, I would never have believed it possible.

I am grateful for the twenty-four months I spent in detention, which gave me a rare opportunity to develop a more comprehensive understanding of the nature of this Party. When in 2011 an interrogator accused me of "maliciously denigrating and defaming the Party and government, and blackening our country's image," I said, "If there is really anyone wasting their time denigrating or defaming the stink of dog shit, or blackening the image of a crow, they must be living under a curse."

My "special exchanges" with the PAP over the course of two years created an almost indescribably mixture of experiences. Meticulously attending to their own interests while facing the sheer power of the totalitarian state, soldiers came to resemble brainless zombies. They seemed to have lost even the most basic desire to prove that they were still human beings, yet they remained animate beings in a state of constant motion aimed at attaining their goals. For example, despite the constant monitoring, soldiers continued to use their cell phones without ever seeming to be caught.

The authorities, in my analysis, worried far too much about the soldiers reading about injustices and rising up in indignation and outrage. The soldiers seemed utterly unsullied by any concerns much higher than a woman's breasts, all of them being busily engaged in intimate online chats with multiple women. Xiao, for example, confided to me that he was chatting online with a total of thirty-two members of the opposite sex, ranging in age from thirty-eight to fourteen, and it was all he could do to keep up with them. He told me that everyone, including officers, was similarly preoccupied, some with even more numerous chat partners.

Discussions between soldiers ninety percent of the time revolved around women, and all too often revealed a disgusting cruelty and callousness. Once Zhou and Ji, both soldiers from Henan, had a late-night conversation in which Ji recounted how early in 2003, a medical supplier who had done business with his family for years had transported more than ten tons of Isatis root, an ingredient in Chinese medicine, to their city. At the time, no one wanted to buy the stuff, even at 2 *yuan* a kilo, so the supplier stored it at Ji's home for the time being. Who would have guessed that just a couple months later, hysteria over the spread of SARS would drive the price of Isatis root up to 300,000 *yuan* per ton. The owner of the Isatis root hurried to claim his goods, only to die in a traffic accident on the way. The Ji family, suddenly in possession of a windfall, managed to show some consideration for the dead. The two-year-old daughter of the deceased Isatis root owner was now an orphan, so Ji's family made a donation to the child's orphanage based on the *pre-SARS* value of the Isatis root stockpile. Zhou's response to this dubious generosity was to say, "If I was you, I would not have given any money to that kid. Instead, I would have brought her to my house, raised her, and then started screwing her daily once she turned twelve. And after I finished screwing her, she could clean my house." Finding this talk intolerable, I jumped in and said that the lack of beliefs or even a basic moral bottom line is dangerous not only to others but also to oneself. Zhou was infuriated: "I can't stand being around that old fart. I would love a chance to finish him off." Ji's response may have saved my life: "There is no point bothering with people like him." They ignored me from then on.

The army leadership constantly warns soldiers that international and domestic anti-China forces are sharpening their knives against China's rising prosperity, and that the army's main responsibility is to protect the hard-earned happiness of China's people. After rising in the morning, the first thing PAP soldiers must say is, "We must always remember the grave situation that we're facing, and remember the sacred mission that we carry forth." At the start of every meeting and study session, everyone has to recite, "Maintain your vigilance every waking hour and even while asleep."

In my observation, the CCP ruling cliques' sense of security is no stronger than that of the average colonial occupier. Soldiers told me that ever since 2007, PAP soldiers in Beijing and Tianjin have been placed on the second highest state of alert in the three days before the Nobel Peace Prize is announced in October of each year. Soldiers are required to eat and sleep in their vehicles so they can respond at a moment's notice to the provocations of the international and domestic anti-China forces. Soldiers are also on high alert on each and every historically sensitive date, searching frantically for the ubiquitous enemy like restless dogs.

Some soldiers understood what was really going on. In the Fifth Squadron, two college-age soldiers commented that for all the flowery language about righteousness and morality, the behavior of officials shows that they know exactly how the Chinese people feel about them. Every year when the National People's Congress and Chinese People's Political Consultative Conference meet, the government mobilizes hundreds of thousands of soldiers to protect the delegates behind multiple lines of defense, as if at war. When the CCP is holding a more "important" meeting, over a million soldiers could be mobilized for defense. Who could have imagined that a few thousand members of a political party would need such heavy defense in their own country? But I told them that such incidents reflect the unfiltered reality of China today. I asked them, "Do you ever think about who all those mobilized soldiers are directed against?" They laughed without giving me a direct response.

A number of soldiers also shared with me their experiences around June 4th each year. They told me that once the morning of June 3rd arrives, officers from every unit are sent out onto the streets of Beijing in plainclothes to track anyone dressed in all black or all white. If such an individual approaches Tiananmen Square, the situation must be immediately reported to one's superiors, after which the suspect is interrogated. Plainclothes officers likewise monitor the purchase of candles. Other government institutions are also required to assign people to watch for suspicious activities during such sensitive times, and soldiers estimated that a few million people could be involved in such work around that time of year. Soldiers told me that the environment is so tense that high-level officers in the military and the police cannot get a moment's sleep.

During my detention, I repeatedly witnessed the constant vigilance and rapid response arrangements at these "sensitive times," with blaring horns and sirens sounding whenever a suspicious individual was spotted. On the morning after June 4th in 2010, some soldiers told me they had been mobilized in the middle of the night as part of a region-wide response to a report that the overseas artist Chen Weiming had created a miniature sculpture depicting the violence inflicted by soldiers on the city. Supposedly, the sculpture was to be covertly transported to Tiananmen to stir up unrest among the uninformed masses.[16]

Soldiers laughed as they told me about the official arrangements for the 2009 National Day parade. Anyone watching the parade would have seen large groups purporting to represent "the masses," yet these seemingly spontaneous crowds were heavily infiltrated by the secret police and military to prevent anything unexpected from happening. In addition, three-deep rows of PAP troops surrounded groups of college students marching in the parade. Some soldiers said that in private discussions, the college students called the PAP dogs who had been called in by their masters to watch over the students, while the soldiers retorted that the students were surrounded like pigs in a pen. One soldier laughed and remarked, "Whether you're a dog or a pig, in either case you're not treated like a human being."

A soldier by the name of Chen told me that recognizing that rank-and-file soldiers were nothing but dogs in the eyes of those in power allowed you to move forward without the worry and distress that those who saw themselves as human might face. He told me that everyone in the PAP knew a popular rhyme that went some like this: "PAP soldiers are dogs, following wherever they are led; PLA soldiers are bricks, sticking wherever they're placed." Once when Guo Tong and Liu Wei were watching over me, Guo Tong shared a saying that is popular among rank-and-file soldiers: "If you hate someone, send him off to be a soldier; if you want to see someone become an animal, send him off to be a soldier in Beijing; if you want to see someone prefer death over life, send him off to be a PAP soldier in Beijing."

Many college-age soldiers told me they had watched military-themed movies and had begun to feel that the motive behind such films was to trick young people into joining the army. "Compared to the military lifestyle I saw in the movies, we seem to have suddenly descended from earth to some type of hell," said one soldier. He explained that he was not at all scared of strict training or

---

16. TN: Chen created the sculpture in 2009, and it was displayed in Hong Kong in 2010.

rigorous demands, but he found that these did not exist for the purposes of effective training or normal discipline, but rather for brainwashing and "stability maintenance" games.

For example, Guo Tong, who always followed the rules and acted in a very cautious manner, made the mistake of shifting in his seat a little bit during a study session and was called out to "have a talk" after class with the class monitor, Fatty Chen. Fatty Chen ordered him to put his hands behind his head and kneel on the ground, which was humiliating enough, but then Fatty Chen started playing with his cell phone, which was a serious violation of the rules, and finally fell asleep for a full two hours, during which Guo Tong had to remain on his knees with his hands behind his head. It was during those two hours that he began to truly understand what life was like as a soldier, as well as the kind of person Fatty Chen was.

Another college-educated soldier, Zhao Zhizhong, said that when his older sister came to visit him during training, she was made to wait outside until a break, when the soldier in charge of new recruits took Zhao to see her, sitting with them the whole time and never giving them a moment of privacy. He told me, "They're afraid of new soldiers running away, and they're even more scared of someone exposing the darkness of military life. I felt like I was being held hostage, and not because of something I had done, but because of things they had done!"

An officer known as "Dumpling Cai" had long been waiting to visit his family and was finally granted leave for the Lunar New Year Festival in 2011. One day, everyone noticed Cai looking unhappy, but when asked what was wrong, he said that the situation was a state secret and he could not share it with anyone. Later another officer revealed that the Central Military Commission, as commanded by Hu Jintao, had ordered an emergency halt to any and all leave for all members of the PLA and the PAP due to the "turmoil" ongoing in distant Egypt that winter. Apparently, China's top officials were afraid that anti-China forces at home and abroad would create chaos just as rioters had done in Egypt, and all soldiers were required to sacrifice their leave in order to guarantee the Chinese people a happy and peaceful New Year.

In terms of my living environment, my time with the Beijing PAP was my most inhumane experience over the past decade. The first issue was the blazing summer heat mentioned before, but another issue that was never resolved was the overwhelming moisture in the underground room in which I was being held. The mountainous region where the detention center is located gets a lot of precipitation, and combined with the lack of circulation in my cell, once autumn arrived, my clothes and blanket became so damp that I could wring water out of them, and they were covered with mold. For the simple right to hang my soaking wet blanket and socks outside to dry a little, I engaged in a back-and-forth with the authorities for the entire time of my detention, without result.

Once when Guo Tong and Liu Wei were watching over me, I looked forward to finally taking a shower, which was only allowed once every three weeks. Troubled by the fact that my blanket was never dry, I wanted to hang it in a different part of my room, but my guards told me I could not change its location without obtaining approval from their superiors. Later, in mid-summer of 2011, the condition of the blanket reached a point at which it was completely unusable. When Chief Fatty from the Sixth Squadron was standing guard, he secretly took it outside to air it while I was in the shower. When I later complained that the blanket had been left outside too briefly to have any real effect, he just gave me an uncomfortable look and said it was the best he could do.

But the most unforgettable discomfort in this round of detention was the cold of winter. There was basically no heating during my first winter in detention, and I had never in my life experienced the type of freezing cold that tortured me that winter. I am not exaggerating in the least when I say that the pain produced by that inescapable cold far surpassed anything that I ever experienced in torture. It was as if everything around me was made of ice. I have memories of life in extreme poverty, but even then, there was never a time in which all of my thoughts were occupied by the cold. That cold stuck to me with a depth and tenacity that I could have never imagined. When I covered myself during the day with my blanket, Deng Quanying, an officer with seven years' experience, came in and told me I could not use the blanket during the day until he obtained instructions from his superiors. I told him that unless he was able to magically rid my room of the cold, this most basic human need for warmth was non-negotiable. Finally, my guards turned a blind eye to my use of my blanket. The fact was that the soldiers watching over me were also cold. They told me that the person responsible for running the furnace was an elderly man who came to work every day at 12:30 p.m. and left promptly by 2:30 p.m. The only reason heat was supplied for two hours was to ensure that the water in the heaters and pipes did not freeze. Soldiers who stood watch over me said their entire bodies went numb. Some of the soldiers finally took matters into their own hands by adding a little coal to the furnace before they started their night shift, and gradually, everyone started doing the same. Some particularly thoughtful soldiers even began adding coal to the fire when they finished their shift. By the second winter of my detention, a system had become established wherein particular soldiers were responsible for adding coal to the heater every night, finally resolving the problem of these freezing cold nights.

At this moment, reflecting back upon these experiences, I remember some of those soldiers quite fondly for the humanity and kindness they showed me. Some of them really went out of their way, and after learning who I was, would add meat or eggs or other treats to my food at meal time. Others, at the Mid-Autumn Festival, would secretly bring in a moon cake for me to enjoy.

In my cell, there was one corner that was not being video monitored, because interrogators cannot be videotaped according to legal procedure. This corner brought me a few occasional joys during my imprisonment. Soldiers were not allowed to share their deployments or transfers with me, but many would come to see me before they left to say goodbye, sometimes with tears in their eyes. They would say things like, "Old man, what they are doing to you is wrong. Good things will come to those who are good. I am leaving and can no longer look after you, so please take good care of yourself." Some were even brave enough to play music for my entertainment in the last few shifts prior to their departure. Those responsible for monitoring behavior in my prison cell looked the other way and let this go on. Little Zhou, one of the soldiers responsible for watching me, said he would visit my family after he was discharged and tell them how I was doing. I stopped him, because I did not want him to do something so dangerous. Every year when soldiers demobilized, I would be up all night thinking about the wonders of human emotion, and how it overcame the obstacles the authorities produced to prevent us from recognizing our common humanity.

As for more complicated cases like Chief Fatty and Deputy Commander Song, comparing their behavior to the suffering other military officers put me through allows me to also remember them fondly. Neither of them had any really bad intentions toward me, and never actively tried to create problems for me.

I had quite a few conflicts with Liu Fei, not because I felt he was a particularly bad person, but because he was simply too shallow. He never liked any of the new soldiers who came in to stand guard with him, and I could not bear how he picked on them. Since I could not address this directly, I used the unreasonable constriction of my space of movement in my cell to start an argument with him. Liu sounded the alarm, and Chief Fatty came in. He immediately reprimanded Liu Fei and then assured me that if anything was bothering me, he would do his best to resolve it. Taking advantage of the opportunity, I told him about being denied my rightful space to move around and be active. "Why can't soldiers treat me more like a human being?"

He said, "You're right. We're not just talking about space but about treating each other like human beings. We need to abide by the rules and not make random adjustments." From that point on, he designated a particular area in my cell in which I was free to move around as I pleased, and the soldiers were no longer able to further limit that space, as they had done before.

Later, I passed a message to Liu Fei that my sole intention that day had been to get him to stop picking on the new recruits. Eventually, we got along quite well. His main motivation for becoming a soldier was to avoid serving time in prison. This was a very common phenomenon among the ranks, with many of these cases coming from Sichuan and Henan. They would tell me, "Most of the guys I used to hang out with are now in prison. If I didn't come here to serve, I would probably be in prison by now as well."

Deputy Commander Song got his name because he had spent more time at that lockup than any of the other officers and men. A few days after he left, an intense conflict occurred between me and Glasses, and soon afterward, Deputy Commander Song was transferred back to that location. He came into my cell several times, but we never spoke. His eyes were kind, and he never added to my misery, and that was enough for me to consider him a friend. At least compared with Deputy Political Instructor Li, Deputy Commander Song was an intelligent person.

I never hated Deputy Political Instructor Li, who racked up merits through keeping watch over me, but I was disgusted with his callousness toward the soldiers; his unprepossessing appearance hid a conniving mind. He was distinguished by the energy and thought he devoted to his tragic role in this dark politics, whether out of impotence or pure stupidity. He never engaged in face-to-face conflict with me, always baring his teeth in a smile, but his unhappiness and anxiety were revealed in his eyes and in his facial expression, which made him look much older than his years.

One incident reflects his callousness and lack of inner peace. Some soldiers discovered stray dogs living in the hills, among them an adorable puppy less than half a year old, which they caught and brought back. One night the puppy began barking furiously while Deputy Political Instructor Li was on duty. Li squatted down and placed his electric cattle prod next to the puppy in its cardboard box and patiently shocked the puppy until the barking stopped. A sentry witnessed the entire cruel process. After Li left, the sentry walked over and found the puppy foaming at the mouth, its body trembling uncontrollably. On the third day, when Squad Leader Gu came in to stand guard, he said the puppy had died and that they had buried it. Apparently, after being shocked, the puppy had suffered from diarrhea and had refused to eat or drink, and saddest of all, whenever anyone came near it trembled with terror. Squad Leader Gu loved dogs and had told me many stories about the puppy and its playful relationship with the enormous police dog, which had protected it. Regrettably, dogs are sometimes better than people, especially in today's China.

The soldiers were always talking about Deputy Political Instructor Li, and I could fill half a book on him if I cared to waste the ink. Several months after he left, when I was proving "uncooperative," Glasses telephoned him to discuss the problem, and a soldier told me that Li gave Glasses the following advice: "Don't engage in direct conflict with him, don't give in to him and don't let him be comfortable."

This time while I was secretly imprisoned, apart from my conversation with the top military commander the Ultimate, there were three other exceptional conversations worth mentioning. I cannot recall the exact dates, but the first conversation occurred during the Spring Festival in 2011, when Zhang Xue talked to me on behalf of his "patron," Yu Hongyuan. Zhang Xue was Yu Hongyuan's most trusted lieutenant, and this made him unbearably conceited and unprincipled, as if everyone else were beneath his consideration.

That day, my cell door opened, and Zhang swaggered in.

"How's it going, Old Gao?" he said before he had even sat down.

"I am still alive, as you can see," I answered.

"What is on your mind these days? Director Yu sent me to have a chat with you."

"I have had things on my mind for a long time. That is why I'm locked up here, as you know."

"Sounds like you are still pissed about it, too. But sulking isn't going to help you. Haven't I told you? Just give up and be more realistic and you can get yourself out of this mess. All that bullshit about democracy, freedom, transforming China—is that practical? Just talking about that stuff gives me a goddamned pain. All these years you have been wrung out here, not dead and not alive. Just look at you! Is it worth it? Old Gao, I didn't come here to negotiate with you, I just wanted to pass on the message that these few years you have gotten in my patron's way." (What he meant was that my refusal to go along with Yu Hongyuan had blocked Yu's advancement in the ranks.) "You know what I'm like—whoever causes problems for my patron is going to have problems with me, and whoever makes my patron uncomfortable is going to feel uncomfortable because of me. Maybe I will make you wish you were dead. You think you can overthrow the Communist Party? You think you can rely on the Americans? Don't make me laugh! Our Chairman Hu Jintao visited the US recently, and didn't the Americans welcome him with smiles on their faces? The American government spent $300,000 to completely renovate the White House South Lawn to receive our Chairman Hu. Nobody could care less about someone like you sitting here in a cell. Hurry up and find a way out for yourself."

The more he talked, the more agitated he became. I said, "In fact, your world isn't all that perfect. I can see you're not happy with your life."

"What do you mean? I don't understand what you're saying."

"We have been meeting for just over eight months, but you seem to have aged ten years overnight. It looks like the smiling reception from American politicians hasn't brought boundless improvement to your world."

"Yeah, thanks to guys like you screwing things up. Someone who switched sides recently was talking about people like you. He said you guys are worse than murderers, because a murderer only hurts people physically, but people like you mess up people's thinking."

"Then I guess you should keep your distance from me—the farther away, the better." Concluding that no miracles would result from further conversation, Zhang left in a huff.

The hatred Zhang Xue and his beloved patron Yu Hongyuan felt for me was evidenced by their consistently cold-blooded treatment over these past ten years. But I pity them more than anything and rejoice that I have not become like them. The truth is that they are tragic products of this system, the process of fulfilling their ignominious roles in this dark regime causing them to lose the many good things unique to human beings—inner peace and tranquility, a feeling of moral pride, conscience, and love.

I had another chat with Zhang Xue in May or June 2009. The pride he took in having a patron like Yu Hongyuan was evident in his words and actions, while he overlooked how his blind devotion to serving as the instrument of Yu's cruelty foreshadowed a tragic fate. During this second chat I learned that Zhang Xue's wife was having a baby just at the time that his patron was entrusting him with overall responsibility for the location. Zhang was not even allowed a trip home for the birth, yet he was endlessly grateful to his patron: "I consider it an honor and point of pride to sacrifice myself for the sake of the happiness and safety of a multitude of families and households."

Even so, whenever Zhang and Yu talked of their children, you could see from their eyes that gentleness and love truly existed inside them. Whenever a child had some small illness, their concern made them into completely different people, and Zhang also clearly loved his wife.

The other person I conversed with here was Zhang Xue's patron, Yu Hongyuan. The timing of this conversation was not long after the conversation with his star pupil Zhang, and it could be that Yu put in an appearance after deciding that Zhang was not capable of turning me around. Yu was obviously anticipated the prison environment, wearing not only outdoor clothing but even a scarf around his neck. Right after entering my cell, he scowled and shook his head and asked if he could open the window, saying, "The air in here is disgusting." It had been at his order that the window had been sealed shut, and now that he wanted it open he found that a polyethylene sheet had been nailed over it. Shortly after sitting down, Yu opened the conversation by rubbing his hands and saying, "It's tough for you, Old Gao. Is this shithole fit for a human being?"

I said, "People made it this way."

"Don't give me that, it's a dump. But changing your prison environment and changing your fate are both in your hands. Whether the change is big or small is also up to you."

I said, "You talk like I have become your leader. In that case, you should hurry on home."

"What do you mean? Old Gao, I traveled a long distance to come here today and give you a chance. Speaking frankly, it's your last chance. You've reached the point where you need to seriously consider your way out. Don't stick with your foolishness and keep refusing to listen to good advice. There aren't going to be any meat pies dropping from the sky, and even if there are, they won't be for you. They gave the Nobel Peace Prize to Liu Xiaobo, but so what? He gets a pile of cash, but he can't even spend it, stuck in his prison cell. They ordered the Communist Party to release him. What do we care? Has that changed the Communist Party? No. Who gives a shit about the Nobel Peace Prize? What is a piddly country like Norway? Our Foreign Ministry spokesman rightly said that our Party has never been ambiguous about defending China's national interests. Let me state it clearly: If the Communist Party was going to become extinct tomorrow, I would kill you tonight. The moment it looks like the Communist Party is finished, the last thing I will do is liquidate you. Then you'll know that whatever is bad for me isn't going to do you any good, either." Yu was panting with rage.

I said, "My continuing to live is proof that every time you have wanted to kill me, I have survived, and I will live until China changes."

"Old Gao, you are not all that smart, much as you might dislike hearing it. I thought I was the only one who knew that, but recently I had a nice talk with XX,[17] and when your name came up, XX said, 'Gao not only has absolutely no political brain, he can be considered completely brainless.' Did you hear that? And here you thought I was the only person who thought you were simple-minded. Just look at XX—he knows how far to take things. That is what I call a guy with a brain. We had a great talk, and he was willing to stay in contact

---

17. TN: Here Yu names a well-known dissident writer, but given that Yu may be lying about this individual, we have protected his identity in this translation.

with us. I said I hoped that from now on whenever he published a non-academic essay or book he should give us in the government a look at it first, and he very quickly agreed—it went a lot smoother than I expected. I give a little, you give a little. But no matter how much we compromise on benefits, you never seem to listen. Do you think it does you any good to back us into a corner? Don't we still hold the knife in our hands? Old Gao, you are just too stubborn, and that is the main reason your fate is so tragic. After we have worked you over, do you think there will be anything left? We give you a way out, but you have blocked one good opportunity after another, and here you are stewing away. In fact, with a soft word and your head down, we go out and buy an electric heater and the problem is solved. Why should we kowtow and beg you for this? Recently we went to see XXX,[18] and he said intellectuals can spend ten years revolting and not get anywhere—when in history have intellectuals staged a successful revolt? Now that's what I call a strategist! Anyone else is willing to sit down and talk with us; an American can talk, Chiang Kai-shek can talk, what can't we talk about?"

"It's a historical fact that the Americans and Chiang Kai-shek could talk with China," I said, "but could they be talked into accepting the communist system? Another historical fact you know very well, which is that they never reached an agreement with you Communists."

"I originally planned to talk with you for an hour today, but I cannot stand it [referring to the cold], and in any case it seems there is no point. Old Gao, I will leave you with these last words: We're waiting for you to write us a letter or pass a message to us, but you don't have unlimited time. I'm going." With that, he stood and left. This was the last time I saw Yu Hongyuan.

Yu was typical of officials in this system, with his unrestrained corruption and lack of principle, callousness, and craving for official promotion. Corruption is undoubtedly the inevitable product of this system, but he treated it as a matter of course and had no scruples about acknowledging it even if to an enemy like me. He could go to any luxury hotel and use the best suite whenever he wanted to. Before I was detained, he always had me brought to either to a high-class club or a fancy hotel, and sometimes I would see Sun Di or Zhang Xue come in a special car with the person Yu was sleeping with that night, even though he could have easily arranged for them to arrive a few minutes later to avoid my eyes. But, as with Zhang Xue, Yu's love for his daughter softened my

---

18. TN: Yu names another dissident writer here, whose name is withheld for the same reason as above.

heart toward him, and I genuinely hope that he turns his life in another direction before he is punished for what he has done.

Another contradictory quality in Yu Hongyuan was that even with the lack of light in his heart, he prayed to the gods and to the Buddha. I have become acquainted with many officials who are "believers" like Mr. Yu, going to the temple to burn incense and knocking their heads on the ground before their gods, their hands clasped as they muttered incantations. Even without believing in God, a person needs goodness and light within him. If a person lacks those two things, all the riches in the world will never make him happy.

Another conversation occurred at a time I cannot remember clearly, but my impression is that it was one afternoon before the Mid-Autumn Festival in 2001. My cell door opened, and the sentries withdrew, followed by the entrance of a person who resembled the Mount Liang outlaw "Stumpy Tiger," Wang Ying, in the classic *The Water Margin*. Most people who came to talk with me would sit down before starting to talk, but this fellow came in with his hands clasped behind his back and shifted his short, thick legs in a trip around the cell, and then with his back to me he suddenly said, "Old Gao, how can you stand it in here? How much longer will you be able to put up with it?"

"I can live to be ninety-four," I said.

He made another turn around the room. "Ah, good man. Ninety-four? That is too bad. Spending the next half of your life in this environment will require special skills. You're forty-eight this year, aren't you?" He continued pacing the room in high spirits and said, "Can we talk?"

"We're already talking, but if there is nothing new to talk about, it becomes a meaningless process, so is it worth the effort?" He left soon after that.

Another interesting phenomenon worth mentioning about this imprisonment was the meals delivered to me every day.

The handling of the relationship between the PSB and the PAP was rather delicate and direct. First of all, although I was handed over to the PAP to be locked up, the PSB had arranged a monitoring room where they carried out airtight monitoring of the daily contact between PAP personnel and me. The PAP, for its part, also had their own monitoring room to keep track of the situation in the prison cell, and established a strict visit registration procedure. Ostensibly I was in a military lockup, but the arrangements for the detention and the cost and arrangements for the board and lodging were the responsibility of the PSB. For the PAP, meals arranged by the PSB gave rise to safety concerns, so when the PSB brought the meals to the prison, the PAP actually delivered each meal to the cell. They also took the food away and stored it in the refrigerator to ensure its freshness, discarding it after twenty-four hours.

This gave rise to the abnormal phenomenon of a person whom the authorities regarded as Enemy No. 1 and referred to as a beast being given such elevated protective measures.

On the night of December 14, 2011, someone shook me awake. I opened my eyes to see the leader of the Sixth Squadron, who said they had received an urgent notice from above to get me up for a talk. Shortly after that, three men came in, among them Demon No. 1 and Demon No. 2. The third person, who looked like an officer, stood across the desk from me, hands behind his back. Demon No. 1 carried handcuffs, and Demon No. 2 held a black hood in one hand. They said nothing, but motioned for me to stand and then pushed me down onto the bed and patted me down. I was then hooded and cuffed and propelled out of the cell and up some stairs. I could tell I was outdoors, the first time in twenty-one months, as a coolness washed over my body, and I heard the grave, full-toned barks of the patrol dog "Little Limpy."

A two or three-hour drive followed, and when my hood was removed, I found myself in a large hospital lobby. Demon No. 1 once again pushed my head down rudely and yelled while a group of people walked toward me, followed by some policemen, video cameramen, and photographers. The lead person was an old man who was looking quite gentle and cultured. I later learned that he was the director of this big hospital. "Everyone is here. Let's go upstairs," the old man said.

On the second floor, I was un-cuffed and taken to a desk, where a woman wearing a gauze mask said she was going to draw my blood for tests. I finally understood that I had been brought out for a physical exam, and that arrangements had been made for it to be carried out when no one else was around. All proceeded without incident except in the Otolaryngology Department, when a female doctor suddenly asked in surprise, "How did this man's vocal cords become like this?" Everyone stared at me until I said, "I have hardly spoken a word in twenty months."

After the exam was finished, I was hooded and cuffed again, and after a bumpy ride I once again heard Little Limpy's familiar barks. The return trip had taken a lot longer, probably due to traffic, and by the time I reached my cell, it was already afternoon. A guard quietly asked how things had gone and said that many soldiers were worried about what might happen to me.

I prepared myself for another long period of imprisonment, but that night at bedtime, an officer told me a phone call had come from above instructing me not to go to sleep. Around ten o'clock, my door opened and the same three men from the night before came in. The lead officer spread a few pieces of paper on the desk, and then the two "demons" held my body while grabbing my hands and pressing them onto a black inkpad. My hands were then pressed onto the pieces of paper to leave finger and palm prints, for what purpose I still do not know.

Just after breakfast on December 16, 2011, my cell door opened again and the same trio came in. Again they searched my body, cuffed and hooded me, and propelled me out the door. I did not know at the time that this was the end of my secret detention, but I had once dreamed of such a scene, and the guard in reality was the same Hunan soldier called "old hero Zhou" as in my dream.

Once again I heard the outdoor noises and experience another long, painful drive with my head between my knees. Finally the car stopped, and my hood was removed before I got out of the car—an unprecedented exception! Demon No. 1 snarled, "Bastard, don't you dare lift your head or you will see the consequences!" Even so, from the corner of my eye I noticed lights flashing on both sides of the street, and as I looked up I saw that we were entering a building while surrounded by dozens of uniformed policemen and the occasional blue or black Western suit and badge. Before I knew it, I was inside a small courtroom, and the policemen took me to the defendant's table. Several "judges," all women, sat upright and still as a bailiff removed my handcuffs. A "judge" asked my home address and then said, "This court is now in session!" Everyone rose to their feet, and immediately the ruling was read. It said that during my suspended sentence, I had shown lack of repentance and had violated prison regulatory provisions, as a result of which the Beijing PSB had applied for my suspended sentence to be replaced by a custodial sentence in prison. As soon as the judge finished reading, she ordered me to sign the ruling, and then I was escorted out. The entire process seemed to take no more than two or three minutes.

None of the normal steps under a rule of law process had been followed, nor had I been given an opportunity to respond to the "ruling." I could see Yu Hongyuan's law-blind silhouette behind the entire procedure. I once said at the outset of a lawsuit, "In China, the highest concentration of people blind to the law resides in the Party's legal cadres, and among them the most law-blind group is the Party's treasured law experts and professors."

The Secretary of the Central Political and Legal Affairs Commission, Zhou Yongkang,[19] headed up the special task force for my case, but he merely set the tone and scope, leaving the actual execution to Yu Hongyuan. Most disheartening is how China's "judges" abandoning due process under the manipulation

---

19. TN: Prior to this, Zhou was the Minister of Public Security from 2002 to 2007. After retiring in 2012, Zhou was put under investigation for corruption in 2013. In 2015, he was sentenced to life in prison for bribery, abuse of power, and intentional disclosure of state secrets.

of a cruel and ignorant secret police chief. What lack of integrity and damaged personalities must they have?

As soon as the "trial" was over, I was escorted into the car, cuffed and hooded. I held the court ruling tight, because I had not had the time to read it, and when they had difficulty snatching it from my grip, someone squeezed my handcuffs until the unbearable pain caused me to open my hands and the document disappeared.

After another interminable drive, my hood was removed and I was escorted into another building, surrounded by uniformed video cameramen and photographers. The two "demons" pushed me into a room full of police officers, marking my transition from an unnamed hell to one with a name.

Before moving on to this new stage of my incarceration, I would like to mention some insights I gained during my twenty-one months with the PAP.

The PAP as an Instrument of Violence

I had spent twenty-four months in PAP prisons being guarded by the CCP's secret police, who receive a small share of the proceeds from their theft and oppressions. The PAP soldiers act purely out of their obligation to serve the evil regime. That is why the CCP controls the two groups in completely different ways: the police through profit-sharing and almost infinite privileges, and the PAP troops through benefits to the cadres and naked oppression of the soldiers.

Pillage is the foundation and purpose of CCP power, while the gains of pillage are ultimately consolidated into specific benefits. The soldier population is way too massive, while violence is an inexhaustible resource that costs nothing.

In my two-year observation of this "mighty army," I found that it performs three "jobs" year-round. The first is to constantly fawn over and express loyalty to the CCP; the second is to use its "spayed dogs" to control the army and maintain its "stability"; and the third is to serve as the iron fist of the forces of evil in the overall stability maintenance process.

As a tool to prolong the system of tyranny, if the army's own "stability" becomes the main goal in its daily operation, its capacity as an army is greatly reduced. Whether it is powerful enough as a defense force for the "state" is anyone's guess. When Saddam Hussein's "elite" Republican Guard came under fierce attack, the only capability the troops demonstrated was the ability to flee.

When facing unarmed peaceful citizens, however, they are supremely powerful, as when they massacred unarmed students in Tiananmen Square. While the American army shattered Saddam's "elite" military units, those same units killed 5,000 Kurds in one night. Likewise, as a tool of violence for China's evil regime to maintain control over the country, this "mighty army" is powerful after all.

Soldiers told me many examples how this "mighty army" cruelly cracked down on people's opposition. I cannot recall the specific locations, but there were instances in Hunan, Anhui, and southern Gansu Province. From what I heard, these cases had several points in common: The first was that troops were assembled from multiple points to carry out the crackdown. The Anhui case resulted from mass outrage when a wealthy businessman killed a child with his luxury car. After the man expressed indifference to the death, the angry crowd began smashing and looting his supermarket. Dozens of PAP troops were transported to Anhui from Beijing, Jiangsu, Zhejiang, Shandong, Henan, Hunan, Hubei, and Jiangxi to handle the "sudden incident."

The second characteristic was that troops were amassed without delay, regardless of the cost. The third characteristic was that once the troops arrived, the crackdown was carried out swiftly, and every effort was made to prevent the situation from escalating.

The fourth characteristic was that the crackdown was carried out in a violent, gangster-like manner. According to those who had participated multiple times in "handling sudden incidents," the majority of officers and soldiers wore plain clothes and micro voice headphones and mingled with the crowd, waiting for the opportunity to make a move. Some even played the part of agents provocateur to change a peaceful gathering into an "unlawful riot" or a "vandalism incident" as quickly as possible. The fear was that if people were allowed to gather and express themselves peacefully, more and more might join in, and the situation would become uncontrollable. Once the agents stirred the crowd into a frenzy, their comrades-in-arms would immediately carry out a violent crackdown, but some of the arrested "rioters" would be rewarded instead of punished. One soldier said he "got a pocket full of high-end luxury lighters" for the Anhui "riot."

Ghosts

Another unbelievable thing I learned during my two years with this "mighty army" is how powerless it is in negotiating with the supernatural world.

On the surface, the CCP denies the existence of gods or ghosts. This is not only their ignorance but also their misfortune, and is a major reason why so many of my countrymen have become moral degenerates. Anyone knows that God is a source of comfort and strength for human souls, and that without faith, human life lacks all foundation and direction. More importantly, a person without faith lacks the ability and impulse of self-restraint.

Denying people the right to religious faith creates multiple-personality disorder for the CCP's personnel, many of whom burn incense in their homes all year round. I once visited the home of the Party secretary of a well-known state-owned enterprise in northern China and discovered that in his bedroom incense was burning beneath a portrait of the leader of the Falun Gong spiritual movement, Li Hongzhi, even though he was in charge of banning Falun Gong in his work unit.

I mentioned previously that the office building where I was being held had been built on a Ming dynasty gravesite and was considered haunted. But encounters with the spirit world were by no means limited to that location. PAP soldiers and officers told many amusing stories about their "struggle" against gods and ghosts. According to the soldiers, "weird phenomena" began to occur after Jiang Zemin became General Secretary of CCP, and "demonic sightings" were reported everywhere. From 1990 onward, PAP units in all provinces were plagued by hauntings, and only after all kinds of experiments did they find a way to effectively deal with the problem.

A soldier reported standing sentinel and suddenly finding himself in the basement, while the surveillance camera went completely blank. Another sentinel spent two hours walking down from the second floor without reaching the first floor. Female soldiers sleeping in upper bunks would leap out for no reason, sometimes injuring themselves in the process. Sergeant Zheng Jun spoke of many strange encounters, including once when he was standing sentinel and saw a woman emerge from the rice field carrying a young child.

Ghost sightings in the National Archives terrified soldiers with reports of eerie weeping, laughter, and screaming. Once a surveillance camera captured a woman in white standing next to a sentinel. Duty officers who rushed to the scene found no woman physically present, and the sentinel himself denied any awareness of a woman standing there, but he was still issued with a demerit for "chatting with a strange woman while on duty."

In the National Archives, the army responded by posting double sentries and scattering peach branches around. (They kept a stack of peach branches in my prison cell because soldiers often reported supernatural sounds or apparitions there, but I never had similar experiences.) For a while, they hung a large plate with the national emblem above every regiment or squadron's door, saying that the national emblem, as a symbol of righteousness and colored a bloody red, must be able to banish evil, but the haunting only increased.

Some troops troubled by frequent "haunting" simply painted the entire barracks red. When this appeared effective, an order was telephone to the entire army (nothing was put in writing) to paint all PAP barracks red. But before long, the "haunting" resumed.

The eventual success came from an experiment by some female soldiers who tried their luck by placing a small stone lion on each side of their dormitory door. When the hauntings stopped, this method was promoted throughout the PAP (again by telephone, not in writing), and the haunting finally ended.

It is said that the successful banishing of ghosts so enthralled top leader Jiang Zemin that he kept bringing it up in conversation. Soon all national ministries, major banks and enterprises, and local governments at all levels were placing stone lion statues next to their doors, and stone lions became a boom industry.

The CDI and Corruption

During that period of my prison life, another major insight I gained from PAP officers and soldiers was about the CCP's CDI. Previously, like most Chinese people, I knew that the CDI has a "double-designation" system, but never realized that this extra-legal internal discipline system was implemented with such savage disregard for laws human and divine.

Judicial sovereignty is an important part of state sovereignty, and unified scope of law means that the same substantive law applies to the entire territory, with procedural law performed by the specialized legal investigation, prosecution, and trial departments. Anywhere in the world, depriving a person of his or her personal liberty outside the state's judicial power is a crime against humanity. The CCP's CDI system, however, handles cases outside the judicial system established by the Constitution and has no procedural legitimacy. Under this system, the CDI detains Party members and cadres by force, holds them in a secret location, and prevents any information getting back to their families. During such custody, the detained person is deprived of all basic human rights and dignity; torture and humiliation are routine, and sleep deprivation is a common interrogation tactic.

One soldier said that when one mid-ranking officer was uncooperative after being taken into custody, the soldier normally standing guard was withdrawn and replaced with goons who took the man off to a different room. When he was brought back a week later, his face was swollen beyond recognition and he could no longer stand by himself.

The soldiers said that CDI case-handling locations are always in luxury hotels located at scenic tourist sites. For example, the Central CDI rents a huge luxury hotel in Beijing's Mangshan resort area. Combined with the cost of manpower for these investigations, the CDI spends money like burning paper.

Soldiers said that each location is equipped with several arrest teams comprising PAP soldiers. Each time a new suspect is apprehended, the teams are frantically busy for days on end, sometimes not even having time to sleep at night. The detainees are not limited to Party members and cadres; after a suspect is detained, his or her spouse and children are usually brought in to "assist the investigation." Next come the suspect's lovers, bribers, relatives, and any others who might be involved. In gang-related cases, 100 or 200 people might be detained, each person locked up in a separate room.

Sometimes a person is apprehended purely for the sake of maintaining confidentiality because he or she happened to be present when the suspect was arrested. When it comes time to publicize the case, the relevant personnel will have a talk with that person, who once released will keep quiet and not demand redress. For example, when Chen Shaoji was arrested, the secretary who accompanied him to Beijing for the "meeting" was held for six months in order to maintain secrecy, but was not questioned even once.

The CDI sets the tone for corruption cases through its verbal instructions to the procuratorate and court leadership. No questions are to be asked about the amounts involved or about anyone the CDI has not already named.

"Ruling the country by law" has long been written into the Constitution, along with human rights, liberty, rights of ownership, but the government's actions openly prevent citizens from enjoying their constitutional rights. Meanwhile, any mention of "constitutionalism" is criticized in Party media as "anti-Party" or "defaming China."

Three years since Mr. Xi's anticorruption campaign started, we see no sign of any move toward "rule of law." Officials held at a "designated time and place" usually reappear in a year or so under the label of "corrupt officials" to raucous acclaim that conceals the fact that the cases have been handled gangster style. "People get the government they deserve"—this is the crux of China's problems, compared to which overthrowing the Communist dictatorship is only a technical issue.

In fact, after three years of Xi's anticorruption campaign, the following conclusions can be safely drawn: He has no desire to introduce due process of law, and the main goal is to maintain the CCP's dictatorial status and eliminate rivals; a sincere anticorruption campaign would subvert the regime. In the history of the CCP, only two top leaders, Hu Yaobang and Zhao Ziyang, did not "kill" colleagues in order to establish their own power, and look what happened to them. I will not go into the details of Mao Zedong's heinous cruelty. Deng Xiaoping took down three Party chairmen in a row, all incumbents. Even the weak, inept Jiang Zemin and the slimy, indecisive Hu Jintao engaged in petty intrigues to take down Politburo members. Today some people are placing

Mr. Xi on par with Mao, who inflicted countless humanitarian disasters on the Chinese people, and Deng, whose reforms resulted in the universal corruption that plagues China today.

Many people who hold a sense of responsibility for China have realized that Mao's Cultural Revolution and the Deng-style reform are both catastrophes, the only difference being that one is political and the other economic. The elite, in the name of reform and opening, turned the state-owned assets accumulated through years of people's blood and sweat into the private property of officials, creating an insurmountable gap between rich and poor and destroying the environment, morality, and social justice. On the surface, Deng's reforms seemed to reject the Cultural Revolution, but brought about the practical consequence of thoroughly restoring bureaucrat privilege. Today, the CCP bureaucrat group's privilege and corruption damage is greater than that of any other time in history, but Deng Xiaoping's "reform and opening" is still touted as the Party's success.

Today, corruption has reached all ranks and all fields. But Mr. Xi's anticorruption campaign includes no "top-down design" on key elements such as a power-monitoring mechanism. With Mr. Xi's intelligence, he must know clearly that the heaviest-hit area of corruption is Party central, and the most corrupt elements are members of the CCP Politburo and its Standing Committee. As far as power monitoring is concerned, there is almost none at the level of the Politburo, none whatsoever of the Politburo Standing Committee. What family of past or current Politburo Standing Committee members is not as rich as a small nation? In the end, whether it is Mao, Deng, or Xi, in terms of political logic, motives, and modus operandi, they are birds of a feather, and the result is a continuation of historical disasters.

The state's anticorruption targets and operation are controlled by the Party's internal institution, in itself a betrayal of the spirit of rule of law. Completely forgoing the state's legal procedures, letting a group of Party officials whose power is not monitored handle everything, and then having the judicial organ package it up at the end—what is different from the situation when Xi Jinping's father was persecuted during the Cultural Revolution? If there is any difference, it is that their methods today are more insidious, and that the fate of an official under "internal investigation" is even darker. After all, official political victims like Mr. Xi's father were eventually rehabilitated; there would be no such hope today!

I myself have participated in the defense of some of those accused of corruption, and those cases let me perceive some common patterns.

First, not a single corruption case has been uncovered as a result of the normal operation of the anticorruption mechanism. Second, such cases have been exposed due to accidental factors or power struggles between groups of corrupt officials. When the power struggles remain at an equilibrium, everyone remains a "leading comrade." Once the equilibrium breaks, the losing side becomes the corrupt, and the winning side becomes the anticorruption hero. In fact, these are actually cases of the heinously corrupt arresting the corrupt, and the corrupt that are still in power arresting the corrupt that have been sacked.

Mr. Xi says he wants to fight corruption, but he does not change the dark politics that universally produce corruption, and he refuses to establish an independent anticorruption judicial system. This is evidence of his clear mind. If he really fought corruption through to the end, he and the rest of his regime would be thrown into prison.

II

The Named Hell: Imprisonment

On December 16, 2011, my nearly four years of imprisonment in the CCP's unnamed hell ended for the time being, and my three years in the named hell began. That day, after two hours bouncing along the road (which followed the two or three minutes of "court trial" and the "demons" snatching my "ruling"), I was escorted into a room full of police.

This was the first time I met the administrators of the named hell. The handover procedure was no different from in the unnamed hell: I was stripped naked, but this time it was a bit more "civilized" and very brief. Afterward another group of policemen took me to the "Beijing prison transit station."

This "getting to know you" routine again involved me being stripped naked. The police explained that this was not directed at me personally; it is a traditional practice carried out on all prisoners at all prisons. After my clothes were stripped off, I was told to put on the prison uniform. The process was conducted in a large room, and I always had at least six policemen surrounding me at all times. The room contained a single bed with chairs arranged around it, and after I changed into the prison uniform, they let me sit on that bed, while the policemen sat in the chairs, one of them wearing earplugs and carrying a mini video camera.

After sitting down, I again requested the return of my "ruling" that had been snatched away, and they promised to look into it. I had no idea what arrangements were being made for my "term of imprisonment." When it comes to deliberately creating a mysterious atmosphere, the CCP justice system belongs in the same league as the secret police.

For the time being, I sat on the bed and listened to the policemen chatting about pay raises, promotions, and home purchases. I continued to request the return of the "ruling" and my personal assets, including my house keys and the box of books that DomSec personnel had plundered during my secret detention. Each time, the police politely promised to look into it, but I eventually realized they were only stalling until the next day, when none of it would concern them anymore.

During that time, someone brought in a novel entitled *The Muslim Funeral,* written by Huo Da. The sight of any book was a miracle to me, as I had not been allowed to see the written word for nearly two years. I had already forgotten a lot of Chinese characters in spite of my strenuous efforts during detention to recall words and form phrases with them in my head. Any book would help me restore my relationship with the Chinese written language, so I persuaded them to allow me to take the book with me. Once I arrived at Shaya Prison, however, the book was locked up in a warehouse, and in spite of at least a hundred requests for its return over those three years, I was never allowed to read it.

I spent all day on December 16th and until the morning of December 17th in my bed surrounded by policemen. They were superficially more than polite, but unfortunately showed little understanding the substance of courtesy. Their shift changes during the night were always noisy, and worst of all was their endless loud chatter next to the bed where I was trying to sleep. I do not think they had any malicious intent; it was simply a bad habit they had formed as a consequence of handling prisoners over a long period.

Before dawn the next day, someone woke me up for breakfast, and shortly after I finished eating, a large group of policemen came in. The leader announced that they were under orders to escort me out of Beijing to a different locality, but he would not tell me where. He also stated that as a prisoner in transit, I would be required to wear shackles from now on. When he finished speaking, two officers squatted down on each side of me and fettered my ankles.

For the first time in my life, I had to walk dragging foot shackles. The Beijing authorities were "polite" enough to provide a chain more than one meter long, which allowed for a decent stride, but even so, walking in shackles is truly difficult. After I was put in handcuffs and foot shackles, two men held me and we proceeded, with great difficulty, to walk out of the building. It was already broad daylight outside; everywhere I saw high walls with electrified wire grids. This was the first time in years that I had seen the sky and earth, but it was only for a moment.

Several identical Iveco police vehicles were parked in the yard, the first few having no glass windows except in the driver's cabin. I had seen such vehicles before, but never figured out their use. Now I finally understood: they were used as personnel carriers for the PAP.

I was loaded into a police car, but for the first time they did not put the black hood on my head. Ahead were several police cars clearing the way, and before and behind my car were several PAP vehicles carrying soldiers. When my convoy arrived at the train station, I saw it also included a number of luxury vans with their curtains tightly closed. We eventually drove up to the train station platform, and here a black hood was pulled over my head and I was unloaded from the police vehicle. After we walked a few feet, one of the men with me said, "Lift your feet. Get on the train." I felt soft carpet under my feet and sensed that we had entered a private compartment. My hood was removed, and I found I was sharing the compartment with four policemen. One of them told me that I could eat two packets of instant noodles per day, that I could only use the compartment toilet, and that I could read light reading material.

The curtains were tightly closed, but the Uyghur decorations on them indicated where the train was headed. When I asked a policeman how long it would take the train to reach Xinjiang, he was obviously taken back, but when he saw me staring at the curtains, he quickly said, "The train running the Xinjiang line does not mean we'll end up in Xinjiang. There are many stops along the way, and who knows, maybe we will even go to the northeast." I knew he was talking nonsense, trying to hide the "secret" that I had spotted.

We were on the train for nearly 40 hours. To reduce the need to use the bathroom, I drank little water except when I ate some instant noodles. I have always believed that shyness is one of the many emotions endowed by God, and the thought of relieving myself inside a train compartment in front of the policemen and their video cameras was intolerable, even after my years of special experiences and hardship. But eventually, I had to have my first experience of going to the bathroom with my head covered, feet shackled, and hands cuffed. It was hopeless. Anyone who has been in a train bathroom knows how small the space is, and three people going in together had to be setting a record. But the policemen were human beings after all, and they became my "eyes" and their words became my "sight." After I was guided to the "right position," one of my hands was uncuffed and the handcuff was immediately locked onto another man's wrist. When I squatted down, each of my knees pushed against their legs. I could also sense that the bathroom's door was open; there was probably a video camera outside as well as other policemen standing guard. Going to the bathroom was always a major event during these years, but this instance was especially ceremonious.

On the train, the policemen switched shifts every few hours. Judging from their conversation, everyone in the carriage was part of my escort. Occasionally, when some of them were looking for each other, someone in my car would say, "Car No. 5 is for senior officers; the rest of the cars are all our people."

The most painful memory of that long train ride is of the foot shackles that became part of my body. At first I did not feel that much, but by the second day I realized how horrendous they were; especially at night, any movement caused heart-piercing pain on both sides of my ankles. The handcuffs were less of a problem, partly because I was accustomed to them and partly because the Beijing judicial police treated me in a more civilized manner than the secret police by making sure they were not too tight.

We arrived in Urumqi on the evening of December 18, 2011. Although they had turned off the train's loudspeaker, I learned from incidental conversation that the train would stop for two minutes at a place called Wulabo. When we arrived at Wulabo around 9 p.m., I was taken off the train. I heard someone say, "Leave him to us," and immediately felt myself being handed over to others.

As Yu Hongyuan put it, "Xinjiang's comrades are really good," and I immediately felt the brute force of the Xinjiang police, which matched the savagery, ignorance, and coldness of that remote place. I could also sense their loyalty to Beijing's leaders and their hatred toward an "enemy force."

The two "Xinjiang comrades" propelled me over the uneven ground, and unable to see anything, I could only stumble forward in the direction they pushed, repeatedly falling down in the process. Perhaps the Beijing police felt they were being too rough, because I heard them shout, "Hey you, slow down!" But that failed to deter the two "Xinjiang comrades," who finally dragged me into what seemed to be a van and pushed me down into a seat. By then I was covered in sweat from head to toe, and the two living creatures on either side of me were also perspiring and gasping for breath. Adding to the problem was the vehicle's heating, which was turned on full blast. I could feel sweat streaming down my face like a river.

The vehicle seemed to bounce endlessly along the road, and I tried hard to shift my attention to reduce the physical discomfort caused by the stuffy heat, just hoping we would reach our destination as soon as possible. Finally we arrived, and I felt myself being taken through a doorway, where people crowded around me and cameras flashed. Then I was half-carried up a flight of stairs and down a hall until I was stopped and someone said, "Strip off his clothes." The hood was pulled off my head, and I found myself surrounded by a group of men wearing peaked caps. Two heavily armed Peaked Caps grabbed my arms from the left and right while several others quickly stripped me bare. As they pushed me down onto the ice-cold floor, I tried to remove myself from the situation, constantly reminding myself to simply observe what was happening.

Several Peaked Caps stood before me with stern faces. Then two of them bent down and parted my legs while another Peaked Cap around fifty years old squatted down to touch me here and there. His eyes fastened on the "private part" between my legs, and after a pause, he reached out and held a pair of testicles in his palm. His expression was quite bizarre, his mouth gaping and his eyes glowing as he seemed lost in contemplation of the testicles. He attempted to lift them, but his pulling hurt me. Still he continued to reverently scrutinize the testicles in his palm. I was tempted to blurt out, "Are they edible?" but fought back the urge.

Then I noticed that standing nearby were two "bigwigs" wearing the epaulettes of high rank. My personal appendages had followed me for nearly half a century before finally enjoying this moment of glory. But of course the grand occasion ended when the bigwigs ordered my underwear discarded. "Throw them all away. Switch to ours," one said, and the fate of my underwear was sealed, as if he were throwing away his own things.

After some waffling, I was taken to a room around 60 feet square, where my moment of glory on a cold floor caused the less pretty situation of a stomach spasm followed by diarrhea. Unfortunately, the taps were not working, and they never turned on right up to the time that I was escorted away early on the second day.

I knew nothing of my whereabouts except that I was somewhere in Urumqi, and this small room was my prison cell. The door opened only twice a day: at dawn to remove the foam mattress and blanket that served as a bed, and again in the evening to return them. In the daytime, the only movable object allowed in the cell was the prisoner himself.

A face was always pressed to the peephole in the door, watching my every move. This seemed excessive, given that there were already two cameras on opposite walls of the cell to monitor all I did. This insistence on watching me with the naked eye suggested a sense of unease on the part of my captors.

On the second day, December 19, 2011, I was shouted awake at dawn. After I made two requests, two swarthy Peaked Caps carried in a bucket of water, but the inside of the bucket was disgustingly filthy. When I protested, one of the policemen returned with a superior, who bent over to look at the bucket and said, "It will do for washing in," then stalked off.

Just after breakfast, a voice came through the door: "Put your clothes on, you are going out soon." The door opened a few minutes later, revealing a crowd of Peaked Caps, and I realized this was no routine outing.

I was hooded and dragged downstairs and outside, where I felt snow underfoot. Then I was loaded into what seemed to be a van, and as the hours passed I sensed we had left the city. As I dozed on and off, I half-heard those around me eating and drinking: "Stewed meat, help yourselves," "I have got eight-treasure porridge and Red Bull, anyone want some?" I had been fed two steamed buns and some corn gruel that morning. Someone shouted for me to let them know when I was thirsty, but I had decided not to drink until we arrived.

The shackles placed round my ankles in Beijing had made it difficult enough to walk, but the brave men of Xinjiang had replaced them with another set two or three times heavier. The iron rings around my ankles were about two centimeters thick, the links in the chain between them as thick as a thumb. The cruelest thing was the heavy chain running between the handcuffs and the foot shackles, so short you could not bring your hands any higher than your stomach. If you wanted to eat you had to bend over or sit down to allow hand and mouth to meet.

I went to the toilet only once in a journey of almost a whole day, hoping to avoid the inevitable drama it entailed. Even that single trip to the toilet caused enough commotion, and I am sure that no esteemed personage urinates with as much pomp and ceremony as I did. Apart from the final biological act, which remained mine, all other arrangements were handled by the peaked caps.

"Forward a bit . . . bit more . . . okay, okay, let 'er rip."

I often have strange thoughts, and as I urinated one came to me: Surely no other state power in the world becomes so intimately involved in the urination of its citizens. Certainly, it was unimaginable that this modest biological function required the mobilization of so much state power.

When I was returned to the vehicle, my hood was removed so I could eat. Perhaps the people from Beijing had spoken to them overnight, as there was a lot less roughness than on the previous day, and they had stopped berating me. I saw we were in a service station in Keche, in the Akesu region of Xinjiang, but I still had no idea where I was being taken to "serve my sentence."

I caught a glance of something I probably was not meant to see, which was Sun Di climbing into a Xinjiang Public Security vehicle with an unidentified person. The secret police had handed me over three days earlier, on December 16th, so there was no reason for Sun Di to be here, with the prison apparatus in charge. And yet I had seen him where he should not have been.

Sun Di's official status within the vast Party apparatus, as head of a detachment in Beijing DomSec, was so minor it could almost be overlooked. But for the clique of gangsters known as the Communist Party, his work was vital to sustaining their reign.

Yu Hongyuan once joked, not without some smugness, that "as long as Beijing stamps hard and fast on the dissidents and activists, the whole country will be calm. But if even a little control is lost there, the consequences would be disastrous." Yu is crueler and more ignorant and callous than any normal person, which is why he valued Sun Di, who had the viciousness and lack of conscience required to carry out such work.

During the time that Sun Di became was an important part of my "life," I was able to observe at close quarters both the man himself and the logic of the power he represents. Sun Di occupied the very bottom of the Communist Party's hierarchy of privilege, but that still meant vast and unfettered power. For example, Sun Di had an official car, was permitted to use any license plate, and was exempt from any penalties. He had an endless supply of cigarettes costing 700 or 800 *yuan* a carton, and his habit whenever he sat down was to pull out a pack of those cigarettes and slap them down on the table for anyone to smoke. He himself chain-smoked, very elegantly. When away from Beijing he would stay in the finest hotels and eat the best food, helping himself to public funds.

Sun Di was clearly a favorite of Yu Hongyuan's, but not completely trusted. (The one Yu really trusted was Zhang Xue—not because he was better at his job, but because he was more obsequious.) But seeing Sun Di in Kuche left me stunned. I had thought I would at least have a few years of peace from that devil incarnate. Yet more proof of my lack of political prowess.

Apart from the sighting of Sun Di, what astonished me even more was the huge force of Peaked Caps escorting me on my journey. I had gotten a vague idea of the size of the convoy from a section chief named Wu responding to a query over his radio: "I don't know, there is three vehicles in each group, I am in charge of Groups 2 to 5, past Group 5 I don't know. The Xinjiang prison vehicles, the public security people and the armed police have got their own groups." But now seeing the turnout with my own eyes, I was speechless.

Someone tore off a piece of bread for me and passed me a bottle of water, and I ate under the watch of the policemen in the van while armed police officers guarded the front of the vehicle and the doors. This grand sight and all those staring faces, all for me.

Before we had left, in the early morning of December 18th, I'd had a dream, lasting no longer than three seconds, of my wife, Geng He, missing her right leg below the knee. She was leaning on two canes, her face pale and bloodless. I could not bear the thought of Geng He and our children suffering, but after twenty-one months with no word of me, they would soon be informed of my imprisonment, and that would be a huge blow to them, especially Geng He. This had left me in low spirits over the past two days. Now the sight of this massive entourage cheered me somewhat. What reason is there to be depressed, after all, when the dark forces of the all-powerful Communist Party turned out in such numbers to validate my work?

The convoy started to snake its way back onto the road while I was still eating, and for the time being, at least, my hood was left off. After about an hour, we left the expressway and turned off at a signpost for Shaya County, and I began to suspect that I was bound for Shaya Prison. As soon as we left the expressway, the hood was put back on.

I knew a little about Shaya, but a colleague at the Xinjiang Xinghe Legal Practice had been deputy head of the Shaya Justice Bureau before quitting to join my firm, and he had described Shaya as a poor, remote, and unpleasant place. I was never able to see it, however, as I arrived there hooded and left in the black of night.

After about two hours, we reached our destination, and I went through the usual process of being unloaded and taken inside. When I was stopped in place and had my hood removed, I found myself in a solitary confinement cell of about seventy-five square feet, with rubber flooring and cushioned walls and a dim ceiling light. Two of the Peaked Caps knelt to remove my shackles, after which I was stripped naked for my handover. Of all the strippings I had endured from Beijing to Shaya, this was the least barbaric.

A tall Uyghur prison guard, who I later learned was the head of Block 16, solemnly read out a list of rules and regulations for prisoners. Once the formalities were over, the bustle and grandeur left the cell, and the door was locked from the outside. Finally I was alone and could have a good look at the cell that was to be my home for the next three years.

A foam mattress took up perhaps a quarter of the space, and there was a squat toilet set into the floor and a tap on the wall next to it. A red warning line near to the door marked off an additional square meter of space. That left me with about four square meters to move around—about the size of a double bed. I would later learn that I was not even allowed to use these four square meters at will.

Video cameras were set into each corner of the ceiling, and a small speaker set inconspicuously into the door would perform its own wicked mission over the next ninety-six weeks. An iron door in the front wall opened onto a dim corridor outside of the cell. It had a small hole for passing meal trays in and out and so the guards on duty could look in. Another door on the back wall, meant to bring China into line with "international standards," opened onto a thirty square foot space that was supposed to be open to the sky and provide ventilation for the cell. In China's jails, these are purely for show. I never once heard that door open in any of the adjoining cell, nor was mine opened at first, and when I asked the guards about it, they said those doors were never opened. Months later, in a meeting with the block head Anwar and Prison Governor Ma, I reminded them that the right to ventilation and light is included in China's Prison Law, and finally the prison agreed to open the door for fifteen minutes each morning and afternoon.

For humanitarian reasons, every prisoner is also guaranteed a certain amount of outside exercise every day, but despite three years of requests I was never able to enjoy it.

When the deliberate restriction of fresh air eventually caused me breathing problems and headaches, the prison doubled the length of time the door was open, and during those times I was able to move around in the ten square foot space behind the door. By then, however, a roof had been added, making it just a small room. I protested that this was in breach of international treaties that the Chinese government has signed up to, as well as going against the spirit of the government's own laws and Constitution. Finally, around March 25, 2012, I heard the sound of welding coming from outside, and looked forward to fresher air and less gloom in the cell. But in my naivety I had once again underestimated their low cunning. Instead of removing the covering, they had made it moveable, with a rope tied to it and attached to the bars of a window on the second floor. During my half hour of ventilation, one of the other prisoners was responsible for lifting the covering up, after which it was replaced and the darkness resumed.

When I asked one of the guards why they went to so much trouble for a shameful and illegal result, he laughed and pointed out, "We have no shortage of manpower here."

Every cell had a small glass window looking out onto the passageway so the guards could see inside, and this naturally improved the amount of light in the cell. But the next day they pasted over those windows with a Uyghur-language newspaper.

I had not been there long when the slot in the door was opened. "A2, meal time." As I was the only resident of the cell, I knew I must be A2. (Who could China's prisoner A1 be? It had to be Liu Xiaobo, who had entered prison before me. "A" is China's designation for "a criminal who endangers national security," and the number following "A" is determined by the Party's ranking according to a unified sequence for heavyweight political prisoners. This gave Xiaobo the place of honor, indicated by the code A1. Everything concerning me there, all paperwork, correspondence, phone calls, everything, was noted under the A2 designation.)

Half a bowl of boiled cabbage was passed in through the slot, followed by two steamed buns. The cabbage looked fresh enough, but over the next three years I would repeatedly argue with the guards over whether or not oil had been added. The guards all seemed sensitive about the topic and got worked up when I raised it. The second day, just after I had finished eating, the door opened and two officers walked in. One had a bench slung over his shoulder and said he wanted to talk with me. I later learned that one of them was an official surnamed Zhou and the other Chen Fan, deputy head of Block 16. In this "conversation," if it can be called that, Zhou did all the talking while Chen remained silent.

Zhou sat down on the bench, legs crossed, and stared at me sitting on my stool.

"Do you know where you are?" When I did not reply he kept going: "Do you know where this is? Well? Do you know or not?"

I just kept staring back at him.

"Not talking? Then I'll tell you. This is a prison, and you are a convict. You're not on vacation. We reform criminals here, and you need to accept what your role here is. You're going to eat prison food. Being rehabilitated and eating prison food isn't easy, but that's the way it is. The state budget for a prisoner's food is 138 *yuan* a month, not enough to buy two sacks of flour. There's no money left over for vegetables and oil, and anyway, the government gives us the flour, not the money. We grow the vegetables ourselves, outside the budget. So don't go thinking this is some kind of health resort. Everything here is compulsory; we don't negotiate, we're in charge." And with that, he stood up and walked out.

After breakfast on the third day my cell door opened again and Ma Bing, the guard charged with looking after me, appeared in the doorway flanked by a group of other guards, along with some policemen with cameras and video cameras. Ma and one other guard came in, put a hood over me and handcuffed me, then I was taken out of the building and driven off for what I eventually learned was my physical.

I do not know how big Shaya Prison was, but I know that Block 16 held more than 300 people, and with a minimum of 16 blocks, there must have been 5,000 prisoners. Yet this hospital was tiny and had a staff of only five: Director Young, Director Hu, a Dr. Han, and two other doctors. The only two up-to-date tests they did were an X-ray and an ultrasound. Everything else was what you might expect at an ordinary clinic. Over the coming years, I learned that three of the doctors were usually stationed in the block clinics, giving injections and selling medicine. A transfer to the prison hospital was permitted only for life-threatening illnesses. It can only be imagined how well this hospital, staffed by only a director and a medical technician, was able to treat patients.

The prison authorities did everything they could to stop me from seeing or hearing anything, but I had my ways of obtaining information. And it was not just idle curiosity—I was stuck here, after all, so I might as well learn what I could for possible future reference. My prison handbook told me that convicts have full health care provided by the local government, but I learned that all medical expenses incurred outside the hospital are borne by the prisoners themselves. It is of course good that hospital treatment was free—but getting admitted to hospital was a Herculean task (because every prisoner was a source of profit, as I will explain later). One guard I talked to about this joked, "The main treatment method at the prison hospital is refusal to admit patients." For whatever reason, I was given two medical exams—this one and another the following day.

After that I started to slowly become accustomed to the hellish life of compulsory rehabilitation. For several months I was kept alone in my cell, until I was taken out for half an hour in March the following year for a family visit.

According to China's Prison Law, convicts are normally accommodated in communal cells, and isolation cells are reserved as the most severe form of punishment for convicts who break prison rules. The law clearly states that solitary confinement may not exceed fifteen days, because such a punishment is simply too cruel. According to a prisoner's handbook produced by the Ministry of Justice, even long-term confinement alongside other prisoners can cause serious physiological and psychological changes. That is why prisoners have to have access to ventilation, light, and the chance to associate normally with others.

Prisoners are terrified of solitary confinement, and I often heard those being taken to the solitary confinement cells begging for a chance to make good. If your only source of space and light is your eyes, your experience of these is greatly reduced. And worst of all, others can place you in darkness. But if you have that space and light in your heart? Those are infinite, and cannot be taken.

The Party's prisons use solitary confinement cells to isolate political prisoners as well as "cultist criminals," most of them Falun Gong practitioners. Prisoners who admit their crimes at admission are kept with other prisoners, but political prisoners and cultists who do not admit their crimes are kept in solitary confinement for three months, and if a confession is still not offered, this induction is extended for a further month.

The handbook I was given mentioned a prisoner in Hebei who broke prison rules and accumulated an extra thirty years in sentences—and during his first ten years in prison spent a total of four years in solitary confinement, "setting a new record for the Chinese prison system." In July 2014, a guard at Shaya told me privately that in that prison, at least, it was unheard of for anyone to be kept in solitary for three years at a stretch, yet I remained in solitary confinement for three solid years.

The whole process of keeping someone in isolation is complex and requires patience and care—all in the cause of utter subjugation. During routine checking of the cameras and microphones in my cell, I would be temporarily moved to another cell to wait, and in this way I was able to see three different cells and identify how mine was unique: Mine was the only one to have a microphone, and the others had one camera, while mine had four.

Most surprisingly was that the other cells all had a shower head, fixed directly onto a pipe. After spending some time in Shaya Prison, I became sure those were not for prisoners to wash under but were an instrument of abuse. I had often heard of "disobedient" prisoners or detainees being forced under cold showers, and as ordinary prisoners of Shaya Prison did not have access to showers, it was unlikely the authorities would offer the worst-behaved any special treatment. In any case, the showers were connected directly to the cold water pipe.

If all the solitary confinement cells had the same provision for such brutal treatment, there must have been a deliberate choice somewhere within the system. There would have been a meeting to discuss it, reports to superiors, a new accounting item, design, funding. However it came about, no matter how grand and lofty an idea it was made to sound on paper, the goal is simply persecution, a blatant act of inhumanity. I could never comprehend how such a thing could be discussed and agreed upon, around meeting tables and under state auspices, and then implemented. (In late summer 2013, those shower heads were removed.)

The extra trouble of keeping people in solitary confinement did not worry the prison: convicts in solitary, except for me, were managed by selected trustee prisoners, identified by Red Vests. These were treacherous men, much like the collaborators you see in Communist movies about the war with the Japanese, selfish, cowardly, and cruel, fawning to the guards and cold to their own kind. They acted as substitute guards in almost all situations. I thought of them as the Red Vests.

The construction of the cell block meant it was freezing in winter and sweltering in summer, but the stench was a year-round constant. Each communal cell was meant to hold twenty people, but actually held at least thirty or forty, along with a duty guard. Every morning and evening a bucket of water was supplied for drinking.

With no hot water, the prisoners never showered or washed their feet. Your first encounter with that stench was soul-destroying, but as I often joked with the guards, you can get used to anything, and after several weeks I did not notice it any more. It was tougher for the guards, who went home after their shifts and then had to get used to the smell all over again upon their return.

I assumed that the prison guards used the Red Vests in order to improve their own circumstances. The day-to-day jobs of controlling and keeping an eye on prisoners, passing on messages, and maintaining order were carried out by Red Vests, as was delivery and distribution of food, the collection of bowls and utensils, and the provision of water and haircuts. As a buffer between the guards and the prisoners, the Red Vests took the brunt of the guards' brutality, and while obliged to accept it, they took out their frustrations on the ordinary prisoners.

The Red Vests also managed the prisoners in solitary confinement—one stood at the door to each cell to ensure the rules were enforced and to prevent self-harm or suicide.

The only object permitted in the cell during the day was a hard plastic stool about a foot high. Whether by design or not, the seat of the stool was dome-shaped and therefore uncomfortable to sit on (these were replaced in 2013 with new, flat-seated stools). Any other items, personal or practical, were strictly forbidden. The Red Vests removed the blanket and mattress first thing in the morning. They delivered food and drink through the hole in the door, watched you eat, and then removed the crockery and utensils when you finished.

The paths to be taken when using the toilet or collecting food from the door were marked on the floor in red paint and were not to be crossed. After you finished urinating or eating, the loudspeaker would bark for you to return to your stool to "study." That meant sitting ramrod straight on the stool, hands placed neatly on your knees and feet placed within two footprints painted in yellow on the floor. Any movement risked punishment.

In those years I suffered three things crueler than torture. One was the heat and humidity of the cell in summer. The second the cold in winter. The third was the constant sitting in contemplation of my "crimes."

No matter how great your inner strength, we all have our physical limits. The most unforgiveable thing about the Party is that they disregard the limits of those they punish. Much of their oppression goes far beyond those bounds, with the very aim of causing physical pain, and the "study sessions" were a significant element of that oppression.

Other prisoners never questioned the requirement to sit all day on the stool, but I refused this inhumane treatment and asked to sit on the mattress, as well as to have some time every hour to move about and relieve myself. Ultimately, the authorities made a minor concession, allowing me to keep my mattress and sit on it. But sitting on the mattress was awful as well, since it was only about six inches thick. There were a full fifteen hours between getting up at 7:30 and going to sleep between 10:50 and 11:00 p.m., and apart from the three meals, it was all sitting. Later they allowed me ten to fifteen minutes to move around every hour, but the position in which you sat and the length of time was enough to cripple you.

I refused point-blank to sit on Sundays. One Sunday in March 2012, Anwar, the block head, came over and looked through the door. "You won't study on Sundays?"

"No. Six days is already illegal, there is no way I will do it on Sundays too."

He glared at me for a while before disappearing. In the end I was able to win one day of rest for the other prisoners as well.

The designers of this system had wherever possible removed all legal and human rights for those in solitary. All the legally given rights normal prisoners had were not for us: no visits, no letters, no open windows, no exercise, no television, no choosing our own activities on holidays, and no sports or weekly "improvements." I became aware of many things that the authorities would have preferred to have kept secret. The most important, and what the prison would most regret my learning, was the use of electric shock torture on prisoners, and the inhuman and illegal treatment of those in solitary.

The Party's Central Political and Legal Affairs Commission assigns rehabilitation targets to the Ministry of Justice, which in turn sets targets for provincial prison systems. Targets are then set for each prison, and the prison will set specific rehabilitation targets for each guard. Nobody who has not experienced this rehabilitation process themselves will be able to imagine how wicked— there is no other word for it—this system is. No normal person can conceive of the values such a system creates. Absolute terror is used to ensure absolute obedience—and the absolute terror is brought about through the use of electric shock torture.

In the two weeks prior to Ma Bing coming to threaten me in April 2012, I heard electric shock torture being used nearby on four occasions. I was amazed this was taking place within the prison system. It may be why God had me sent here. The cries of someone being shocked and electrocuted differ from those of any other physical pain. I have been electric-shocked many times, and I know what those cries sound like. They are animal-like, constant, and impossible to control. After arriving at the prison, I had assured the authorities that I would respect the prison rules and not cause trouble as long as they acted in accordance with the law and protected my humanitarian rights, but at the sound of those cries, I paced back and forth, angry and unsettled. I did not know who those cries belonged to, but I knew it was a human being and that someone wearing the state insignia was administering those shocks—not a criminal, but a guard with criminals to rehabilitate.

Knowing the system, I could say with certainty that countless people wearing that same uniform must be carrying out that same conscience-destroying work at the same time, all over the country. But hearing it happening with my own ears was a blow to my own conscience and to my sense of justice. I knew how little I could do when faced with such cruelty, but I could not bring myself to do nothing. I started to think of what action I might take and also, selfishly and naturally, of the consequences for me.

In the morning of January 4, 2012, when the crackling of the electric cattle prod and the cries of a human being sounded once more, I stood up without permission. The door soon opened and Ma Bing entered, hands folded behind his back. "Did you hear something?"

"I was just about to ask for you. That's the fifth time I've heard that. You shouldn't be doing it."

Ma interrupted me. "So what if you did hear it? You need to mind your own business."

"I know there's nothing I can do, but you're breaking the Prison Law."

At this point someone arrived outside and beckoned him away.

I continued to pursue them on this point to the very end, although I believe my efforts had no effect. This is part of a systematic wickedness, and eradicating it is the only way of changing that system, but having witnessed it, I had no choice but to act according to my personal values. In the coming month I spoke about this face to face with the block chief Anwar, Kang Jianhui, the head of the education office, surnamed Li, and Governor Ma. Anwar fervently denied it, while the various office heads just stared at me quietly and said nothing. Governor Ma, after hearing my concerns, chewed his lower lip for a full half minute, then lifted his head and replied: "Ordinarily we wouldn't do this, we should reason with people. But reality is complicated. Sometimes we're dealing with the mentally ill."

"Mr. Ma, if that's the case it's even less appropriate. Under China's penal code the mentally ill are not responsible for their crimes and shouldn't be in prison. And if they are here, you shouldn't be knowingly rehabilitating them like this."

"Maybe it is an intermittent illness," he replied.

"That's not what we're talking about, Mr. Ma. Treating anyone like this is a crime against humanity. This is not your fault personally, or even that of the prison or of the prison system as a whole. It's an inevitable outcome of your rehabilitation policy. It would be a great kindness if you could just reduce the frequency of its use, or even stop it happening."

It was an instinctive and emotional appeal, but I knew I was powerless. Later developments proved this: the noises were as frequent as ever, but now muffled. They were gagging the prisoners before shocking them. All I could do was pray for them, and continue to make my representations.

The sole outcome of my interest in torture was that every prisoner now had to sign a form once a month to say the prison was not torturing anyone. Of course, nobody dared refused.

One day I asked for the block chief, Anwar, to ask them to stop the torture, but he flatly denied it was even happening. "I would not do something like that. I have got children, a degree in psychology, you think I could do that? But if children misbehave, then parents have to educate them, maybe hit them a few times; it is all out of love. It is the same in here; if someone's disobedient I have to scold them, just like my kids."

I just shook my head as he talked. Unbelievably, he had grown up in a religious household and was still surrounded by religious people. This only increased my contempt for him.

Anwar had developed different sides to his personality as a result of his work in officialdom, and he was also quite conceited. But he was not as sophisticated as the other officials, so eventually he was transferred away from me. I would rather have dealt with him than with the other block chiefs, who were cold, cruel, and conniving. Anwar had his cunning side, but at least he was not good at hiding it.

The cell was terribly cold my first winter there. I wore thermal long johns and padded cotton trousers, which would have been enough if any kind of activity had been allowed. Anwar came into the cell once a day to check the temperature. There was a layer of frost around the iron door two or three centimeters thick, which made for stunning scenery, but was not ideal for living quarters. Some days he would visit several times, muttering. "Gao Zhisheng, you're suffering here, you've come to Xinjiang to suffer." And as he muttered he would bend over to test the temperature of the floor with his hand.

The floor of my cell was heated, so when the cold was too much to bear I would sit directly on the floor. The guards turned a blind eye to this, except for Chen Fan, the deputy block chief, who rushed in to stop me as soon as he noticed. I would tell him the cold in the cell was unbearable, and he would tell me there was nothing he could do about it—he was merely responsible for ensuring I obeyed the prison rules.

I had some unpleasant dealings with Chen Fan in my first days at Shaya. He was Anwar's deputy, twenty-four years old and with a single bar and star on his epaulette indicating he held the lowest rank, yet he has been promoted over other guards who had two bars and two or three stars. I often wondered if this was because of some connections he had, or if he was simply better at his job—even if it was just the crueler aspects of it.

During my induction to the prison he was responsible for my "cultural education," so I dealt with him more than anyone else. Once or twice a week he would come in carrying a long bench to "tutor" me. Over the five-month induction period I was forced to repeatedly read an induction handbook of no more than 20,000 Chinese characters—short enough to finish in a day or two. There was nothing in the book's language or content that would have challenged a junior middle school student, but I had to sit up straight and attend to my lessons.

At one point, Chen read from a part of the handbook that said some criminals appeal their convictions on the grounds that they regard their actions as illegal but not criminal. He berated their foolishness: "It is hilarious how ignorant of the law they are, saying what they did was illegal but not criminal." Of course, any student of law knows that while criminal behavior is always illegal, it is possible for an illegal act to not be criminal. It was that obvious Mr. Chen had no legal education.

Chatting, I learned that he had become a guard in 2007, when he was only nineteen. This made me curious about his background and I asked what he had studied at college. He said he hadn't gone.

"May I ask what education you have had?"

"Technical school level."

"Then how were you able to become a public servant?"

"There's nothing special about that in Xinjiang," he said.

"Well you are special, at least. You are the assistant block chief when there are plenty of others with more years served and higher rank."

"Yes, plenty of public servants, but not many of them can get leadership jobs."

On my third day in Shaya, he and the block chief came in to introduce themselves. Chen stood facing the wall for some reason as he spoke: "Gao Zhisheng, you'll come to understand that no matter how important you were outside, in here you are nothing, and you have nothing. You're a smart man, you don't need me to go on, do you?" He was talking to me, yet not looking at me.

On my third day, when they were pretending to give me a physical, he sat with legs crossed and yelled at me for not standing correctly—clearly showing off in front of all his superiors. I had only been there a few days and nobody had told me how I was meant to stand. He would often find fault with me when his superiors were present.

Before he was transferred away, he would always give me the obligatory haircut every two weeks. The other prisoners had their hair cut in the hall by the Red Vests, but there was no power supply in the solitary cells, so I had to go to the interview room on the ground floor. And he was not just ignorant of the law—he was a nasty piece of work.

Every time I had my hair cut I would be hooded and taken from my cell by two guards. I would complain this was illegal, and when they said there was no law against hooding a prisoner, I immediately refuted this, but only drew blank looks for my trouble. This is a prison, I was told, and you do not get to argue.

Some of the older guards warned me not to provoke Chen—he was known for his cruelty, and that was why he was favored. Chinese prisons produce two kinds of personalities, both deformed: puffed-up and hypersensitive guards, and numbed and humiliated prisoners. An entirely harmless joke, normal and welcomed among ordinary people, could not possibly be made among guards and prisoners, as I found out.

Ordinary prisoners could go to get water for drinking twice a day, but my water was delivered by a guard. One day Balati and Nuerai came to fill my cup. As Nuerai poured water from the kettle Balati spoke: "There you go, kid." And as I took the cup, I followed suit: "Thanks, kid." I never meant to cause offence, and in the case of an ordinary prisoner, the guard would have restored his dignity by hurling abuse or administering a beating. With me things were a little more complicated, but the matter still could not be allowed to pass.

At noon the following day, Ma Bing and Gao Jianjun, the head of the education office, had me taken to the interview room, telling me that Governor Ma had sent them to speak with me. The reason left me speechless: Addressing the guard giving me water as "kid" had deeply wounded his self-respect. The slight had been reported to the prison administration, with a request that I be reminded that this is a prison and I should not forget I am a prisoner, and that this heinous event had never before happened in the history of the prison. I pointed out that this indicated a severe lack of humor, but they disagreed. Over time I got used to this difference—because we were genuinely different.

Time passed, and I got to know the prison better, despite the best efforts of the authorities to prevent me from seeing or hearing anything. Their plan for my three years of imprisonment also became clear: First, hold me in isolation; second, prevent me from seeing or hearing anything; third, feed me like an animal; fourth, do not torture me; fifth, deny me any of my legal rights as a prisoner; sixth, make sure I came to no harm and caused no trouble during my time at Shaya. However, achieving these aims was no easy task, and over those three years I saw how they struggled. The prison had only one method of controlling prisoners: violence. But as I had been convicted through due legal process, in name at least, the prison was unwilling to torture me.

Some of the arrangements for me caused difficulties for the prison. For example, the permanent solitary confinement, removal of all my rights, harassment via the loudspeaker in my cell, preventing me from seeing or hearing anything, were all added complications. I was privately told that the prison itself was merely following special orders from the Xinjiang Prisons Bureau.

Their own induction handbook talked of the importance of labor, saying that imprisonment alone is inhumane and the usual method internationally is to give prisoners some kind of work to do. It added that China is a socialist nation, and human rights are best protected in socialist nations. Therefore, the government allows prisoners to work in order to protect their human rights. But I was imprisoned for three years with no opportunity to work.

In response to a suicide attempt I had made in protest the day before, I was visited by the heads of the prison administration and internal investigation departments on June 10, 2012. They told me this incident would be recorded as a breach of discipline, and then patiently read me some regulations. The intent was to signal that the prison was being restrained, and that I was being spared many of the more extreme measures. A tougher regime would mean only two meals a day, consisting only of two steamed buns; a cell lit only by a five-watt light bulb; no rests on holidays, no bedding, no ventilation, no cultural activities, no visits, and so on. The intent was to make clear the prison was already taking care of me.

In fact, the solitary confinement caused me no harm—physical restrictions do not affect me. There are bigger spaces, after all, than those we can see. For anyone of faith, infinite light and freedom await us when we close our eyes. I hoped for solitary confinement, as the disorder of a communal cell would have been unbearable and, most importantly, the constant battling with other prisoners destroys all dignity. I also wanted to make full use of this predicament, this humiliation, to improve myself, to raise myself above it. In my experience, it is these difficult circumstances that bring me spiritual strength, not the times of easy living. And as I look back today I find it impossible to overstate the extent to which that period of solitary confinement improved me. It gave me the ideal environment in which to connect with my God. It was not loneliness the walls of that cell enclosed. It was tranquility.

One of the favorite tests of the prison authorities was to ask me what year it was, what month, and what day. I would often reply in two parts: First, I would point out that unless the questioner was a new arrival to the planet, this was no real question. Second, I would tell them the date, and also the time of day. That usually left them stumped. It was not easy to keep me uninformed. But this was a prison, and the building was full of other prisoners.

They were fairly successful in preventing me from seeing anything, but not completely successful. Block 16 looked west, and my cell was one of fourteen rooms on the west side of the first floor. I was at the end of the corridor, in Cell 14. Opposite me were three communal cells, numbers 8, 9, and 10. According to the guards, those had been emptied prior to my arrival. Until early April 2012, the prison authorities prevented me from seeing anyone except prison guards. And they had good reason to segregate me like this. In about early April 2012, apparently as the prison was full and there was no other option, prisoners were placed in those three cells opposite mine. Over the next three or four days, I witnessed clear breaches of law and inhumane treatment. When department heads Li and Kang were talking with me, I told them what I had seen. Neither commented, but that night I heard the sounds of metal beds being moved. This went on for some time. The next day, when they opened the door as usual to remove my bedding, I saw the prisoners who had for those few days been my neighbors were gone. The mystery of where they had moved to was soon solved: I could hear roll call for other cells, and now each had fourteen people rather than twelve. The extra two prisoners slept on wooden boards that were delivered every evening and taken away every morning, for two and a half years. Due to my presence the adjoining cell, Cell 13, was used instead as temporary storage for those wooden boards.

After that brief period of having neighbors I saw nobody until the day I left, other than guards and the man who gave me haircuts.

According to the Prison Law, convicts may not grow their hair long, but there are no other rules regarding hair. However in practice, at least at Shaya, it was obligatory to have your head shaved every two weeks. I regarded this as a technicality and did not protest too vehemently.

After Chen Fan transferred out, one of the other convicts took over cutting my hair, giving me a chance of contact with him over the next two years. But this was no human contact in any meaningful sense, as we were not allowed to speak. While I was happy to ignore their rules, I had to consider the trouble I might cause my barber, so I simply greeted him when we met and thanked him as I left, and he smiled in response.

The process never took more than five minutes, usually in mid-afternoon, but it was a major event that required sacrifices from everyone in Block 16. First, the duty guards would order the Red Vests to close all the ground floor windows (which were opaque) so I could not see anything outside. The televisions in the hall, which otherwise seemed to be permanently on, were turned off. Then everyone apart from the guards and my barber was sent outside, or to the hall on the second floor if the weather was bad. They could not return until I was back in my cell.

If I was taken for an interview, meeting or medical exam, the prisoners on the ground floor would be moved to the second floor, regardless of what they were doing. Whenever I left my cell, the entire place was quiet.

After the prisoners were removed from the cells opposite, one-third of the north side of the floor became my exclusive territory. A red line was painted on the corridor floor, and crossing it was regarded as a grave breach of discipline.

Off to the side, but not visible to me, were three cells. My only contact with the prisoners in those cells was when I heard them—roll call, the guards disciplining or abusing them, and the singing of revolutionary songs on a Thursday evening. But most of the time there was nothing but silence.

The other prisoners got up at 7:30 in the morning and usually went off to work no later than 8:30. They returned for lunch and dinner breaks of no more than half an hour each, and went to bed sometime between 10:50 and 11 p.m. after a quick wash. And so the building fell silent again. There were never more than three hours in a day in which they might be in the cell making noise. The remaining twenty-plus hours were "my time."

According to the law, prisoners should be allowed to listen to the news every day, but this right was as good as ignored in Shaya. In three years this happened on no more than ten days, between April 9 and April 17, 2013. Even on those days, the forces of darkness shut down the loudspeakers on my side of the building, preventing all the prisoners there from listening.

Prior to early 2014, there were no televisions in the cells, but one in each hall. The prisoners could watch television on Sunday mornings and evenings, and as there were always guards in the hall the television was left on, except for when I was having my hair cut. Once they either forgot, or were so keen to watch a sporting event that they did not bother, but Chen Fan noticed and immediately ordered it turned off. I heard it was treated as a disciplinary matter, with the guards involved being fined and the TV being removed. When I first arrived, the prison would play popular songs over the loudspeakers on holidays, but that stopped when Chen Fan took charge.

In order to segregate me from the other prisoners, the area around my cell was only cleaned if someone higher-up was visiting or on certain holidays. The prisoners doing the cleaning were not allowed to use mops, but had to bend over and walk backward as they scrubbed the floor with a handful of cloth strips.

If my recollections of Shaya feel disordered, it is because there was very little to distinguish one day from the next and form a linear narrative. Likewise, I have no way to describe Shaya Prison itself, because apart from two family visits totaling an hour, I spent all my time isolated in my tiny room. I have read that South Korean dissident Kim Dae-Jung could see the stars from his cell, and Taiwan's dissident writer Li Ao could see the sun from his. I cannot tell you how envious I am. I came in hooded and I left in the dark, so I saw nothing that I can describe.

From what I could gather from the guards, Shaya Prison mainly holds Uyghur criminals serving long sentences. Chinese prisons are classed as high, medium, or low security, and are also classed as suitable for prisoners serving long or short sentences, or as ordinary prisons. Prisons for those serving long sentences are of course high security, and these high-security prisons are secretly used to hold special prisoners: "political prisoners" and "cultists." This was part of the reason why I, with a sentence of only three years, was sent to Shaya. Of all of the Party's jails, conditions are worst and the regime strictest in those for prisoners serving long sentences. Block 16 was where political prisoners and cultists were held.

Shaya was in the Akesu region of southern Xinjiang, in the Tarim Basin and close to the Taklimakan Desert. This region is only barely habitable. The climate is arid, freezing in winter and scorching in summer. There are dust storms every March and April, with the sun hidden by dust for days, perhaps more than a week. Even my closed-off cell did not keep the dust out—sometimes in the morning, after the bedding was taken away, I could see the outline of the mattress in the dust on the floor. Sometimes this would go on for over a week, and even in my dreams I would smell the dust and sand. It was not the ideal place to live, but a fine spot to build a prison. To the south of the prison a vast expanse of desert stretched hundreds of miles. In my three years I did not experience a single decent rain.

Although it was impossible for me to learn much about the prison through what I saw, during those three days when the prison was so full they used the two cells opposite mine to hold prisoners, I had a chance to observe firsthand how the prison worked.

I found that prisoners were classified and identified with different colors of badges. The guards told me that the different colors indicated the degree to which the prisoner had acknowledged his crimes and his attitude to reforming. Prisoners were marked for either strict or lenient treatment, with each category being further divided into two levels.

Those allowed to wear a badge were the lucky ones. The least fortunate were the political prisoners and cultists, who wore pieces of yellow cloth on their chest and back, making them stand out from the rest of the prisoners. Political prisoners were marked on their back with the letters "WG" for *weiguo*, an abbreviation of the Chinese term for "endangering state security." I forget what letters the cultists were marked with. Conditions for the prisoners were terrible, but the plight of the political prisoners and cultists was most distressing. No matter what color of badge another prisoner wore, they could treat those two categories of people like dirt, without any risk of consequences.

Although prisoners were denied lawful rights such as the ability to exercise outside, watch TV move around, or chat, I never saw them make even the slightest protest, even when mistreated by other prisoners.

All prisoners in a jail are allocated to "teams" of three that almost become a single organism, eating, drinking, defecating, and urinating together. They watch each other and report on each other, and are all punished for any breaches of discipline that are not reported.

Each group has another job, which is to watch and report on the political prisoners and cultists. Broadcasts over the loudspeakers in their cells relentlessly targeted these particular prisoners, and there was daily discussion and criticism of them. A guard entering a cell always asked first if there was anything to report on those prisoners, and everyone vied to give their overnight reports. That discrimination and abuse seemed to be a daily occurrence, the murderers and rapists elevated by the very presence of political prisoners and cultists.

In such circumstances, maintaining dignity is a struggle for anyone without faith. But most frightening is that people in general have no idea how to maintain their own dignity. For example, the food at the prison was minimally adequate, but every time a bucket of steamed buns was placed down, the line that had formed would degenerate into a free-for-all. Here was an opportunity to maintain some dignity, yet everyone, when faced with steamed buns, acted shamefully.

The number of people held in Chinese prisons has always been highly classified. My personal and conservative estimate is that the number cannot be less than 15 million. China has far more prisons than universities. (It was only after years of working as a lawyer that I found out that there are more than 5,000 detention centers used for holding those on remand, including those under the Xinjiang Production and Construction Corps, the railway authorities, and the army and navy.) And this system does not rehabilitate or help people or provide them with the education they need. It does not teach them to recognize their errors and to develop a conscience and love and responsibility. It just pursues a so-called rehabilitation through violence and oppression, with no sense of duty toward society.

The prisoners live in a state of constant fear. One example is the roll call system. There is always one roll call in the morning, but others are held at random through the day. When roll call is announced, there is momentary chaos as everyone rushes into place. Once lined up they stand at attention, scarcely breathing and fearful of what is to come: roll call, head counts, beatings.

Each prisoner has to shout out his number in Mandarin, which is intimidating to those from remote villages who do not speak Mandarin well. If a number is called incorrectly, a beating is administered and the count begins again. One floor can hold 200 people, and mistakes are always made. Head count and beating, then head count and beating again. A guard told me he knew of young prisoners weeping whenever roll call was announced.

Roll call is followed by another round of terror through the delivery of reprimands to the group or to individuals. Humiliation or beatings are administered entirely dependent on the mood of the guard on duty.

I was the only prisoner exempt from these processes, but I felt for the prisoners who faced the daily uncertainty of whether they would be beaten or humiliated. There was no dignity there, and the political prisoners and cultists received the worst of the humiliations. But in a sense, was not everyone a political prisoner? On induction to the prison everyone received a handbook listing the prison rules and the punishments for breaching them. One of the grave breaches of discipline listed was a failure to maintain the "four basic principles," of which the first was "support the leadership of the Party." Every day there were five points at which the prisoners had to recite oaths including language such as: "I am grateful to the government and Party," "I give thanks to the Party and government," and "I support the leadership of the Party."

The list of major breaches of prison discipline includes the heading "Illegal Religions." And it is only in prison that you can see it is not "illegal religions" the Party opposes, but all religion. Under that heading of "Illegal Religions" was "Carrying out, or covertly carrying out, the namaz" (the namaz is an Islamic prayer), "inciting others to carry out the namaz," "praying or covertly praying," "inciting others to pray," "washing in the Muslim fashion," "touching the face in the Muslim fashion before or after meals," and so on. Each of these is aimed not at "illegal religions" but at religion itself.

I once asked several of the guards, one of whom was responsible for education on religious matters, what exactly an illegal religion was. None of them was able to answer. I then asked what legal religious acts they sought to protect, and they said there were no legal religious acts in prison. "Then why ban 'illegal religion' and not all religion?" Again, they could not answer.

There is no population anywhere in the world more in need of religion than prisoners. Let them find meaning in their suffering and use religion to light their darkness, and then in that light plant kindness, love, honesty, and responsibility. This would only benefit the prison, yet the authorities blindly fight against the prisoners' own hopes for something better.

Of course, the even more urgent task is to bring the light of religion into the heart of those who run the prison; they are in need of saving even more than their charges are. It is they who lie without thought or regret as part of their job.

Special days at Shaya Prison, when inspections or visits are carried out three or four times a year, involved an unbelievable amount of effort. Dress rehearsals would start two days prior to such an event. The corridors and halls would be decorated, with the usually dull corridors further brightened with colorful lights. According to the guards, most impressive was the scene in the yard outside the main building, which was large enough to hold all 1,000 prisoners from the three cell blocks. It was divided into three sections, each with its own performance. One was the drums and gongs of Han culture, loud enough to make your ears ring. According to the guards, the most spectacular part of this was the dancers, their heads clad in colored silk. Even more visually impressive was a tai chi performance, with its participants in bright clothing, their movements synchronized to beautiful music. The third was a traditional Uyghur drum performance with a large troupe of dancers. Closing your eyes in the midst of all that, perhaps you could forget where you were.

On such days lunch would be good enough to remind us the world outside still existed, and when the guards bought me my meal I would joke about being back in the real world. They would laugh without comment. As soon as the inspection or visit was over all would be restored to normal, our meals far below the standard a pig or dog might expect.

Once, when the food fell too far below even the most minimal standards, I complained to the block authorities. The block chief Kang Jianhui came to speak with me (Kang was still head of the education department, but as Chen, who had replaced Anwar, had repeatedly clashed with me, Kang acted as temporary block chief from October 2013).

Kang had someone bring me the menu posted on the wall of the main hall. There is no way to describe the amazement with which I stared at that masterpiece of fabrication. On paper, we had the good fortune of egg soup every morning! And steamed rolls and noodles every day!

I had heard in the past that prisoners in most of China's jails actually ate quite well, because although government provision was very poor, it was possible to supplement meals with income from the prisoners' work. The poor quality of the food at Shaya never ceased to amaze me. At least the steamed buns were good, and there were enough of them to eat your fill, but twenty meals of steamed buns a week were enough for anyone. And then there was the endless torment of the boiled cabbage, the very smell of which made me retch.

Nominally there was one "highlight" a week, Uyghur hand-pulled noodles accompanied by the usual boiled cabbage and maybe some pea-sized lumps of chicken skin. It seemed that they just butchered the chicken and threw the raw meat in with the boiling cabbage, making it smell like a butcher's worktable. Twice I simply handed my meal back to Ma Bing untouched.

The sneakiest trick of all was played on major holidays, when we got stuffed buns. The stuffing was our usual boiled cabbage—but far less of it than we would normally be given. You had to take several bites of the bun before you saw any sign of it.

Readers may think I focus on the failings of the prison, but I am just presenting the problems encountered in one prison as an example of the problems in the prison system as a whole. I bear the prison authorities no malice. If anything, I empathize with them—they bore me no malice either, but were merely tools of their superiors, who certainly did. The prison authorities who actually dealt with me were often pragmatic and flexible, and I am grateful for that, but it does not mean I should avoid talking about the problems

I encountered, which are representative of issues with this system and of our society and times.

"Property must not be public, rights must not be private." This is hard-won knowledge, but disappointingly our nation has not yet accepted it and continues to ignore common human experience.

During my three years in Shaya Prison I realized that accusing them of trampling over the law actually gives them more credit than they deserve. The law is an outcome of human civilization, and the problems in Shaya Prison stem from its place in relation to that civilization.

The greatest fruit of human civilization is a love for our fellow man and the trust and reverence borne out of that love. Without it, an individual, a community, and even a nation becomes a base organism. Both the oppressor and the oppressed suffer for it. The oppressed are stripped of dignity—but did the oppressors ever have it? China's civil servants have more power than any others, yet they also suffer more from a lack of dignity and respect. If they were ever to feel shame, they could no longer go on.

I once sought out Li Jianfeng on a number of occasions to discuss the overworking of the prisoners. During our last conversation, sometime in November 2013, I said something like this: "Officer Li, since September you have not been allowing the prisoners to rest on Sundays. I originally thought this was due to the cotton harvest, but the harvest is finished and the prisoners are now working indoors. I would like to request that you refrain from overworking the prisoners, respect their basic humanitarian needs, and at the least allow them to rest on Sundays. I have already raised this issue with you a number of times."

His response was immediate: "They all volunteer to work on Sundays, they all want to. The more they work, the more they earn."

"Officer Li, do you actually believe what you just said?"

In any case, from that week onward the prisoners got Sundays off.

The prisons of an autocracy are home to the most primitive of systems: slavery. There is also a primitive type of freedom at work—unrestrained state power, and it is wielded for only three purposes: to obtain funding from the state, to maintain order through violence, and to turn prisoners into generators of profit for private benefit.

I had heard in the past that prisoners worked hard in exchange for better conditions—specifically better food. But in Shaya, at least, the prisoners' labors benefited only those employed at the prison.

Profits were generated year-round processing work and cotton farming. Part of the profits went to the prison guards; a guard once told me the block paid bonuses of at least 300 *yuan* monthly from processing income alone.

Under this system, there was no need to encourage the guards to make the prisoners work—they were already keen to defend the system.

Some may ask about prison regulators and the prison's own superior body. There are of course prison regulators—but this just means the spoils get spread more widely.

According to the guards, there are farmers in Shaya making millions of *yuan* from cotton farming. The large-scale farming practiced by the prison will be even more profitable, as it does not pay for electricity, water, seeds, or labor. The prisoners do get a monthly stipend of 8 *yuan* each—but that comes from taxpayers. So any prison in Xinjiang holding several thousand convicts could be making tens or even hundreds of millions of *yuan* just from cotton farming.

Where does all the money go? I asked one of the older guards, who just laughed and did not reply. A few days later, he told me about the prison's chicken farm: "The prison got another 6,000 or 7,000 chickens this year. The prisoners look after them, they eat grain grown by the prisoners, and where do all the eggs go? The prisoners eat them, of course. Don't believe me? It is all in the accounts, in black and white. You prisoners eat all the eggs and the chicken meat. That is what it says in the accounts."

Extrapolating from what I had seen from my own meals, I told him that it would be an exaggeration to say that each prisoner ate even a fifth of an egg over the course of a year, and nowhere near a tenth of a chicken. He was explaining that the part of the prison's income that was being siphoned off was accounted for as spending "to improve prisoners' standard of living and buy extra tools and materials." But the fact was that those tools and materials are paid for by the taxpayer. I believe the vast bulk of the income earned by those slaves go to the prison authorities and their provincial superiors, with a very small part going to the Ministry of Justice and perhaps another very small part contributed to state coffers as profits.

Over the three years, I gradually came to understand that over time people's morals and conscience had been sold, exchanged for profit. The changes happened slowly and were imperceptible to those undergoing them, just as a frog in a pot does not notice the temperature gradually rising.

One guard, a university graduate named Mao Ruijian, arrived at Shaya the same day I did. As is my habit, I greeted him, and during the first six months, he returned my greeting. During the next six months, he only grunted in acknowledgment. After that, he ignored me. I joked that he was now a proper guard. He did not understand my meaning until I explained how he had changed. He said he had not noticed. It happened to all the graduates assigned to the prison, even though they did not know it.

I often discussed this change with the guards, including with Zhang Xue in Beijing. Zhang Xue told me sometimes this was necessary, and recalled his first day as a police officer. He was interrogating a thief who refused to confess for over two hours. Zhang's superior came in, struck the suspect twice, and sat down. The suspect confessed. Likewise, the guards all thought the prisoners, murderers, and arsonists that they were, would ignore anyone who did not mistreat them.

It is easy for people to submit to the realities of their environment, and so become a part of it. The state of affairs in the prisons is entrenched, the natural outcome of unrestrained power. There is no more hope of changing things under the current system than of picking yourself up by your collar and hurling yourself into orbit.

I was once told off by one of the guards, Bai Liping, for taking too long to wash my face: "You have taken more than five minutes. The other cells have over a dozen people and they only get ten minutes."

"Ten minutes for over a dozen people, how's that possible?" (I was deliberately provoking him) "You are pulling my leg."

That annoyed him: "Of course not, it has always been that way, and why would I want to fool you anyway?" Later I saw for myself that this was, for a change, not a lie. When the two cells opposite mine were occupied for those two days, I noticed that none of the prisoners cleaned their teeth, and nobody spent more than forty seconds in the toilet.

Later a guard explained to me in private that this was because we were in Xinjiang. Muslims have a particular method of washing their face, saying prayers as they do so, and the prison was concerned that time spent washing would be used for illegal religious activity. This guard was himself raised in a Muslim home.

The prison was home to two completely different groups—the oppressed and the oppressors. The oppressors could not understand at all that the oppressed might have basic human needs. We were living in different worlds, even in terms of the water we drank. The prisoners' water came from wells and had an odd color and taste to it. Guards told me that the prison knew the water was not fit for drinking—trees watered with it died. An urgent request for assistance had been sent up, with an extra five million *yuan* being allocated to solve the problem (I was told this by a guard shortly after my arrival, when I complained about the water, and Li Jianfeng confirmed it). But I saw no change in the three years I spent there. As a guard said, once they had the money they were not in such a rush to help.

Numerous aspects to life there left me speechless. One was the poor quality and high prices of the goods you were permitted to buy through the commissary system, which I was told made millions each year. (And you do not need to be told who made those millions.)

I paid thirty *yuan* for a t-shirt that would have cost at most ten *yuan* outside the prison, and it was falling apart within a week. A high-necked shirt I bought to keep my neck warm at night turned into a short-sleeved and low-cut dress after being washed, and the long johns were no longer long although I had bought the large size.

When I spoke to Ma Bing about this, he said there was nothing he could do— all the prison purchases were like this. I gave up and did not wear my new clothes. Every penny I spent had been sent by my family, who had labored hard to earn it. I felt that burden with every purchase, yet everything I bought was an utter disappointment.

During the Chinese New Year of 2012, the light in my cell failed. As it was a holiday, they could not find the proper twenty-watt replacement, but put in a six-watt bulb as a "temporary" measure. This made the cell even gloomier, but I was assured that the bulb would be replaced after the holiday. But in spite of my repeated requests, nothing was done for more than a year. Someone explained that the bureau was in charge of my light bulbs, and the prison was allowed to reduce the wattage, but not increase it without the bureau's approval. Finally on March 17, 2013, a second six-watt bulb was installed, which was their way of "solving" the problem without going against the bureau's orders.

(By way of contrast, when I was still being held by the PAP in late 2010, the head of operations for the Beijing PAP visited the location where I was being held and immediately decided that another security gate had to be added to the corridor outside my cell in order to "further reinforce the Party's status." This grand project was quickly approved and passed up to a deputy unit commander. At least ten different soldiers told me how the cost of the project snowballed as it passed up the bureaucratic line, reaching 20,000 *yuan* at the unit level, and no one knew how much at headquarters. To top it all off, the project was listed as one of the PAP's "ten major achievements" for that year.)

The bureau had planned for me to "completely abandon my reactionary stance and join the progressive side," but it was the Ministry of Justice that decided what means would be used to that end, and that meant the bureau could not use torture, greatly reducing their choices.

Under the Prison Law, prisoners are entitled to borrow or buy books, but thanks to the special attentions of the bureau, prior to March 17, 2013, my reading matter was confined to such offerings as *Jiang Zemin's Important Three Represents Theory* and *Deng Xiaoping's Theory*. Chen, the deputy block chief, laughed as he handed me a heavy tome entitled *A Compilation of the Theoretical Work of Jiang Zemin*, arguably humanity's most egregious waste of paper.

In May 2012, after repeated representations and after bureau approval, the prison gave me a copy of Lao Tzu's *Tao Te Ching*, which I read for the next five or six months. And even that came with conditions: The bureau wanted me to write weekly reports on my remorse, on my thinking, on my breaking with the past, on my confessions, and on my determination to make amends. These were weekly tasks for all political prisoners and cultists.

I did actually write the reports several times, although the content caused some anger at the bureau. For example, on one occasion I wrote a single sentence for each report. In my report on my remorsefulness, I wrote of my remorse that I had not done a better job of exposing and criticizing the dark forces at work in China. In the report on my thinking, I told them of how I spent every day thinking of how I could end China's dark system. In my report on how I was to break with the past, I told them how determined I was to break with dark forces at work in China.

In the end, they stopped requiring me to write these reports but said I had to write a report on what I had learned from each book I read. I agreed, since this was open enough that I could choose my topics, but apparently a reactionary sitting alone in his cell reading books made them nervous, and once I had finished with the *Tao Te Ching* I was not given any more books.

Having been deprived of the chance to read for such a long time, even the worst of reading materials offered the chance to reacquaint myself with the written word, so asked if I could read something by Chairman Mao. Mao is a decent writer, and the first four volumes of his *Selected Works* are of historical value. They found this an appropriate choice and provided the first four volumes, but not the fifth, despite repeated requests. Perhaps they did not like my book report.

On completing the first four volumes, I wrote a twenty-six page long report on what I had learned. In Chinese terms, there is no doubt Mao was a success, but ultimately history will regard his era as a tragedy for the totalitarianism it inflicted on China, and which remains in force today. This conclusion to my report on what I had learned from Mao's writings left the prison authorities unhappy. "This is not what you have learned, it is just accusing the government."

After that they just gave me one piece of paper for each report, out of fear of what I might write. But then they decided it was too dangerous even to give me that one piece of paper, claiming that I was using these reports as an opportunity to "continue my reactionary stance." Finally they just stopped giving me books.

I remained in frequent conflict with the prison authorities: I was in solitary confinement, not allowed to work, not allowed to read. All of this was in breach of their own laws. All I did was request they obey their own laws. After I spent several months insisting on my lawful right to reading material, they reluctantly presented me with a copy of *Educational Readings on the Core Values of Socialism*, which described breakthroughs in political theory by 500 of the Party's greatest thinkers.

My views on this compendium of moral midgets once again enraged the prison authorities. What did these "breakthroughs" consisted of? Let me make an analogy:

There is a sexually transmitted disease, genital warts, which at the point of outbreak resembles a peach blossom. Describing a horrible disease such as that in terms of a beautiful flower—that's a "theoretical breakthrough." It might look as lovely as a flower, but it is still a disease.

The prison authorities demanded to know if I thought I knew better than those 500 experts. It was not, I told them, a matter of numbers; every summer the outdoor toilet of my childhood home would crawl with maggots, but I never saw them come up with any breakthroughs. The head of the prison's investigation department described this attitude as "brazen refusal to rehabilitate." So no more books for me. I was told many times in private that this was a bureau decision and there was nothing they could do.

Beginning on March 17, 2013, there seemed to be an improvement—at least they started giving me books to read, although they were dull and given only with extreme reluctance. They also started restricting the time I could spend reading, which led to arguments with the prison authorities and a hunger strike until they made some small concessions. Even so, they just gave me *Chicken Soup for the Soul* or books on how to get rich—all rubbish, at least as far as I was concerned.

In the end, once they had decided I was not going to abandon my reactionary stance, they stopped having me write about what I had learned from the books, but the truth was that I wanted to write about problems with the books.

For example, one book of a series of lectures given at Peking University, by a man who described himself as "more advanced than the scholars of the Academy of Marxism" and expressed hopes that "China will be forever Marxist," was riddled with basic errors. Perhaps this is why Peking University was so fond of him. In the most amusing example, he told his pasty-faced charges that the world rotates at 30 kilometers a second. He also repeated a theory of Lao Tzu, that the world makes a noise as it rotates, but that the noise is so great that it has no sound. Apparently, the students were all well trained enough not to challenge him on any of this.

The nastiest of all the experiences that the bureau created for me in that difficult period was harassment via the loudspeaker in my cell, which showed that those in the bureau knew exactly what would nauseate me the most. A few items were mindlessly repeated over the course of ninety-six weeks: a list of thirty activities banned as dangerous to national security, a lecture on the theme of "Socialist victory is inevitable, while capitalism will die out," and a patriotic education piece. These were broadcast nonstop on a loop, despite totaling less than ninety minutes.

The list of banned activities was shouted out by a man with a high-pitched voice, and the other pieces by a woman in a hysterical pitch reminiscent of the madness of the Cultural Revolution. The speech on the inevitable elimination of capitalism changed as it went on—by the end it was not capitalism that would die out, but capitalist countries. In one five-minute period, the word "socialism" was mentioned more than sixty times. The female voice became so agitated that it could have belonged to a toddler in mid-tantrum. I find it hard to believe even she loved socialism and hated capitalism so much.

I complained endlessly about that loudspeaker, which was turned on without warning when you were not expecting it, and not turned off when it should have been. Worst of all was when they suddenly turned up the volume.

After repeated failed attempts to resolve the situation, I cut my wrists to protest their wickedness. My suicide attempt was not successful, and they realized they had finally gotten to me; they had the staff and would use any number of them to "protect" me, their enemy. I was watched around the clock, with at least ten guards on duty at any one time. At any sign of trouble, they would storm into my cell.

My actions only worsened things. Originally the loudspeaker had only been turned on for one period each day, from when I woke up to noon. From the day I cut my wrists, this was increased with an extra broadcast in the evening.

Privately I was told that the prison did not want to take such a pointless course of action—the bureau had orders from the ministry to carry out the important "political task" of giving Gao Zhisheng several thousand hours of political indoctrination. As long as the officials could report this achievement, it was all fine.

Despite my attempted suicide, the use of that loudspeaker as weapon continued until my constant objections finally wore down those charged with carrying out this sacred mission, and on April 9, 2013, the recording was changed to one about the consequences of not admitting to my crimes. Amusingly, they came to see me after this to tell me how much effort this had entailed and asked if I could return the favor by writing a few sentences of praise. I may not be an official, but I know how their minds work; I suggested that they write their own praise and I would sign it.

Unlike me, they were unable to put themselves in my position and understand me. That inability to understand is an outcome of overrigid political thinking and forms a shell around a person, and when there is no need to have any consideration for those you interact with, that shell becomes permanent.

For example, Xinjiang is a cold place, and the Uyghurs tend to wear hats. Outside of the big towns, you will never see a Uyghur man without one. In the prison fortnightly haircuts were compulsory, but then should not the prisoners at least be given hats in winter, especially for when they took outside exercise? I asked the guards why a few prisoners did have hats—they said these were given to prisoners who kept overnight watch, as these prisoners were also responsible for sweeping the yard in the morning. Of course, the guards had hats for the winter—just like they had short-sleeved uniforms for summer, which were denied to the prisoners.

The groundwater used for washing in the prison was icy cold, even in summer. One time I complained to Gao Jianjun in the hope that prisoners could be provided with hot water to wash with in winter. Gao was thirty-one, but had sixteen years of work experience (including twelve years as a soldier, having signed up at the age of fifteen) and had only been in charge of education at the prison for a few years. He explained "It's like the process of national reform, it's all gradual. We can't do everything overnight."

Of course, the guards had access to hot water for showers, yet we were forced to wait. Their power meant they enjoyed better conditions than we did, to the point that they could not imagine our experiences. And in fact, they had already accepted the idea that there was a difference between the guards and the prisoners.

The summer heat and humidity in my cell was sometimes worse than that in my underground cell in Beijing. I was locked up in there like an animal, stripped of all ability to do anything about my discomfort. And to rub salt in the wound, for some reason I started suffering rhinitis. On July 11, 2013, after repeated and reasonable representations, I made a final ultimatum: if they did not provide ventilation by the 14th, I would take extreme measures. They knew I always stuck to my word. I was told my cell was not actually hot—they had measured the temperature, and even included it in a report to their superiors. I asked Li Jianfeng to repeat the measurements and sometime after ten o'clock the next morning he arrived with Feng Yongsheng in tow. Even though it was not yet the hottest part of the day, the thermometer reached 28 degrees within five minutes—at least, that is what he told me. I was not allowed to see the actual thermometer. Finally they admitted the cell was much hotter than they had thought, and on the 14th they started allowing me some ventilation. This reduced the heat somewhat, but did nothing to help my rhinitis, which always started as soon as I walked into the cell and ended as soon as I left. On August 7, 2014, when I was removed from the prison, the rhinitis I had suffered from for three consecutive summers cleared up, never to return.

Another admirably wicked act of the Communists during my imprisonment was to ignore my rights to letters and visits, rights enshrined in black and white in their own laws. Almost every letter sent to me by Geng He and others during my three years in that prison was confiscated. I was given only one letter each from my two brothers, and only after they had been opened and read. As one guard said, "You can only get reasonable letters that do not attack the government and the Party."

My replies to those letters were confiscated, and when I demanded to know why, the prison administrators informed me that my letter had "revealed state secrets." Specifically, I had written that my letter would take the long way round, as it would be sent to Beijing to be read by some high-up official before reaching my brother. I had also said that hearing my name, or hearing me speak a few words of truth, was enough to make the entire regime shake. And I had said that my letter would be full of spelling mistakes, as it had been years since I had read or written much.

Xu, the head of the prison administration department, told me that the decision to confiscate the letters was not made by the prison: "As you wrote in your letter, it had to go the long way round, to Beijing. And the official who read it found lots of problems."

When it came to visits, the Party's forces of evil were on guard against all possible dangers; if external pressure obliged them to arrange a visit, they proceeded with a trepidation beyond all reason. According to their own legal regulations, an inmate could have a family visit once a month. In reality, this only applied to ordinary prisoners and not to political prisoners and "cultists." During the three years I was incarcerated in Shaya Prison, Beijing gave me permission for only two visits lasting a total of one hour.

At each visit, my family members would arrive at the visiting room, and then I would be brought to them from my cell. The visit was prefaced by warnings not to attack or slander the Party or reveal state secrets or rehabilitation methods, not to ask about negative news and not to speak in code or dialect. It had been almost three years since I had seen any of my family and even longer that my family had been living in worry and despair, not even knowing where I had been taken or whether I was alive or dead. The first visit was by my father-in-law and my oldest brother, and the scene was truly wretched: two graying men choking back sobs.

The second visit, in 2013, was by my father-in-law and fourth younger brother, with whom I had always been closest. Tears were rare with him, but when he saw me, he began to cry.

A prison guard once asked me for my impressions of Shaya. I said that compared to being locked-up gangster-style in the past, Shaya Prison was a pretty tolerable kind of hell, but it was still a hell. The paradise of power is the hell of rights. I was at Shaya Prison for three years, and my feelings toward the prison and its staff were pretty complicated. I found the guards' treatment of other prisoners monstrous, but they generally treated me fairly well. The prison administrators had to complete the task of oppressing me, but did not want to let conflict with me get out of hand, so they could be flexible and pragmatic. For example, they could not give me hot water for washing, but they could give me a pair of latex gloves. I could not eat cold steamed buns, so the prison brought my food in an insulated lunch box. Since there were no bath facilities for the prisoners, following the evening meal on Saturdays, they would bring me a thermos of hot water for that purpose. When I began suffering from leg cramps in October 2012 due to a calcium deficiency, the prison agreed to buy milk for me outside. In short, apart from a very few individuals who would deliberately give me a hard time, things were more or less alright, and I could sympathize with them: Much of what they did was under compulsion. Except for some matters of principle, I made an effort to control myself and get along with them peacefully.

While I was locked up in this signature Chinese Communist prison for three years, three groups never forgot me: my family, friends in China and abroad who cared about me and about China's fate, and most of all, the Party's forces of evil. On the afternoon of July 22, 2014, the door of my cell opened and I was told they wanted to have a chat. Three men were waiting for me in the reception room, and one of them gave me a big grin and called out, "Old Gao," but they refused to identify themselves beyond saying that they were from Beijing and Xinjiang. I got up and turned to go. "Your government sent you to talk to me, this is your signposted legal venue and with armed guards and police all around, but you do not have the guts to give me your names and job titles. Yet this is what your own law clearly stipulates for a conversation to take place between public officials and citizens." This is what I said to Section Chief Kang when he came hurrying over. It was a stalemate.

He came twice that afternoon to see me, saying these men had come all the way from Beijing and regretted not being able to give their names and titles, but he hoped I would be accommodating. I firmly refused. Before dinner, Section Chief Kang came in again, hoping I would accept the compromise of being told their work units and titles, so I agreed to talk again after dinner.

When I got to the first floor reception room after dinner, my opponents had changed tactics, standing up of their own accord and extending their hands for me to shake: "Director Ren from the Public Security Ministry's First Department, and this is Section Chief Zhang from the Xinjiang PSB." The two sat down across from me. "Our colleague should not have acted as he did this afternoon, so he is not joining us this time; that way we can create a better atmosphere." The one who said he was Director Ren said, "Old Gao, you have been here a few years. Things are very different on the outside now, with Xi Jinping's ascent. The whole country calls him Xi the Bold. There's a huge anti-corruption effort and big changes in government. I hope when you get out you will have the chance to hear and see how it is," Ren said.

I asked him, "Are you familiar with my case and the circumstances under which the Beijing PSB has been dealing with me all these years?"

He said, "I am not, because I was transferred from Hubei to the ministry not long ago. But I don't agree with the way you were treated in the past, and the people who treated you that way have been dealt with, including the one surnamed Yu. He has gotten what he deserved." He was referring to Yu Hongyuan, but in fact Yu was promoted from deputy bureau chief to head of the Justice Bureau overseeing lawyers, so I do not know how Ren could say this. "Even Zhou Yongkang has stepped down. His four secretaries have already been detained and Zhou is next."

"Zhou's arrest is just another tragedy under this system, but I have no doubt that he will be facing trial for crimes against humanity after 2017. So let's get to what you came here to talk about," I said.

"You are talking about that event of 2017 [meaning my visions of the collapse of the Chinese Communist Party]. But there are still four years to go, right? And I can say you have definitely got it wrong there. The Party still has a good forty years of life in it. Let's talk about your plans after your release, Old Gao," Ren said.

"If you're really interested, my plan is to go back to Beijing and live happily ever after," I answered.

"You can't go back to Beijing; the Ministry sent me here in hopes that we could reach a consensus on this issue at least."

"I either return to Beijing or I go back to prison. For me the Communist Party is my prison," I said.

He just stared for a moment and then said, "Old Gao, you should give more consideration to your family, let them live a quiet life for a few years. If we could let you go back to Beijing, why would I have to come here to talk to you? Apart from that, tell me about any problems you have, and we will deal with them as long as it is within our power. Living expenses, work, anything can be solved, and you can live anywhere you want except for Beijing." (That was a lie.)

"What problems do I have? You sentenced me to three years and I've been locked up for nearly seven. I was dragged out of my home, and there are a lot of things at my home in Beijing that need doing—all kinds of fees and expenses to be covered. Our house keys are still in the hands of Beijing PSB and—totally absurd—they have recently changed the locks. So should I negotiate about all this or not? Then there's my health—in the six or seven years I have been in your hands, I've been able to take medicine only for colds or minor complaints. For the rest, including serious dental problems, you have done nothing. If I ask to see my regular dentist in Beijing, is that in some way unreasonable or unlawful?"

He was silent for a while and then said, "All this is easily handled, but you can only see a dentist outside Beijing."

"I have to go back to Beijing to see about my teeth," I insisted, but ultimately he would not compromise about returning to Beijing. I agreed not go back to Beijing for the time being, but rather to visit my in-laws in Urumqi, and after seeing to my dental problems in Xinjiang or Xi'an, I would return to my old home in Shaanxi. He agreed to this plan, but facts later showed that he was lying about everything, and he completely denied what he had said to my face.

I was scheduled for release on August 7, 2014. I knew I would not be leaving prison in the normal fashion and that I would not be truly free. At 4:00 a.m. (around 2:00 a.m. Beijing time), I got up and began washing my bedding. This was something I had decided on the first day I came to prison. When I entered prison, the bedding issued to me was filthy, with a very obvious body-shaped stain on one side. I reminded myself that although I was powerless to change my environment, the one thing I could do was wash the bedding clean before I left, in order to spare the next prisoner the same vexation. When I finished washing the quilt I began cleaning the cell, including the squat latrine, as I had done every day for three years. Refusing to resign myself to slovenliness was part of my daily round of keeping my spirits up. I did not need anyone to force me. This perplexed some of the prison guards, including Li Jianfeng, who repeatedly said that when he opened other cells the stench hit him in the face, and mine was the only exception. I told him this was part of maintaining a positive attitude and confidence toward life.

I originally thought that they would release me in the morning, and that after passing through the prison gates, I would take a walk around the area. After three years in Shaya, I was curious about the customs and people, and most of all I dreamed of going straight to a Uyghur restaurant and eating a bowl of hand-pulled noodles. The food in prison tasted utterly unlike what I remembered of the food ordinary people ate, and sometimes I would daydream about the leek and egg dumplings Geng He used to make for me and just go crazy. I had to remind myself, "Old Rabbit, you are in an environment where you have no power to satisfy physical yearnings. The more you want, the greater will be your disappointment." Not eating their food again was the only way to avoid disappointment. Eating a bowl of Uyghur noodles had long taken shape as a totemic fantasy for me, but only a fantasy after all.

Sometime after five, my cell door opened, and I was told someone was outside to meet me. The plane was at 8:00 a.m., so release procedures had to be moved up. As I walked out, I felt a faint reluctance to leave the gloomy cell that had been my world for three years, and my heart bid it a silent farewell.

Once outside, I saw several police cars parked at the side of the dark road. A section chief from the Ministry of Public Security's Domestic Security Bureau, surnamed Li, and a "brigade leader" from the Midong District of the Urumqi Municipal PSB were in place, and after a very brief process, I was put into a car. We arrived at the airport about an hour later, and as we got out of the car and walked into the airport, I suddenly felt a dizzying pressure, as if there was nothing under my feet. For five years I had been living in tiny cells where my feet never touched earth, and I had completely lost the ability to live in the world. I knew this was a reaction to going from the small world of long incarceration to the wide open spaces, but it was quite earthshaking.

We did not join the hustle and bustle of the crowd in the airport waiting area, but were taken to the luxurious so-called VIP room. Filled with wonderful light, the place was a great waste of energy. A hundred yards of plush carpeting covered the floor, but all that morning we were the only two people there; the ministry "leaders" were accommodated elsewhere. In the restroom mirror I saw a face that had been become strange to me, and it is no exaggeration to say that it terrified me. Anyone with some experience of life would have been taken aback by what they saw, "a record of hell in a face."

Once the airplane reached Urumqi, the "brigade leader" drove me from the airport, and when we entered the city limits he suddenly told me he could not take me home for the time being, and that we had to report to the police station. I immediately started opening the car door, intending to jump out as we sped along the highway, and he turned pale with fright. "I never thought you would be so uncooperative! If something happens to you, I will be in big trouble."

"I don't want to cause problems for you, so stop the car alongside the road and I will get out. If you don't stop, I will jump out, and that is a fact!"

"Old Gao, please don't put me in a spot," he said anxiously. "I'm following orders. If I take you straight home, won't I be reprimanded by my superior officer?"

I said, "Have you ever considered my feelings or my family's feelings? They are waiting anxiously for me after not seeing me for five years, and here you are making these inhuman arrangements! Why do you need to take me to the police station?"

"There is nothing I can do about it. I am required to keep you under the control of the law," he said.

I said, "You're wrong. The law is supposed to ensure my safety and protect my right not to be interfered with. Enough arguing. Stop the car or I am jumping out!" He finally agreed to take me home first and then explain it to his superiors.

When I reached my father-in-law's home, my wife's elder sister, Geng Qing, wept when she saw me. "Gao, how thin you have gotten!" The whole family talked for a long time, lamenting what they had been through over the past few years, and I could only listen silently.

Just as we finished lunch, there was a knock at the door, and two policemen came marching in, saying they had to perform their legal duty by having a talk with me. I forcefully objected to their intrusion and demanded to know what was so urgent that they had to burst in on my family less than two hours after my arrival. The two police officers said all they knew was that their senior officer had ordered them to rush over to interview Gao Zhisheng. They recorded my refusal in their notebooks and withdrew, but I knew it would not end there; even if the local police did not want to keep disturbing us, the Xinjiang PSB would never let up, especially Section Chief Zhang.

Less than two hours after I had sent the two local police officers packing, Section Chief Zhang from the Xinjiang PSB and Section Chief Li from the Public Security Ministry's First Department came knocking at the door, accompanied by a swarthy-faced young man said to be the youngest department head in the Xinjiang public security apparatus. I had met Section Chief Zhang several times before, including with Director Ren of the Public Security Ministry's Domestic Security Bureau during that last visit in prison. I decided that he must be from his department's First Section, which denotes Domestic Security, since the others he accompanied also headed sections with that designation.

The DomSec apparatus is not unique to China but originated in the former Soviet Union and then rapidly spread to other communist regimes. The Communist Party wields the secret police in this as its lethal weapon to ruthlessly suppress dissent. In the words of PAP officers, DomSec is like the notorious secret police under the eunuch faction headed by Wei Zhongxian under the late Ming. Historical patterns of autocratic regimes show that the closer the regime is to extinction, the more frenzied and savage its eunuch faction becomes, which accelerates the demise of itself and the autocratic apparatus. I once discussed this phenomenon with a relatively sympathetic veteran DomSec officer, and he said there was an unwritten standard for recruiting people into DomSec; in particular, "They have to be not very sensible, like children, and to have no human feelings, and they have to be willing to hit people and hit them hard, and most important, they must be absolutely obedient to their superiors." I summarized this to him as: ignorant, callous, savage, and slavish. He said, "I didn't say that."

Xinjiang's Section Chief Zhang left a very bad impression on me with his overbearing attitude, which was no doubt meant for the benefit of the "leader from the ministry," but seemed to leave an equally bad impression on Section Chief Li. I was actually quite favorably impressed by Section Chief Li; at least in our contacts over those few days, he was polite and rational, and when there were differences he was willing to calmly discuss them. The promises he made to my face (like, being able to get dental treatment outside of Beijing) disappeared along with him, but I knew he was only the messenger.

Section Chief Zhang, however, was a product and tentacle of the system, a two-dimensional personality ignorant of the law, as I had observed during our conversation at Shaya Prison. Zhang no doubt regarded accompanying a "leader from the ministry" in negotiations with me as a rare opportunity to ingratiate himself, not knowing how to find his own way through the bureaucratic apparatus. Within two days of my returning to Urumqi, he arranged for the police to knock on my family's door four times for a "visit." Later, someone told me that Zhang's capacity for long-term strategy should not be underestimated, and that his real objective was to force me to leave Xinjiang. Clearly, Xinjiang's "stability preservation" situation was unusually grim, and my remaining in Xinjiang meant nothing but trouble, first and foremost to Zhang. It therefore made sense that his greatest wish was for me to leave Xinjiang as soon as possible, and the Yulin police later expressed the same views to my face.

My original intention was to return to northern Shaanxi after seeing a dentist in Urumqi, mainly in hopes of keeping my family from seeing my horrible appearance until I'd had some time to restore my health. Given the extraordinary "enthusiasm" of Section Chief Zhang and the others, however, I decided to wait and see a dentist in Xi'an instead. The Xinjiang police readily agreed to my plan and said they would report it immediately to Beijing, and they even became more civil, no longer bursting into my family's home but meeting me among the trees downstairs. When my Xinjiang relatives saw what my face looked like, they thought I was concealing major health problems from them and could not relax until I had a physical examination in their presence. I knew that in fact my body was internally sound, always believing that, physiological laws notwithstanding, a positive attitude and perseverance go far toward resisting illnesses. But in order to placate my relatives, I underwent a full physical examination in Urumqi, and my health was found to be excellent, which was as I expected, but surprised my adversaries, at least two of whom privately said to me that I looked ready to drop dead in my tracks.

While dashing from one hospital to the next during those few days, I did in fact fall in my tracks, but I also got back up again. I tumbled from a spell of vertigo while hurrying to a bus station, which alarmed my in-laws, but I assured them I would be back to normal within a month. Following my physical examination, I looked forward to having my teeth looked after in Xinjiang.

One day, the "brigade leader" who had escorted me to Urumqi from prison arrived at my sister-in-law's house with a copy of *Global Times*, which had an article under the byline Dan Renping about "Western countries promoting 'rights defense lawyers.'"[1] The no-doubt pseudonymous Dan Renping was clearly the government's parasitic hatchet-man, the kind who screeches away with his face concealed, and he accused me of "radical ideas," although only China's enemies would oppose the systemic modernization I advocated. In any case, even a "radical idea" is ultimately only an idea, and criminal laws target only acts that endanger state security, not thinking.

The real implication of Dan Renping's article was to send a warning to me and my sympathizers: "We won't allow you to cause mischief anymore." The Dan Renpings of China and the corrupt officials they serve oppose constitutional government, rule of law, freedom, religion, universal values, democratic elections, judicial independence, and all other things universally acknowledged as good, and anything that is not conducive to their corruption is labeled the erroneous ideological trends of the West. In fact, justice is justice, and does not distinguish between East and West.

I would like to add here that when this evil regime falls, there will be a squaring of accounts. Investigating and punishing evil is one of humanity's most common methods for protecting justice, but we likewise know that without forgiveness there is no hope for tomorrow. The people of South Africa were able to implement social reconciliation, and Chinese can as well, but certain individuals, such as Jiang Zemin, Luo Han, Hu Jintao, and Zhou Yongkang, cannot be included among the ranks of the forgiven if they do not convince the world that they have reformed. Likewise, Party mouthpieces like Dan Renping should be treated like Leni Riefenstahl, who extolled Nazi Fascism in works such as *The Triumph of the Will*.

Apart from that incident with the newspaper, the two weeks or so that I spent at my sister-in-law's home after my physical examination passed in the blink of an eye. I felt as if I had gone to another world, returning to a life of dignity

---

1. TN: The Chinese article can be read at http://opinion.huanqiu.com/shanrenping /2014-08/5099388.html, and an English summary at http://www.cefc.com.hk/china-news /press-meeting-highlights-december-17/ (accessed March 30, 2016).

and respect among those who loved me after years of being called a beast and dog shit. In that caring environment, supplemented by Geng Qing's cooking skills, I gained more than sixteen pounds and my complexion greatly improved.

The dates I kept setting with the Xinjiang police to go to Xi'an to see a dentist were repeatedly postponed, however. They blamed the Beijing authorities for delaying a decision, but I later learned that it was due to wrangling between the Xinjiang and Shaanxi police. The Xinjiang police wanted to hand me over to the Shaanxi police in Xi'an to get me off their hands, but the Shaanxi police, who were in no hurry to take me on, demanded that the Xinjiang police hand me over at Yulin, and they kept going back and forth.

Finally someone from the Yulin police said to my face, "No one is willing to take you to Xi'an to see a dentist. This should be left to Beijing to handle; the costs for your case are in their hands. Why should local authorities cover the costs for all those people in Xi'an?" On August 25th, the day before I was to leave Xinjiang, the brigade leader told me that after arriving in Xi'an I would fly that same day to my family in Yulin, and would have to wait until later to see the dentist. Since it had all been arranged, I could only go along with it.

I arrived at Yulin Airport under escort around 6:00 in the evening on August 26. My eldest brother, fourth brother, and cousin were all outside the airport waiting for me, but several vehicles full of personnel from the provincial, municipal, and county PSBs were there to pick me up. There was an unpleasant exchange in the vehicles. My fourth brother's home was in Yulin City, and his family had prepared dinner for me that night. I protested, "My family has not seen me in five years, so why can't I have dinner with my brother and other family members?" The commander said, "We are just following orders, so it is no use complaining to us."

Instead, I was escorted to my eldest brother's home in the countryside, where people who were obviously secret police roamed around the courtyard of the compound. Within two days of my arrival, the police burst into the cave dwelling where I was staying four times. Knowing my temper, my eldest brother shadowed me wherever I went, but conflict was unavoidable, and eventually even he could not stand it anymore. On the third day, he flew into a rage and telephoned the head of the local police station, demanding that they either detain me again or desist in their harassment.

A practical issue after I returned home was the problem of seeing a dentist. I had not had dental care in a long time, and combined with long-term malnourishment and the torture I had undergone in April 2010, most of my teeth were loose and painful and needed immediate treatment. But the attitude of the Yulin police was that they had to get money from higher-up, otherwise they could not do anything, and they would not let us go to Xi'an on our own.

I was certain that Jia County was too backward to handle my dental problems, but when the pain became unbearable I finally steeled myself and went to what I was told was the best dental clinic in the locality. The clinic had no disposable implements, and when the dentist pulled a tweezers out of a blood-stained bowl to extract my tooth, I backed off, feeling I would be better-off losing all my teeth than being treated at that clinic.

Scaling back my expectations, I asked if the doctor could prescribe some medicine for dental pain, and he pulled a pile of bright yellow pills from a piece of paper in his cabinet and spread them out on the table.

"Don't you have any bottled medicine?" I asked him anxiously.

"This is how we prescribe medicine here. Do you want it or not?" He was starting to look irritated. So my experiment with seeking dental treatment in Jia County was a failure.

The pain was finally so great that I felt I had no choice but to go to Yulin, even though this required overcoming the psychological hurdle of my elder brother negotiating with the local authorities. I had objected to the local authorities demanding that I telephone the police station every day when they were surrounding me around the clock, and they finally agreed that I could simply report to them when I planned to go outside the village. Even so, both sides were unhappy, and the stalemate had my brother constantly on edge. Behind my back he told the authorities that he would step forward to negotiate whenever I needed to leave the village. I expressed my objection to him, and he rejected my objection, and that is where matters stood.

At least Yulin was a prefectural-level city with a carapace of civilization, but it turned out to be just window dressing. While waiting in Xi'an for our flight on November 28, 2009, PAP squad leader Han, who had rushed over from Yulin to "receive" me, had asked me, "What is your impression of Yulin?" I said everyone who lived there was poor, but he said Yulin was now the wealthiest prefectural-level city in Shaanxi. He said, "In the past, when we went to the provincial capital for meetings, the Yulin leaders always sat in the most inconspicuous spot in the back row, but now we sit in the front row. Yulin's people can stand tall now." I said poverty was more than a matter of money; you could not find a single news stand in the whole city, and its bookshops did not sell any books on religion, philosophy, sociology, or natural sciences, and this was worse than having no money. After being silent for a moment, he said that was a real problem.

After the trouble of gaining permission to go to Yulin, my dental treatment there also ended in failure, and the process was truly hair-raising. Chinese who have become accustomed to this kind of thing may think I am making too much of it. I am aware that over the years I had become removed from the medical environment of ordinary people, and in Xinjiang or in Beijing I was always able to get medical treatment for myself and my family in a clean environment and without having to wait in line. We were part of China's social injustice in terms of medical treatment. It was while seeking dental treatment this time that I realized how hard it is for the vast majority of China's people to obtain decent medical treatment.

I went to Yulin's largest hospital, which I was told was also its best, but I will not name it here because the problems I saw are pervasive in China, especially the lack of social ethics and proper deportment in a public environment. I found myself in a large ward with maybe twenty examination tables lined up on each side and separated by a narrow corridor. There is no way to describe the sense of chaos, crowding and racket, and the doctors, nurses, and interns had to have been distracted by the clamor around them as everyone vied to talk first. I gently complained to my doctor and nurse, about the unbearable noise, some of which was being produced by the medical professionals themselves. The nurse carelessly remarked, "It is a state-run hospital—they are all like this."

Ultimately, this simple tooth extraction became a discouraging problem, as the bleeding continued for days afterward. The trouble involved in going to Yulin the previous time made me reluctant to make a return trip, and I thought the bleeding was sure to stop within a few days. I managed by holding a cotton ball in my mouth during the day, but at night the blood flow was frightening, and one night I had to turn on the lights and get up several times to deal with it. My brother slept on the same heated brick bed with me, and all this caused him immense worry and convinced him that I was hiding a more serious problem with my health. When it got worse on the fifth night, my brother calmly insisted that I go to the hospital, and I promised to observe it for one more day and go along with his arrangements if there was no change for the better.

To this day I do not understand why this problem arose, as I had never suffered from any clotting disorder or circulatory disease, but by the sixth night, the situation was out of control, and sleep was impossible. My elder brother blamed me for being so stubborn. "I cannot stand to see you begging those evil creatures," I said, disheartened.

"Why are you still thinking about that? We don't have time to care about them. We need to get you to the Yulin Main Hospital right now," my brother said as he began getting dressed.

Although I steadfastly believed that God would not allow me to suffer any serious health problems at this time, the nonstop bleeding was impossible to ignore, so I also started getting dressed. My brother called my nephew, who lived near the county seat, to drive over and pick us up, and we rushed over to Yulin before dawn.

When we got to the hospital, the doctor said he had never come across a case where a wound kept bleeding for an entire week after a tooth was pulled, but he knew how to stop the blood, and his two-minute procedure proved effective. He had me stay at the hospital for observation for half an hour, and during this time, my fourth brother arrived at the hospital and insisted that I remain in Yulin for a couple more days to be safe.

During the subsequent days, I had several intense conflicts with the Yulin police. One was over the fact that I had left the village that night before they had the chance to respond, which meant that I had left without obtaining permission, and that was no small matter for those habitually overbearing authorities. While I was staying with my fourth brother, some rascals kept barging into the courtyard, no doubt to communicate a threat. Another family in my brother's compound opened their door early one morning and found the head of the Yulin secret police, Glasses, standing in the second-floor hallway with a scowl on his face. I had been dealing with that gentleman for quite some time; he had led the group of ruffians into my eldest brother's courtyard in April 2006, nearly ten years before, and every time I returned to northern Shaanxi, I would catch sight of him. When I was detained by the Yulin secret police at the end of 2009 and early 2010, he was the officer in charge of the location where I was held. He had directed my abduction from my eldest brother's home in 2009 and my heavy-handed expulsion from northern Shaanxi in 2006. The years did not seem to have brought any progress in terms of a humane temperament, and his continued engagement in these shameful acts made him an object of pity.

My fourth brother insisted that I stay in the city, because he hated the thought of me living in the village, where the food was basic and there was no proper bathroom and no heat in the winter. I was originally told by the official from the Public Security Ministry that this would not be a problem, but they went back on their word and explicitly stated that they would do all in their power to prevent me from staying in the city. The conflict intensified over what should have been a minor matter, and my younger brother began advising me to return to the village, but I refused. The Yulin police spread the word that they would use drastic measures, but in fact it was a performance. Finally my younger brother resorted to bringing our eldest brother to Yulin.

My gray-haired eldest brother had endured too much humiliation and psychological torment on my behalf over the years, and the suffering of my family members over the past ten years has been a source of almost unendurable pain to me, turning love into a double-edged sword. My eldest brother tried to persuade me for a good ten minutes, and when he saw that I would not back down, he began to sob and said, "Our parents have been dead all this time and we brothers have never been cross with each other. You all have always respected and listened to me, and I have never guided you onto the wrong path. Today your eldest and fourth brother are begging you. After those people have spent all these years doing so many unspeakable things to you, why can't you learn to back off just a little? What difference does it make which brother you stay with? It's not a matter of principle, so why be so stubborn?"

I could not bear to see my brothers weep, especially since God had never indicated to me that it mattered where I stayed. (It later turned out that staying in the village worked out better.) I promised to go along with my eldest brother's arrangements, and while we three brothers calmly talked, my eldest brother told me, "Now I will come out and tell you that I went to see them about this several times and told them that the leader from the Public Security Ministry had said you could stay anywhere but Beijing and that his word should be respected, but they completely refused to talk reason, saying, 'You are not kids. Even if it is written on the paper, not to mention if it is just a verbal promise, if the Communist Party won't acknowledge it, that is the end of it.' Now the higher-ups won't admit promising this to you, and they have explicitly ordered you to live in the village. We are dependent on them, so I am going to do what they tell me to." My eldest brother said that being able to see me alive at his side was more important than anything else. My constant disappearances over the years had left lingering fear in the hearts of my family members.

In this narrative, I have yet to devote a special section to my eldest brother. As I write this behind closed doors, I hear him out in the courtyard chopping firewood for me. We have never had a stove just to warm ourselves, but this winter, my eldest brother bought a "foreign stove" in the city for me, and in order to ensure my safety, he only burns wood rather than coal in it. My stove consumes kindling at a ferocious rate, but every day he provides all the firewood I need, regardless of the weather, and sometimes I can hear him singing while he is out there chopping.

We lost our father when I was young, and in all the hardship we have been through, it is my eldest brother's image that is most distinct in my mind, not my father's. After my father was felled by poverty and hardship, it was my eldest brother who shouldered the heaviest burden. Forty years of endless toil has reduced him from a burly, sturdy man to a small, thin figure. I often think that my elder brother is a living specimen of the fate of China's peasants and a cross-section of the travails of China's lower classes. In a civilized society, the state shields its citizens from the vagaries of life; that is the basic purpose of humanity constructing the state. The saddest part for people like my eldest brother is that the state only adds to their hardship, and their entire lives are an endless struggle that is never directed against those in power.

When I wondered why my brother's two granddaughters were not at breakfast one morning, he angrily told me of how their local school had been closed down, and now village children had to compete to get into a school in the city. Meanwhile, local teachers were still able to draw their salaries from the state payroll as long as they handed over a third of it to the local education department cadres. I wondered why none of the parents had reported this problem. My brother said, "Who would dare? Some parents wanted to go to Beijing to file a complaint, but you know the results—anyone who files a report gets arrested, and even if the complaint was filed, wouldn't it be the education department investigating itself?"

My brother's complaints were depressing, and when I did not say anything, he said, "Brother, we cannot smooth out the world with a razor. The local Party branches do all kinds of damned things, and they could not care less what the ordinary people think about it. Nowadays farmers have to get permission from the police station to buy gas for tractors to plow their fields. In the government's eyes, every farmer is a bandit." I silently looked at my brother, feeling as troubled and powerless as he did.

Many scenes relating to my eldest brother have become part of my life, and writing about them makes these scenes dance before my eyes in rapid succession.

One midsummer's day in 1975, less than two months after our father's death, my brother used his lunch break at the agricultural cooperative to run over to hoe our family's private garden plot. When I carried half a jug of watery rice porridge out to him, I saw my brother laboring away, shirtless, shoeless, and hatless, with sweat pouring down his body and sobbing like a child. The despairing sound of his weeping still rings in my ears decades later. I placed the jug of porridge on the ground, and he looked up at me but did not stop weeping. When he walked over, I thought it was to eat his porridge, but instead he took me in his arms, and the two of us wept until the hills rang with our sobs.

One time in 1976, after my brother and I went to the county seat to sell medicinal herbs, he sent me home first, saying he had other matters to attend do. Passing by the brickyard at Shenjiawan Village on my way home, I stopped to watch a kiln being opened. The heat that poured out of it made me instinctively run away, but in that instant I saw a shirtless man at the bottom of the kiln transferring bricks to a cart, sweat pouring in streams through the dust and ash on his body. When I called out, "Big Brother!," he raised his head. "Get out of here, it is too hot!" he said, and then lowered his head and went back to work. I said, "Big Brother, let me help you." But he said, "Get out of here! There is only room for one person here, and a kid will die of the heat in a few minutes.

Go back and tell Mom that I've finished a kiln of bricks for 5 *kuai*, and I'll be back in time to go to work at the cooperative tomorrow morning, so she shouldn't worry." All I could think was how pitiful and hard his life was. At that time, Father had been dead for more than a year, and the burden of his crushing poverty had been passed on to my eldest brother. I recently reminded my brother of this episode over breakfast, but he said it was common to use the time allowed for going to market to haul coal or do other work for people. "That was back when Dad was no more, and I don't even remember it."

At the end of 1977, our second brother wanted to join the army, and when he came home after his physical examination and our mother anxiously asked him the results, he did not say anything but lay down on the *kang* and wept. My mother quietly consoled him and said he could try again next year. But he sat up and said he had passed the physical, and the recruiters were keen to take him on, but there were too many people who wanted to join up, and they hoped he could exert some influence on the commune's relevant cadre. My second brother asked how much money that required, and the cadre said 20 *kuai* was needed. For our family, that was no small matter, and when my mother heard it, she said nothing more. That night, our eldest brother returned home after working all day, and when our second brother told him how things had gone, he said, "There is no ditch that cannot be crossed. If this had happened at the beginning of the year it would be a big problem, but we are just starting to take in the harvest, and we can sell some rice. If it means going a little hungry next year, that's next year's worry. Let's solve the present problem first." I recently reminded my second brother of this incident, and it still made his eyes shine with tears. "Our eldest brother has always known how to handle what matters," I sighed.

At the end of 1982, I also decided to join the army. When I told my mother my intentions, she said nothing, but after my eldest brother came home that night, she said, "You boys are so hardhearted. Your father has been dead all these years, and your eldest brother has been suffering like a beast of burden, but you boys only think of yourselves, running off as soon as you're grown. How can you let him take all this on by himself?" My brother, sitting on the floor as he ate a big bowl of rice, silently listened and then raised his head and said to my mother, "Mom, this is our brother's opportunity. A person who is destined to suffer can never set that bowl aside; at best you get a break of three years when things are a bit better and then you go back to suffering. I support our third brother going out to join the army." When the new recruits were seen off at the county seat, my eldest brother chased after the truck for a couple of miles across the meandering hills. A mile and a half outside of town, I spotted him still running after us, and he waved at me. More than thirty years later, this image has only grown clearer in my mind, just as I recall him dashing after our fourth brother when he joined the army as well. He saw each of us off, one by one. For those of us going out, the future was uncertain, but there was still hope, while he was always left behind. His love and kindness opened the outside world to us, and likewise by chopping wood for my stove now, he was expressing that word he never said, love.

I have a cousin, Mugou, who is now in his thirties. One time when he had a falling out with a girl, Mugou drank down a bottle of pesticide, and by the time his family found him he was unconscious and his limbs were twitching uncontrollably. My aunt and uncle sobbed to the heavens, which in that closed-off village was like sending up an emergency siren in a military camp. On hearing the news, my eldest brother tossed aside his hoe and ran back to the village, and pushing through the wailing crowd, he saw his cousin Mugou prostrate and twitching on the ground, and he yelled, "Are you all dunces?" Then he went to the latrine and grabbed the sludge scoop, and he stuck it deep into the latrine and stirred it around and then ladled out a sizable portion.

He yelled for everyone to move away, and some people joined in the rescue effort by grabbing hold of my cousin and prying open his teeth, after which my brother poured the ladle of sewage between Mugou's open lips. Mugou gave a huge sneeze that sprayed excrement all over my brother's face. Chaos ensued, but my brother's expression did not change. "Keep pouring!" he shouted, and finally the empty ladle was tossed aside. My brother told the others to let Mugou lie flat, and within twenty seconds, Mugou vomited a mixture of excrement and pesticide onto the ground, filling air with its stench. Mugou opened his eyes. He had come back to life.

Some refined persons may find this story too vulgar, but this is how people have lived for thousands of years in China's peasant society, and people retell the story every time I go home.

Of course, it is better when people become refined and proper. But I feel that my brother's ladle of excrement was more effective than the CCP's socioeconomic principle of "scientific outlook on development."[2] In any case, it reflects the fact that while Chinese have "risen to their feet," our country's rural inhabitants still live in a world where people cannot run to a hospital emergency room, but have to resort to a scoop of sewage to save their lives. These thoughts make me look at my eldest brother with both distress and admiration, but I have not been able to bring myself to discuss them with him.

---

2. TN: The "scientific outlook on development" or "scientific development perspective" was a guiding principle and central feature of former President Hu Jintao's call to create a "harmonious society" in the early 2000s.

My eldest brother has always been clearheaded about major issues of right and wrong, but he also has the poor man's loss of heart. One time when he went to Beijing, a squad leader, from the secret police who had gone to northern Shaanxi several times, had eaten mutton noodles at my brother's home several times, and had taken local products away with him, stuffed 500 *yuan* into my brother's hand, and he accepted it. I never felt the slightest impulse to blame my brother for this, although my fourth brother and I both felt it was unacceptable.

It has been half a year now since I returned to my home village, and I have stayed out of contact with the outside world for two main reasons. First of all, my in-laws and my brothers agreed to keep me in conditions of privacy for two years. This allows time for restoring my health, and I also owe it to them to allow them some peace in their lives. In any case, the authorities repeatedly told my family, "If Gao Zhisheng contacts the outside world, we will adopt the same resolute measures as in the past." My family members are constantly on edge, fearing another clash between me and the authorities and afraid of losing me again, especially after seeing my condition when I returned this time.

Another reason is that I am unwilling to see visitors arrested before my eyes, as happened on an almost daily basis outside my home from 2006 to 2008. I once saw a Japanese friend being forced into a small room that the secret police had commandeered downstairs, and on another occasion, a lawyer from Sichuan, surnamed Li, was confronted in my doorway. When the Party's secret agents shouted at him, "Who are you? What is your purpose in coming to see Gao Zhisheng?," the lawyer calmly asked them, "Who are you? What purpose in visiting Gao Zhisheng is illegal?" They were dumbstruck for a while, having never been so boldly challenged before.

Yet another important reason is that it is been six years since I have been able to read anything worthwhile, so I have buried my head in books. And the final reason is that I have used this time to write as well. First of all, I wanted write about the time from when I was small until the birth of my son. This was at the request of my son, Gao Tianyu, who asked me to tell him stories of my experience growing up, and then suggested that I turn these stories into a book.

I owe my children too much, so once my son came up with this idea, I wanted to spend some time on the project to demonstrate my love for my son and daughter. Once I got started, I spent more than two months and wrote nearly 200,000 words. After that, I set about writing this book, which took more than three months. I have been so absorbed in my writing that it is no exaggeration to say that I even run when I go to the bathroom. I did all this behind closed doors for fear that my writing would cause my brother and other family members to worry about new conflict with the authorities. Whenever someone opened the door, I would hide my pen and notebook and pick up a book to read. More than once, my eldest brother asked me at dinner, "You haven't been writing, have you?" I am not sure when I will tell him that I lied to him.

As is my habit wherever I am, I have quickly established a living pattern. Every day I rise at five o'clock in the morning and read for an hour, and at six o'clock I spend an hour exercising in the courtyard in that unique atmosphere that my "bodyguards" provide. At seven I spend half an hour washing my face and tidying up my room, then I devote half an hour to reading the Bible at 7:30, and from eight o'clock onward I spend most of my time writing until around 6:30 in the evening. I read while I eat at seven o'clock, exercise for about an hour, and then read a little more before going to bed, usually falling into a deep sleep as soon as I hit the pillow.

Some people have managed to track down my brothers and offer me work at a substantial salary, even though I cannot leave the village for now. Gratifying as these offers are, especially in this politically oppressive climate, and welcome as the money would be, I have felt obliged to refuse them.

During my spare time on Sunday, I usually go hiking in the hills behind the village, gradually discovering the breathtaking beauty of my native place, which I had never noticed in past decades. Especially in autumn at break of day, looking out onto the hills and rivers under the red sun I feel heaven, earth and man come together in a mystical contrast, inspiring feelings that cannot be conveyed in words. Then at sunset I experience the land's immovable majesty, and my thoughts soar with the feeling that I am the only man left on this planet, and that my heartbeat is the only sound beneath heaven and earth, until the fluttering of a bird arouses me from my daze before the world is lost to me forever.

Today when I went out to exercise at noon, the earth was weighed down by snow and blown raw by the wind, but plants pushed out new green shoots, indifferent to the harsh remnants of winter. My heart was stirred by this small miracle, which seems beneath notice but can inspire like the greatest philosophy. The harshness and desolation are not death, but the harbingers of a flourishing life to come. The other revelation it gave me was that my homeland has never lacked beauty; all it lacks is our ability to discover or notice that beauty.

Written from December 27, 2014 to March 18, 2015, in the cave dwelling where my mother once lived.

Index